MARITIME TRANSPORT 1986

ORGANISATION FOR ECONOMIC CO-OPERATION AND DEVELOPMENT

Pursuant to article 1 of the Convention signed in Paris on 14th December, 1960, and which came into force on 30th September, 1961, the Organisation for Economic Co-operation and Development (OECD) shall promote policies designed:

- to achieve the highest sustainable economic growth and employment and a rising standard of living in Member countries, while maintaining financial stability, and thus to contribute to the development of the world economy;
- to contribute to sound economic expansion in Member as well as non-member countries in the process of economic development; and
- to contribute to the expansion of world trade on a multilateral, non-discriminatory basis in accordance with international obligations.

The original Member countries of the OECD are Austria, Belgium, Canada, Denmark, France, the Federal Republic of Germany, Greece, Iceland, Ireland, Italy, Luxembourg, the Netherlands, Norway, Portugal, Spain, Sweden, Switzerland, Turkey, the United Kingdom and the United States. The following countries acceded subsequently through accession at the dates hereafter: Japan (28th April, 1964), Finland (28th January, 1969), Australia (7th June, 1971) and New Zealand (29th May, 1973).

The Socialist Federal Republic of Yugoslavia takes part in some of the work of the OECD (agreement of 28th October, 1961).

Publié en français sous le titre:

LES TRANSPORTS MARITIMES
1986

© OECD, 1987
Application for permission to reproduce or translate
all or part of this publication should be made to:
Head of Publications Service, OECD
2, rue André-Pascal, 75775 PARIS CEDEX 16, France.

Photo : Compagnie Générale Maritime

This report was approved by the Maritime Transport Committee and was subsequently derestricted by the OECD Council on 22nd July 1987.

TABLE OF CONTENTS

	Page
DEFINITIONS AND ABBREVIATIONS	8
INTRODUCTION	11
SUMMARY	11

CHAPTER I

INTERNATIONAL SHIPPING DEVELOPMENTS	15
General	15
World Shipping Surplus	16
General Agreement on Tariffs and Trade	16
US/CSG Dialogue	17
United States Affairs	17
EC Shipping Policy	17
The Liner Trades	18
United Nations Liner Code Convention	18
State Trading Shipping Lines	18
United Nations Affairs	19
- Ship Registration	19
- UNCTAD Committee on Shipping	19
- Maritime Fraud	20
- United Nations Convention on International Multimodal Transport	20
- Hamburg Rules	20
Activities of the United Nations International Maritime Organisation (IMO)	20
- General	20
- Maritime Safety Committee (MSC)	21
- Marine Environment Protection Committee (MEPC)	21
- Legal Committee	22
- Committee on Technical Co-operation	22
United Nations Convention on the Law of the Sea (UNCLOS)	22

CHAPTER II

THE DEMAND FOR SHIPPING SERVICES	24
General	24
Dry Bulk Commodities	29
- Iron Ore	29
- Coal	33
- Grain	36
- Bauxite and Alumina	40
- Phosphate Rock	42
- Other bulk commodities	43

General Cargo	45
Oil	49
- Production	49
- Consumption	50
- Seaborne Trade	51

CHAPTER III

THE SUPPLY OF SHIPPING SERVICES	56
General	56
The World Merchant Fleet by Types	58
- General	58
- Tankers and combination carriers	58
- Dry bulk carriers	62
- Liquefied natural gas, petroleum gas and chemical carriers	63
- General cargo and unit-load ships	64
The World Merchant Fleet by Flags	67
- General	67
- The fleets of the OECD countries	67
- The fleets under open registry flags and the development of offshore registers	70
- The fleets of the East European countries	74
- The fleets of the developing countries	75
Size and Age of Ships	76
Tonnage Laid up, Lost and Scrapped	79
Personnel	81

CHAPTER IV

THE FREIGHT MARKETS	84
General	84
Dry Bulk Freight Market	85
- General	85
- Dry bulk voyage and trip market	87
- Dry bulk period (time) market	90
- Prospects for dry bulk rates	93
Tanker freight market	93
- General	93
- Tanker voyage (spot) market	98
- Tanker period (time) charter market	101
- Prospects for tankers	103
- Freight futures market for tankers	104
Liner freight market	104
Bunker prices	104

CHAPTER V

COMMON PRINCIPLES OF SHIPPING POLICY FOR MEMBER COUNTRIES	107
Introduction: The Invisibles Code	107
Instruments complementing the Invisibles Code	108

    The Content and Importance of the OECD Instruments ..   109
    Attachment:
    - Recommendation of the Council concerning
      Common Principles of Shipping Policy for
      Member Countries   113
    - Annex I: Guidelines concerning the Transport
      Activities of Mobile Offshore Vessels   119
    - Annex II: Guidelines concerning Competition
      Policy as applied to Liner Shipping   120
    - Resolution of the Council concerning work to be
      undertaken on the sections of the Code of
      Liberalisation of Current Invisible Operations
      relating to maritime transport and in following
      up the Recommendation of the Council concerning
      Common Principles of Shipping Policy for
      Member countries   125
    - Annex: Procedure for Implementing Operative
      Paragraph 1   126

CHAPTER VI

    DEVELOPING COUNTRY PROTECTIONISM IN INTERNATIONAL
    MARITIME TRANSPORT SERVICES   127

    Introduction   127
    Types of Controls in Maritime Services   128
    - Direct Control of cargoes   128
    - Indirect protectionist measures   131
    Conclusion   134
    Annex I: Inventory of existing discriminatory
      cargo legislation and practices by
      developing countries   136
    Annex II: Direct Control of Cargoes   164
    Annex III: Indirect Measures of Protectionism   165

STATISTICAL ANNEX   167

DEFINITIONS AND ABBREVIATIONS

The following terms are used fairly extensively in the report and may not be entirely familiar to all readers:

-- Gross register ton (grt): the basic unit for measuring the total capacity of a vessel. One gross register ton equals 100 cubic feet. The grt is being progressively replaced by gross tonnage (gt) as defined by the 1969 Convention on Tonnage Measurement of Ships which came into force in 1982 but which contains a twelve-year transitional period.

-- Deadweight tonne (dwt): the basic unit for expressing the weight of cargo that a vessel is permitted to carry. A ship's dwt indicates the maximum weight of cargo stores, fuel and domestic water that may be loaded before her loadline (unless otherwise stated, the summer loadline) is submerged.

-- Very Large Crude Carrier (VLCC): a tanker designed to carry crude oil, with a tonnage of between 160 000 and 320 000 dwt.

-- Ultra Large Crude Carrier (ULCC): a tanker designed to carry crude oil, with a tonnage in excess of 320 000 dwt.

-- Worldscale: an index designed to express the current charter value of a particular oil carrier anywhere in the world regardless of the route on which she is operating. The basic schedule contains calculated US $ per ton rates for a vessel of specified characteristics under defined conditions for virtually all oil shipping routes. These rates are used as the yardstick (Worldscale 100) to express the current charter rate. Thus, W25 indicates that the charterer will pay the shipowner one quarter of the basic schedule rate per ton of cargo moved on the particular voyage.

-- Combination carrier: a ship designed to carry either oil or other cargo normally not concurrently. They include Ore/Oilers (O/O), Ore/Bulk/Oilers (OBO), Oil Products/Bulk/Crude oil carriers (PROBO) and tankers which can also load a limited number of containers.

-- Charter types - voyage or "spot" charter: the vessel is chartered to transport so many tons of cargo at a particular price per ton, regardless of the duration of the voyage.

-- Trip charter: the vessel is chartered for a specific movement on a daily rate (either per dwt or as a lump sum) without reference to the amount or nature of the cargo.

-- Consecutive voyage charter: the vessel is chartered for a number of voyages or a period of time with the cargo transported being paid for at agreed rates per ton.

-- Time or period charter: the vessel is chartered for a specific period of time on a monthly rate per dwt, with the charterer paying the cost of fuel and port charges.

-- Bareboat or demise charter: the vessel is chartered for a specified period of time on a daily or monthly rate per dwt or grt, with the charterer providing and paying for the manning, the maintenance, the insurance and the cost of fuel and port charges.

-- Contract of affreightment: the owner is paid by the charterer to deliver specified parcels of cargo at given intervals over a specified period of time at an agreed rate per ton, without a particular vessel being designated.

-- "Point-to-point" or "door-to-door" tariff: the indication of a single price per ton for a movement between one inland location and another, involving more than one mode of transport (road, barge, sea, rail, etc.) without giving a breakdown of the allocation of the price between the various modes. These are contrasted with "port-to-port" or "range-to-range" tariffs which cover only the sea leg.

-- Unit-load vessels: dry cargo ships designed to receive cargo which before loading has been consolidated into uniform units (packages such as pallets, trailer loads, containers or barges) to facilitate handling and transfer between transport modes.

-- Ro/ro vessels: unit-load vessels where the cargo is moved on and off using trailers normally carrying containers; a common characteristic of these vessels is their intermodal capabilities, i.e. their cargo can go directly into the highway system.

-- TEU: twenty-foot equivalent units. The basic unit for expressing the capacity for carrying containers upon fully cellular, part-container, or ro/ro vessels. The purpose of this unit is to put on a single basis, ships designed to move containers of 20, 35 or 40 feet in length, with a standard height and width of 8 feet.

Acknowledgements are due to the following for certain factual and statistical information used in this report:

Wm. Brandts (Timber) Ltd.
Institute of Shipping Economics and Logistics, Bremen
BP Trading Ltd.
H. Clarkson and Co. Ltd.
Drewry Shipping Consultants Ltd.
Fairplay International Shipping Weekly
Fearnleys
General Council of British Shipping
Hapag Lloyd
Harley Mullion Ltd.
Institute of London Underwriters
International Sugar Council
Intertanko
John I. Jacobs PLC
Journal de la Marine Marchande
Lloyd's List
Lloyd's Register of Shipping
Lloyd's Shipping Economist
The Petroleum Economist
The Platou Quarterly
Seatrade
Shipping News International
United Nations Conference on Trade and Development
United Nations Statistical Office

INTRODUCTION

The 33rd Annual Report prepared by the Maritime Transport Committee covers developments of interest in the field of shipping during 1986 and, wherever possible, the early part of 1987 and sets recent developments within the framework of longer-term trends in international shipping and trade.

Chapter I describes international shipping developments during 1986 in the context of national and international shipping policies. Chapters II and III discuss recent trends in shipping demand and supply and Chapter IV shows how the interaction of supply and demand was reflected in the world freight markets during 1986 and the early months of 1987. Chapter V explains the background and relevance of the OECD Recommendation concerning Common Principles of Shipping Policy for Member countries, which was adopted by the OECD Council on 13th February, together with a Resolution concerning the work to be undertaken on the sections of the Code of Liberalisation of Current Invisible Operations relating to maritime transport and in following up the Recommendation. Chapter VI analyses existing forms of flag discrimination and provides an inventory of existing discriminatory cargo legislation and practices by developing countries. The report is accompanied by a statistical annex which brings together the principal elements of international seaborne trade and bulk commodities, the world fleet and the various freight markets.

SUMMARY

Chapter I considers those developments and aspects of national and international shipping policy matters with which the Maritime Transport Committee and its subordinate groups have been involved during 1986. Although there was a substantial growth in overall demand for shipping services, this was not enough to restore a market balance in the tanker, dry bulk carrier and container shipping markets. The year 1986 started with severe financial problems for Hong Kong's shipping giant Wah Kwong and ended with United States Lines surviving only with the aid of the US bankruptcy code; overall the year was yet another disaster for world shipping -- one of many since 1973.

As in previous years, the Maritime Transport Committee closely monitored all developments directed towards safeguarding and promoting competition in shipping with a view to the expansion of the sector under conditions of transparency and progressive liberalisation. The Committee noted in particular the policy statement agreed upon by the United States and the Consultative Shipping Group, the adoption of a package of measures laying down the foundation of a common EEC shipping policy and the outcome of a GATT summit meeting where Ministers decided to launch negotiations on trade in services including maritime transport. Furthermore, the Committee continued to view with concern the non-commercial competition from certain state-trading liner companies operating as third-flag carriers as well as problems related to cargo allocation bureaux and pre-shipment control of cargoes by developing countries. Once again, some worrying extensions of cargo allocation were reported in West Africa.

The activities of the different organisations within the United Nations has occupied much time for the members of the Committee. The fourth and final session of the United Nations Conference on Conditions for Registration of Ships adopted on 7th February 1986 the UN Convention on Conditions for Registration of Ships and thus brought to an end eight years of work within UNCTAD covering the issue of open registries. In UNCTAD the discussions at the 12th Session of the Committee on Shipping centred on: i) the world shipping oversupply situation, for which it was decided to devote the main part of the 13th Session, advanced to early 1988; ii) the UN Liner Code Convention Review Conference, which the developing countries were reluctant to discuss as they were not prepared to agree a wording ensuring that the Code should be implemented "in conformity with its scope and provisions"; iii) the protection of shippers' interests, a vexed question which was finally resolved by a Resolution setting out a number of issues upon which conferences should consult shippers' organisations; and iv) UNCTAD's work programme for the next two years on ports, multimodal transport, technical assistance and co-operation between developing countries. The 12th Session of the UNCTAD Committee on Shipping also considered the final Resolution agreed by the Ad Hoc Intergovernmental Group on Maritime Fraud and endorsed the establishment of a Maritime Fraud Prevention Exchange Centre.

Within the International Maritime Organisation, regular meetings of the following main Committees were held: the Maritime Safety Committee, the Marine Environment Protection Committee, the Legal Committee and the Committee on Technical Co-operation. After the agreement of both IMO and UNCTAD, a Joint Intergovernmental Group of Experts met for the first time to discuss Maritime Liens and Mortgages. This meeting was primarily concerned with the procedural aspects and there was little discussion of substance. The UN Convention on the Law of the Sea will enter into force one year after 60 states have ratified or acceded to it. So far, only 31 states and Namibia have ratified the Convention. Work in the Preparatory Commission to prepare the ground for the International Seabed Authority continued.

Chapter II reviews the recent trends in demand for shipping services and makes certain suggestions on the directions these may take during 1987. Although total seaborne trade increased by 2 per cent in terms of volume following a zero growth in 1985, the year 1986 showed rather unsatisfactory results for shipowners. Measured in ton-miles, the 1986 results should have been more encouraging as there was an increase of 5.4 per cent against a decrease of 2.3 per cent in 1985. However it has to be underlined that this was almost entirely due to higher crude oil shipments -- 8 per cent above 1985 in terms of quantity and some 16 per cent in terms of ton-miles as most of the additional amounts originated from the Middle East. As regards 1987 the still over-supplied tanker market is entering a further year of uncertainty, because of difficulties in assessing the effects of the December 1986 decision of OPEC countries regarding prices and production levels. Developments in the dry bulk sector, on the other hand, were more than disappointing for shipowners. With a decline in steel production in nearly all major industrialised countries and very substantial cuts in grain shipments, due to higher crops and consequently lower import demand, seaborne trade in the three main bulk commodities -- iron ore, coal and grain -- showed a decline in both volume and ton-miles of about 5 per cent. Other cargoes, including liner cargoes appear to have grown marginally. For 1987 no significant upturn can be expected in the dry bulk markets as none of the major bulk commodities is likely to generate an upswing in demand for shipping tonnage, which could conceivably absorb the tonnage surplus estimated at between 15-20 per cent of the present bulk carrier fleet. For the liner fleet, the 1987 outlook is not much brighter as the gap between available container slot capacity and container transport demand is expected to widen again, in spite of an increase in the amount of cargoes.

Chapter III examines the evolution of the world fleet and its constituent element during 1986. For the first time, there was a significant reduction in the overall fleet, by 2.7 per cent in gt and 4.0 per cent in dwt, mainly due to the record levels of tanker scrapping in 1985 and early 1986, coupled with a rapid rise in the demolition of dry bulk carriers. Nevertheless there is still a substantial way to go before a healthy balance is attained in all sectors of shipping. Unfortunately, the short-term rise in the tanker freight market led in the second half of the year to a virtual cessation of tanker scrapping and an outburst of new orders, many of them speculative.

The fleets under the flags of OECD Member countries fell dramatically and in both Norway and Germany less shipping is operated under the national flag than under other flags. There was increasing competition between the longer-established open registries and a host of newcomers; this was complicated by the rapid expansion of "offshore registers" associated with OECD countries, a trend which is likely to have a very major impact on world shipping in the near future. A small number of developing countries, particularly in South-East Asia and the Far East, increased their fleets, to bring the developing market-economy countries past their target for the Third Development Decade, with three years to spare. Other sections of the chapter consider the changes in the size and age structure of the various elements of the world fleet, the improvement in casualties (other than those caused by war), the fall in layup and scrapping, and the trends to be observed in the patterns of seafarer employment in Member countries.

Chapter IV discusses how supply and demand interacted and were reflected in the principal freight markets during 1986. In the dry bulk markets, shipowners remained far from profitability as voyage freight rates fell to levels well below what could conceivably have been foreseen; in certain cases they were lower than those 35 years earlier. In the tanker sector, rates more or less stagnated at a depressed level until July but by the end of August they had reached a level twice that recorded a year earlier. They continued to increase in September, but the market then collapsed again. Nevertheless, the uncertainty resulting from OPEC price and production decisions caused rates to go up again somewhat at the end of the year. Voyage charters for the carriage of the major bulk commodities were down by about 5 per cent while period chartering dropped even more. On the other hand, a switch by charterers from time charter to single voyage arrangements was experienced in the tanker sector. The long-standing overcapacity in the liner trades once again made rate stability impossible during 1986. On a global basis a continuing slump in freight rates can be envisaged for 1987 and an overall recovery is still a long way off.

Chapter V explains how the common bases for the shipping policy of Member countries have evolved over the years and discusses the content and the importance of the two new Instruments adopted by the Council of the OECD on 13th February 1987. These constitute a new and coherent common approach to international shipping policy between Member countries and their relations with countries outside the Organisation. The texts of a Recommendation concerning common principles of Shipping Policy for Member Countries and a Resolution concerning its follow-up and on work to be done to extend and make more effective the maritime transport sections of the OECD Code of Liberalisation of Current Invisible Operations are annexed to this chapter.

Chapter VI reviews the various types of flag protectionist measures which have been encountered over recent years by the Maritime Transport Committee and lists the countries which have adopted them. A detailed inventory of these measures is contained in Annex I to this chapter, by country. Annexes II and III set out, in a summarised form, which countries operate the various direct and indirect measures of flag-protectionism.

A statistical annex brings together from a large number of sources essential elements of seaborne trade, the development of the world merchant fleet by flag, size and type and the indices which illustrate the various shipping freight markets, both in general for the long-term and in detail for the last two or three years.

Chapter I

INTERNATIONAL SHIPPING DEVELOPMENTS

GENERAL

Although the capacity surplus continues to be a major influence on shipping markets, 1986 saw further progress towards the restoration of a balance between vessel supply and demand. The tonnage of the world tanker fleets continued to fall, although to a lesser extent than in 1985, whilst seaborne trade in oil increased significantly. The rapid expansion of the dry bulk carrier fleet which has occurred in recent years came to a halt in 1986 in response to a substantial increase in scrapping and a reduction in new deliveries. The tonnage of dry bulk carriers on order has also fallen considerably from the high level recorded in the early 1980s, providing the prospect of further reductions in fleet size if scrapping rates remain high.

There were contrasting developments within world shipping markets during 1986. Tanker markets staged a significant recovery in freight rates from the spring in response to the fall in oil prices and the expansion of OPEC production, which resulted in an 8 per cent increase in the tonnage of seaborne oil trade and 16 per cent in tonne-miles, the latter reflecting an extension in the average haul-length. The increase in tanker freight rates led to the reactivation of a substantial element of idle tanker capacity, and laid-up tonnage fell from 36 million dwt to 13 million dwt during the year. There was also a sharp fall in the volume of tanker scrapping from 27 million dwt in 1985 to 13 million dwt in 1986. Towards the end of the year, freight rates fell back in response to the imposition of tighter oil production controls by OPEC and the movement of tankers out of lay-up. The fact that second-hand tanker prices have remained firm, however, suggests an underlying optimism as to the future course of freight rates.

In the dry bulk sector, freight rates were largely unchanged from their 1985 levels after allowing for the fall in bunker prices. Seaborne trade in the major dry bulk commodities fell during the year, iron ore and coal movements falling by about 5 per cent and 2 per cent respectively in response to a decline in world steel production. Grain movements were 12 per cent below 1985 levels due to good harvests in some of the major grain importing countries such as the USSR. However, the contraction in demand for dry bulk carriers appears to have been largely offset by a small reduction in the size of the fleet and by the transfer of combination carriers into the oil sectors. In the liner sector there was a modest overall increase in general cargo traffic during 1986 but the strength of the Japanese currency and the reduced purchasing power of the Middle East oil producers had an adverse impact on traffic volumes on particular routes. More generally, the expansion of container ship capacity ahead of demand has continued to put pressure on liner freight rates in a number of trades.

WORLD SHIPPING SURPLUS

The world fleet fell by a further 12 million dwt (about 2 per cent) during 1986. Tanker tonnage, which fell by 25 million dwt in 1985, recorded a more modest reduction of 7 million dwt in 1986, reflecting a 50 per cent decline in the amount of tonnage scrapped (to 13 million dwt) and a small increase in new deliveries (to 6 million dwt). The decline in oil tanker capacity, together with the increase in tanker demand already noted, represent a further significant move towards the restoration of balance between supply and demand.

Estimates of the size of the remaining tanker surplus tend to vary depending upon the allowance made for slow steaming and additional time spent in port. Upper estimates suggest that the surplus could still be of the order of 70 million dwt, representing 27 per cent of the world tanker fleet. However experience during 1986 shows that demand increases which fall well short of eliminating the excess capacity can lead to substantial increases in freight rates, at least for short periods.

In the dry bulk sector the volume of scrapping almost doubled in 1986 to 14 million dwt. With new deliveries falling below 12 million dwt, the size of the bulk carrier fleet fell marginally, bringing to an end the long period of expansion which had resulted in the fleet doubling its size since 1972. Estimates of the current bulk carrier tonnage surplus range from 38 million dwt to 50 million dwt. If the lower figure is correct, the increase in demand and adjustments to fleet capacity through scrapping required to bring the market into balance would be relatively modest.

GENERAL AGREEMENT ON TARIFFS AND TRADE

At the summit meeting of GATT in Punta del Este (Uruguay), Ministers decided to launch negotiations on trade in services, with the aim of establishing a multilateral framework of principles and rules, with a view to the expansion of such trade under conditions of transparency and progressive liberalisation as a means of promoting economic growth. A Group on Services has been established to develop this programme.

Within the OECD the Trade Committee, the Committee on Capital Movements and Invisible Transactions (CMIT) and the various sectoral committees including the Maritime Transport Committee, will be considering how the Uruguay Round should be related to the OECD's own work on trade in services. These considerations will also include an evaluation of OECD's general conceptual framework on trade in services, and its validity for the various service sectors.

US/CSG DIALOGUE

Following the joint United States/Consultative Shipping Group (CSG) Copenhagen Statement, which affirmed the importance of safeguarding and promoting competition in shipping, agreed in April 1986, the US and the CSG have continued to work closely together in furthering these objectives. Concerted representations have already been made to Peru and Sri Lanka, and further joint action is being considered.

UNITED STATES AFFAIRS

The Federal Maritime Commission continued the process of monitoring the effect of the 1984 Shipping Act by issuing a questionnaire to shippers, shipowners and terminal operators, an exercise which will be repeated annually until 1989. The 1986 Tax Reform Act contained two provisions relevant to shipping: it gave liner conference members the right of independent action on brokerage fees for freight forwarders; and it modified the provisions for taxing income earned by foreign shipowners within the US. Half of the gross income would be considered to have a US source, although bilateral tax exemption agreements with the US remained unaffected.

A system of fees was authorised for users of customs and immigration services. Although the Administration had expressed discontent with the Food Security Act 1985 provision to increase the minimum percentage of food aid cargoes subject to cargo preference from 50 per cent to 75 per cent, no repealing Bill was introduced during 1986.

In the field of bilateral relations, the agreement with Brazil was extended for a further three years, and a treaty with Iceland was approved which provides for the sharing of US military cargoes between US and Icelandic shipping lines.

EC SHIPPING POLICY

1986 marked a historic stage in European shipping with the European Community adopting a package of measures which lay the foundation of a Common Shipping Policy. In December 1986 Member States agreed on four important regulations providing for:

(a) The freedom to provide international shipping services to, from and between Member States. The Community has agreed to phase out by the end of 1992 unilateral cargo reservation laws and discriminatory cargo-sharing arrangements in bilateral agreements;

(b) The establishment of a Community competition regime by laying down detailed rules for the application of Articles 85 and 86 of the Treaty establishing the European Economic Community to maritime transport;

(c) Powers to take concerted Community action to combat protectionism from third countries;

(d) Powers to counter unfair pricing practices, particularly from state trading lines.

The Community States have not yet been able to reach agreement on the liberalisation of cabotage trades and negotiations on this are to continue.

The Member States of the Community have also agreed to move straight to the further development of policies aimed at the harmonization of aids given by Community governments to their merchant fleet and at ways of strengthening the position of the Community shipping industry in world shipping markets.

THE LINER TRADES

The desire of many developing countries to direct cargoes to their national shipping lines and to reduce competition from non-conference lines continued to be a major problem for most OECD countries. The problems of cargo allocation offices and pre-shipment control of cargoes by developing countries were not resolved and during the year some worrying extensions of cargo allocations were reported in West Africa.

The setting up of a "focal point" within the OECD for gathering information on restrictive practices of developing countries should prove valuable for the dissemination of information on protectionist practices and possible subsequent co-ordinated resistance by interested Member countries.

UNITED NATIONS LINER CODE CONVENTION

France was the only OECD country to accede to this Convention in 1986 and did so in accordance with the provision of EC Regulation 954/79. Preliminary work commenced on the preparations for the 1988 Review Conference, both at the UNCTAD Committee on Shipping and in other international fora.

STATE TRADING SHIPPING LINES

As in 1985, non-commercial competition from state trading lines, particularly those of the USSR, remains a cause of concern to a number of western governments and their shipowners. The detailed monitoring of Soviet carryings and freight rates between Northern Europe and East Africa, Central America and the Far East, announced in 1985, was introduced by the Governments of Belgium, France, the Federal Republic of Germany, the Netherlands and the United Kingdom.

UNITED NATIONS AFFAIRS

Ship Registration

As mentioned in the 1985 Annual Report, the fourth and final session of the United Nations Conference on Conditions for the Registration of Ships adopted on 7th February 1986 the UN Convention on Conditions for the Registration of Ships. The Convention is open for signature from May 1986 until 30th April 1987. It will come into force only when 40 states, with at least 25 per cent of world shipping tonnage (in grt) under their flag, have become parties to it. The following six countries have signed the Convention with intent to ratify: Bolivia, Cameroon, Mexico, Morocco, Senegal and the USSR.

UNCTAD Committee on Shipping

The 12th Session of the UNCTAD Committee on Shipping was held in Geneva from 10th-21st November 1986. The meeting was a low-key one with a markedly less political climate than previous sessions. Discussions ranged over a number of important areas and several Resolutions were agreed.

In particular, the Committee urged states to consider taking national measures to bring about a more balanced situation in world shipping and shipbuilding. It invited states to consider scrapping incentives and recommended restraint in the ordering of new buildings. It requested the UNCTAD Secretariat to convene the next session of the Committee in early 1988 to consider primarily the imbalance between supply and demand in world shipping.

The Committee succeeded in agreeing a Resolution on the question of the protection of shippers' interests, which had been left over from the 11th Session. The Resolution sets out a number of issues upon which conferences should consult shippers' organisations and invites the latter to co-operate more closely with one another. States are also invited to encourage the relevant parties to agree upon the calculation and operation of bunker and currency adjustment factors on the basis of equitable cost recovery. The 14th Session is to review the situation with regard to shippers' interests in the light of a report by the UNCTAD Secretariat.

The Committee also adopted a Resolution inviting States to consider signing and ratifying the UN Convention on Conditions for the Registration of Ships, as well as a Resolution covering multimodal transport and technological developments, ports, maritime fraud, model clauses on marine hull and cargo insurance, technical assistance and training and co-operation among developing countries in shipping, ports and multimodal transport.

On the Code of Conduct for Liner Conferences, despite considerable discussion, it was not possible to agree a Resolution going any further than the 1984 Resolution 50 (11). In particular, the Group of 77 was not prepared to agree a wording to try and ensure that the Code is implemented "in conformity with its scope and provisions".

Maritime Fraud

The twelfth session of the Committee on Shipping considered the final Resolution agreed by the Ad Hoc Intergovernmental Group on Maritime Fraud which had met during 1984 and 1985. The Ad Hoc Group had been established by the tenth session of the Committee on Shipping in June 1982 to consider means of combatting maritime fraud. In particular, the twelfth session considered proposals made by the UNCTAD Secretariat for the establishment of a Maritime Fraud Prevention Exchange. These proposals, which were designed to improve the availability and dissemination of ship-related information relevant to combatting maritime fraud, were agreed by the Committee. The UNCTAD Secretariat will monitor progress in this field and participate in the preparatory working groups which will be set up to advance progress and facilitate the early establishment of the Exchange. It is planned that the Exchange will be set up and paid for on a commercial basis.

The UNCTAD Secretariat will also monitor progress on the work on seaway bills, both in liner and tramp shipping, being undertaken by the relevant international organisations. A training programme on measures to combat maritime fraud will be developed by the UNCTAD Secretariat in co-operation with relevant national and international organisations.

The outcome of the discussions on this subject at the twelfth session of the Committee on Shipping was satisfactory to the developed market-economy countries and the proposed future work is practicable and realistic.

United Nations Convention on International Multimodal Transport

The Convention will enter into force 12 months after the governments of 30 states have become contracting parties to it. As of the end of 1986, only four states, Chile, Malawi, Mexico and Senegal, had ratified it and three others, Morocco, Norway and Venezuela, had signed the Convention subject to ratification.

Hamburg Rules

The United Nations Convention on the Carriage of Goods by Sea 1978 will enter into force after the governments of 20 states have become contracting parties to it. As of the end of 1986, 11 states, Barbados, Chile, Egypt, Hungary, Lebanon, Morocco, Romania, Senegal, Tanzania, Tunisia and Uganda, have ratified or acceded to it.

ACTIVITIES OF THE UNITED NATIONS INTERNATIONAL MARITIME ORGANISATION

General

By 31st December 1986, membership of the Organisation had risen to 130 member states, plus one associate member. The Council met twice during the year, in June and November, and as a result of a decision by the November Council, an Ad Hoc Group is to be established to consider a draft convention for the Suppression of Unlawful Acts against the Safety of Maritime Navigation. This Group is scheduled to meet twice during 1987, following which the draft convention will be examined by the Legal Committee before a Diplomatic Conference is convened to adopt it.

During the year, the Convention on Limitation of Liability for Maritime Claims 1976, the 1983 Amendments to the International Convention for the Safety of Life at Sea 1974 as amended, and the 1986 Amendments to the Convention on Facilitation of International Maritime Traffic 1965 as amended, entered into force. In addition, the 1984 Amendments to the Annex to the 1978 MARPOL Protocol entered into force. The 1985 Amendments to Protocol I and Annex II of MARPOL will enter into force on 6th April 1987.

Maritime Safety Committee (MSC)

During 1986 the Maritime Safety Committee held two meetings. A major new item related to Assembly Resolution A.584(14), which requested the MSC to deal with the question of passenger and crew security, following the hijacking of the Italian-flag cruise ship "Achille Lauro". In response to the Assembly's request, the Committee developed and unanimously approved measures intended to assist Member governments when reviewing and strengthening, as necessary, port and on-board security.

The MSC gave further consideration to the procedures for introducing the Future Global Maritime Distress and Safety System (FGMDSS) into the SOLAS Convention and decided that a frequency of 406 MHz should be used and that the carriage of float-free satellite emergency position-indicating radio beacons (EPIRBs) should be mandatory. However the MSC decided that the 1.6 GHz system, if proved to be satisfactory, may be used in certain areas as an alternative to the mandatory 406 MHz frequency of the COSPAS/SARSAT system.

Agreement in principle was reached on the use of ship identification numbers which would be inserted, on a voluntary basis, on ships' certificates. These "IMO numbers" would be based on the Lloyd's Register numbers allocated to ships at the time of inclusion in the Register. The Committee considers that the use of these unique numbers might be helpful for identification purposes in combatting fraud and import state control procedures.

Marine Environment Protection Committee (MEPC)

The major item before the MEPC was work in relation to the implementation of Annex II of MARPOL 73/78. In particular, the MEPC developed "Guidelines for Surveys under Annex II" and "Procedures for the Control for Ships and Discharges under Annex II" and developed Unified Interpretations of the Provisions of Annex II. This work was given priority because of the implementation date for Annex II of 6th April 1987.

Bearing in mind the imminent entry into force of the revised Protocol I of MARPOL 73/78 (on reporting) and the expected fulfilment of the conditions to bring Annex III (dealing with the prevention of pollution from dangerous goods carried in package form) into force, the MEPC continued its work on the identification of marine pollutants and approved an initial list for inclusion in a Code on the matter.

The Committee endorsed the recommendations of an Advisory Group convened for the purpose of providing advice on arrangements for combatting major incidents or threats of marine pollution, in implementation of Assembly Resolution A.587(14). It also continued its work on the anti-pollution manuals and gave initial consideration to the need to identify "particularly sensitive areas" and to whether, inter alia, ships' routing measures need to be adopted near or in such areas, including the possible designation of these areas after identification, as areas to be avoided as much as possible.

Legal Committee

The Legal Committee has continued its consideration of the question of salvage and related issues, in particular the revision of the 1910 Convention on Salvage and Assistance at Sea. The Committee completed its final reading of the Draft Salvage Convention prepared by the Comité Maritime International (CMI), at its 57th Session in October 1986. It is expected that a Diplomatic Conference will be convened in 1988 or 1989 to adopt the convention.

Following approval by both IMO and UNCTAD, the Joint Inter-Governmental Group of Experts (JIGE) met for the first time in Geneva in December 1986 to discuss Maritime Liens and Mortgages. The Group completed its consideration of procedural matters at this Session. The next JIGE meeting is to be held in London in May 1987 when consideration will be given to substantive work, probably based on the CMI draft revision of the 1967 Convention on Maritime Liens and Mortgages.

Committee on Technical Co-operation

The Committee continued with its task of attracting funds from donor countries to assist developing countries to operate and regulate shipping in accordance with the requirements of the various IMO Conventions. There are three main planks to this programme. First is the encouragement of fellowships for developing country nominees to attend courses of training at maritime and other educational establishments in developed countries. Second is the work of donor countries to set up maritime training establishments in developing countries, to assist with the drafting of legislation for maritime safety in those countries and provide expertise in other related safety areas such as hydrographic surveying and the development of technical fault operations programmes. Third is the provision of assistance in the administration of maritime legislation in accordance with the IMO Conventions. Another facet of the Committee's work is to encourage co-operation and funding for the World Maritime University by financial contributions, by the provision of fellowships, by the provision of facilities for on-the-job training and by technical assistance by donor countries, agencies and organisations.

UNITED NATIONS CONVENTION ON THE LAW OF THE SEA (UNCLOS)

The Law of the Sea Convention sets out a comprehensive regime for the regulation of the world's oceans. The 1982 Law of the Sea Convention, which had 159 signatories, had been ratified by 31 states and the UN Council for

Namibia by the end of 1986. It will enter into force one year after the deposition of 60 documents of ratification or accession. At the final session of the Law of the Sea Conference in 1982, a resolution was passed calling for the creation of a Preparatory Commission (PREPCOM), to lay the groundwork for the International Seabed Authority, the entity which will be responsible for the regulation of mining activities on the seabed beyond national jurisdiction.

The discussions in PREPCOM continued. In March-April 1986, the Fourth Session was held in Kingston, Jamaica. Little progress was made on most issues. A Declaration proposed by the Group of 77, declaring the licences for deep-seabed mining issued by the Federal Republic of Germany and the United Kingdom to be illegal, was adopted on a vote. Informal consultations took place between interested parties on conflict resolution (overlap between mining sites). These focus in particular on the Arusha Understanding (AU) worked out in February between the Chairman of PREPCOM, Mr. Warioba, and the four applicants for registration as pioneer applicants under Resolution II, France, India, Japan and the USSR. The Acting Chairman reported at the end of the meeting that, in his view, most delegates believed the AU was a good basis for resolving conflicts but that more consultations were necessary.

The Fourth Session continued in New York in August. It was dominated by the issues of conflict resolution and the registration of pioneer interests. The PREPCOM reached agreement on an understanding which opens the way for registration of the mine sites of France, India, Japan and the Soviet Union at the next session. This understanding takes account of separate negotiations between Belgium, Canada, the Federal Republic of Germany, Italy, the Netherlands and the United States (all of which have interests in the private consortia which have invested in deep-sea mining) and the Soviet Union. At a meeting in Moscow in November, preliminary agreements were prepared for direct negotiations between the Soviet Union and the private consortia.

Chapter II

THE DEMAND FOR SHIPPING SERVICES

GENERAL

1986 -- Growth slower than expected in mid-year

Growth in the OECD area in 1986 was slower than expected. The fall in oil prices early in 1986, reductions in interest rates and the improved pattern of exchange rates did not lead to the optimistic 3 per cent growth that had been projected in mid-1986. However, the 1986 performance of 2 1/2 per cent for the OECD economy as a whole combined with an inflation rate of well under 3 per cent -- the lowest for twenty years -- can still be considered as relatively satisfactory. (1) Employment too grew moderately, however the overall growth of the OECD labour force meant that this was not sufficient to produce a reduction of the overall OECD rate of unemployment which remained at 8 1/4 per cent, the level since 1984. Major current account imbalances were again the key macroeconomic problem facing the OECD economies.

Two main factors explain the slowdown in real GNP growth in 1986, which was much more marked in Japan than elsewhere. Firstly, non-OECD countries exporting oil and other primary commodities cut back their imports from OECD countries much more sharply than expected. The fall in exports to non-OECD countries, and a large increase in OECD imports (especially of oil) from them resulted in an unusually high negative contribution from net exports to GNP growth for the OECD area as a whole, and for most OECD countries individually, including all major countries. At 3.6 per cent, the growth of domestic demand outpaced that of real GNP by 1.1 percentage points. Secondly, a wave of business pessimism, especially in Japan and Germany, led to cut-backs in investment spending late in the year. This pessimism seems to have been related to fears that the dollar would continue to depreciate in a disorderly fashion, rendering some planned additions to productive capacity unprofitable. The weakness in net exports for the area seems by now to have largely run its course, but that in private investment spending persisted into the early months of 1987.

As the increasing sluggishness of demand in 1986 was concentrated in the manufacturing sectors of OECD economies, the impact on the growth of industrial production was more marked than on GNP itself. The OECD index of industrial output rose by just over 1 per cent in 1986 (2.7 per cent in 1985), and a small fall was recorded in Japan, the first time since 1975 that industrial output has declined there. Reflecting the steadily improving competitiveness of US industry, manufacturing output accelerated in the United States during the year, although the year-on-year growth remained modest at 1 per cent. Within Europe, smaller OECD countries generally fared better than the four majors, perhaps because small-country trade with non-OECD countries and with the United States is relatively less important. On average, small-country industrial output rose by 3 per cent, and was particularly buoyant in Turkey, Switzerland and Portugal.

World trade growth continued at about the same rate (3 1/2 to 4 per cent) as in the previous year. Trade in manufactured goods and raw materials decelerated while that of trade in oil rose significantly for the first time for a number of years -- up by 8 1/2 per cent. Within the OECD area, there was a notable decline in the volume of Japanese exports. German exports also fell in the latter part of the year. Due to a general weakening of export markets, a strong home demand and exchange rate appreciation, both countries experienced a substantial loss in export market shares and a sharp increase in imports. On the other hand, exchange rate movements had little effect on US imports as exporters aligned their prices with those of US producers. There was a slow response to the depreciation of the US dollar and the volume of US exports failed to increase. A substantial different between import and export growth existed also for most European countries but this was largely the result of depressed exports to non-OECD regions.

The significant decline in oil revenues meant that oil-exporting non-OECD countries had to cut their imports, which fell in volume terms by over 20 per cent. Countries hit by declining non-oil raw material prices, which fell further than originally expected, also reduced their imports, because of weaker earnings and more difficult access to credit facilities overall. This contrasted with the development in newly industrialised non-oil-producing countries, which recorded a 6 per cent import/export growth. The development of import/export prices enabled the NICs to increase their current account surplus to over $20 billion, whereas the non-oil developing countries as a group recorded a deficit of $10 billion.

The current account deficit for the OECD area as a whole amounted to some $20 billion. Within this overall picture, the most remarkable development was the continued widening of the US current deficit to about $140 billion (plus 19 per cent), compared to the Japanese and German surpluses of $86 and $36 billion respectively. Excluding energy-exporting countries, most European countries registered higher external surpluses or lower external deficits.

Although total seaborne trade increased by about 2 per cent in terms of volume following a zero growth in 1985, the year 1986 was yet another disaster for world shipping -- one of the many since 1973. Measured in ton-miles, the 1986 results should have been more encouraging as there was an increase of 5.4 per cent against a decrease of 2.3 per cent in 1985. (2) However, it has to be underlined that this was almost entirely due to higher crude oil shipments -- 8 per cent above 1985 in terms of tons. As most of these additional quantities originated from the Middle East, the increase in ton-miles for crude oil shipments amounted to some 16 per cent. On the other hand, the development in the dry bulk sector was more than disappointing for shipowners. With a decline in steel production in nearly all major industrialised countries and very substantial cuts in grain shipments due to higher crops and consequent lower import demand (particularly for the USSR), seaborne trade in the three main dry bulk commodities (iron ore, coal and grain) showed a decline in both volume and ton-miles of about 5 per cent. Bulk freight rates remained at extremely low levels and in certain cases were lower than those 35 years ago. Other cargoes, including liner cargoes, appear to have grown only marginally. Faced with these developments, more and more shipowners were confronted with financial crises. 1986 started with severe financial problems for Hong Kong's shipping giant Wah Kwong and ended with United States Lines surviving only with the aid of Chapter 11 of the US bankruptcy code. Overall these failures, as well as the near-bankruptcies that were avoided by debt moratoria or guarantees of various sorts, all involved huge write-offs by the international banking community and other financial institutions.

Table T.2.A summarises the twenty-year trend of seaborne trade, from 1966 to 1986, as estimated by Fearnley's, giving the average annual percentage variations in tons and ton-mile transport performance for both dry cargo and oil shipments. Total shipments and transport performance for total seaborne trade and for each of the main commodities are given in Table T.2.B.

1987 -- Maintenance of growth in the OECD area

For the OECD area, economic growth is expected to expand at annual rates of 2 to 2 1/2 per cent through the middle of 1988, bringing the present recovery into its sixth year. The United States should be at the top of this range with Japan and Europe lower. Such growth rates are likely to do little to alleviate unemployment, which is expected to remain at about 8 1/4 per cent of the OECD labour force (about 31 million people). On the other hand, inflation may remain subdued at about 3 1/2 to 4 per cent. It is also projected that world trade will grow by 2 1/4 per cent in 1987 and by 4 per cent in the first half of 1988. Trade in manufactured goods may accelerate from 3 per cent in 1986 to 3 1/2 per cent in 1987 and to 4 1/2 per cent by mid-1988. World trade in oil, however, is expected to fall early in 1987, largely as a technical reaction to the steep increases during 1986. Thereafter, expansion at a 3 to 4 per cent rate is projected. These forecasts are subject to the usual areas of uncertainty related to exchange rates, oil prices and debt problems in developing countries. Furthermore, any major new protectionist moves could put at risk the projected rate of growth in world trade.

In spite of the expectation of continuing growth in economic activity, the prospects for demand for shipping services in 1987 do not seem to be bright. The 1986 dry cargo recession is unlikely to end in 1987, the oversupplied tanker market is entering another year of uncertainty as to the effects of the December 1986 decision of OPEC countries regarding prices and production levels, and the growing overcapacity in container shipping will face only marginally higher liner cargoes. All these factors suggest that on a global basis a continuing slump in freight rates can be envisaged and that an overall economic recovery is still a long way off. In the long run, market forces will certainly restore an equilibrium but it is for the maritime industry to decide now whether to sit back (as it has done for a couple of years) and wait for something to turn up, or to attack the ship supply side through newbuilding restraints combined with vigorous scrapping of existing tonnage.

T.2.A

THE GROWTH IN SEABORNE TRADE 1966-1986

per cent variation per annum

	TONNNAGE SHIPMENTS			TON-MILE TRANSPORT PERFORMANCE		
	OIL	DRY CARGO	TOTAL	OIL	DRY CARGO	TOTAL
1966-1967	+8	+3	+5	+24	+7	+16
1967-1968	+13	+7	+10	+20	+7	+16
1968-1969	+11	+9	+10	+13	+10	+12
1969-1970	+15	+7	+11	+15	+11	+14
1970-1971	+6	+5	+7	+16	+4	+11
1971-1972	+10	+4	+4	+4	+11	+6
1972-1973	+13	+12	+13	+18	+16	+17
1973-1974	-1	+10	+4	+4	+11	+6
1974-1975	-8	-4	-6	-8	-3	-6
1975-1976	+12	+6	+9	+15	+4	+11
Average 1966-1976	+8	+5	+6	+13	+7	+11
1976-1977	+3	+2	+3	+2	+3	+2
1977-1978	-1	+5	+2	-8	+5	-3
1978-1979	+4	+10	+7	0	+10	+3
1979-1980	-10	+4	-3	-12	+5	-5
1980-1981	-10	+1	-4	-11	0	-6
1981-1982	-10	-5	-8	-23	-3	-14
1982-1983	-5	-2	-3	-12	-3	-7
1983-1984	+3	+10	+7	+1	+11	+6
1984-1985	-4	+1	-1	-3	-1	-2
1985-1986	+8	-1	+2	+16	-2	+5
Average 1976-1986	-3	+3	±0	-6	+3	-2

SOURCE: Calculated from "Review 1986", Fearnleys, Oslo January 1987 and earlier Reviews.

T.2.B.
WORLD SEABORNE TRADE, 1976-1986

in million tonnes

	TOTAL TRADE ESTIMATE	CRUDE OIL	OIL PRODUCTS	IRON ORE	COAL	GRAIN	OTHERS ESTIMATE
1976	3 312	1 410	260	294	127	146	1 075
1977	3 399	1 451	273	276	132	147	1 120
1978	3 466	1 432	270	278	127	169	1 190
1979	3 714	1 497	279	327	159	182	1 270
1980	3 606	1 320	276	314	188	198	1 310
1981	3 461	1 170	267	303	210	206	1 305
1982	3 199	993	285	273	208	200	1 240
1983	3 090	930	282	257	197	199	1 225
1984	3 312	950	297	306	232	207	1 320
1985	3 293	871	288	321	272	181	1 360
1986 (estimate)	3 362	940	310	304	268	160	1 380

in thousand million tonne miles

	TOTAL TRADE ESTIMATE	CRUDE OIL	OIL PRODUCTS	IRON ORE	COAL	GRAIN	OTHERS ESTIMATE
1976	17 023	10 199	950	1 469	591	779	3 035
1977	17 453	10 408	995	1 386	643	801	3 220
1978	16 934	9 561	985	1 384	604	945	3 455
1979	17 513	9 452	1 045	1 599	786	1 026	3 605
1980	16 611	8 219	1 020	1 613	952	1 087	3 720
1981	15 662	7 193	1 000	1 508	1 120	1 131	3 710
1982	13 499	5 212	1 070	1 443	1 094	1 120	3 560
1983	12 580	4 478	1 080	1 320	1 057	1 135	3 510
1984	13 368	4 450	1 140	1 631	1 270	1 157	3 720
1985	13 065	4 007	1 150	1 675	1 479	1 004	3 750
1986 (estimate)	13 765	4 730	1 270	1 620	1 460	875	3 810

NOTE: Attention is drawn to the figures for grain which include sorghum and soya beans (in addition to wheat, maize, barley, oats and rye) for the entire period.

SOURCE: Fearnleys, Oslo, Review 1986.

DRY BULK COMMODITIES

Total transport volumes of the five major dry bulk commodities in 1986 are estimated to have declined to about 814 million tons, approximately 43 million less than in 1985. These commodities accounted for about 38 per cent of the total dry cargo shipping demand and about 51 per cent in terms of transport performance. For 1987, no significant relief can be envisaged. The steel industry, which is the main industry pointer for dry bulk shipping, since it generates most of the coal and all of the iron ore demand, faces an uncertain year; steam coal is expected to remain static or to increase only marginally; and the grain trades will have to face a shrinking market again because of higher domestic production in the major importer countries. The only positive development in the field of bulk shipping during 1987 should be a further reduction in the fleet as a whole but this cutback will not yet be sufficient to correct the gross surplus overhanging the dry bulk market.

Iron Ore

Fierce competition among iron ore producers in an oversupplied and shrinking market characterised 1986 seaborne ore shipments. After having recovered strongly in 1985, they experienced a serious setback and fell to 304 million tons (some 45 per cent of world consumption). Nevertheless iron ore was still the most important single dry bulk commodity in world seaborne trade with about 15 per cent of the volume of the dry cargo trade and about 21 per cent of the tonne-miles. Given the traditional market dominance of Japan and the EEC, this decline was largely due to lower imports to these two areas during the second half of the year after stockpiles had been replenished in 1985 and early 1986. Among other importers there were much less signs of slackness with significant iron ore importing countries such as South Korea, Taiwan and China continuing to increase their steel output.

Following an increase of just 1 per cent in 1985 to some 718.9 million tons, world crude steel output recorded another decline and fell back to an estimated total of around 696 million tons (-3 per cent). Within this global picture, the pattern was the same as that for several recent years, i.e. stagnation and contraction in the traditional steel-making regions of Europe, the United States and Japan and growth in developing countries, particularly newly industrialised countries. The reduction in output was almost universal in the OECD area, the only notable exceptions being Turkey (+20.3 per cent) and Yugoslavia (+17.6 per cent). In North America and Japan, production was around 7 per cent below 1985 levels and in the EEC the decline was even slightly more. Among developing countries, an expansion took place, especially in iron ore exporting countries such as Venezuela (+13.9 per cent), South Africa (+8.0 per cent), Brazil (+3.8 per cent) and India (+2.7 per cent). China, the world's fourth largest steel producer, also produced more and reached about 50 million tons, with most of the additional amounts coming from the new Baoshan steel works near Shanghai. Crude steel output in the USSR increased further and reached more than 156 million tons.

The principal reason for a decline in the OECD area was a lower steel demand inside the area as well as a considerable decline in net exports to the rest of the world. Steel demand in the United States fell by at least 5 per cent while smaller reductions occurred in Japan, some EEC Member countries and Sweden. Among the factors behind those declines were the sharp cutback in oil drilling activity (North America and the United Kingdom), the further deterioration in shipbuilding (Europe and Japan) and a decline in capital spending in the United States. Steel exports by Japan and the EEC to the world's main market -- the United States - were down significantly, partly because of a lower United States demand but also because of the value of the Yen and certain European currencies. There were also considerably lower shipments to China, the USSR and certain counries in the Middle East and Africa. Steel imports into the EEC and Japan, on the other hand, showed a tendency to increase and most of these additional quantities came from developing countries and Eastern Europe.

With the decline in crude steel demand, there were efforts to reduce capacity and costs by restructuring. However, the average rate of capacity utilisation was still only about 70 per cent. Due to plant closures and other developments, employment continued to decline but as a result of low prices, increased competition, especially from developing countries, and accumulated losses, OECD steel mills continued to operate at inadequate profitability levels.

The substantially lower steel production forced Japanese iron ore importers to cut back their total shipments by about 10 million tons to a total of around 114 million tons. Of the main suppliers, Australia and India were most affected by such cuts, losing out to Brazil, which increased its share in the Japanese market. Imports from these three major sources still made up more than 80 per cent of the total. At the end of the year, the stocks kept by Japanese steel mills were about 19 million tons, much the same as at the end of 1985. Of the EEC countries, Germany continued to be the largest single importer, taking about 37 per cent of the 120 million tons imported into the EEC, followed by Belgium, Italy and France. Of the total United States iron ore consumption of about 60 million tons, only about 15 million tons were imported (half from Canada, followed by Brazil and Liberia), although imported ores were significantly cheaper. The reason for this is that a number of major steelmakers have economic interests in US ore mines and consequently prefer these supplies over lower-priced import ores. It is estimated that about 80 per cent of US iron ore mines are directly controlled by US steel mills. Imports into Eastern European countries -- mainly Poland and Romania -- totalled some 55 million tons, the majority of which came overland from the USSR. Shipments to China amounted to slightly over 10 million tons, as they have for the last three years, with three-quarters originating from Australia, while Brazil kept its 20 per cent share. A significant rise in Chinese imports is to be expected upon final completion of the Baoshan steelworks.

With the start of the Brazilian Carajas project, exports increased by about 4 per cent to some 95 million tons, of which almost half were taken by Japan and Germany. The remainder went to 40 other countries all over the world. By the end of 1986 shipments from Carajas were running at 15 million tons per year and are expected to increase to some 35 million tons when total capacity output is reached in 1988 or 1989. To secure purchasers for these quantities, a number of new long-term supply agreements were negotiated and it is reported that these were successfully concluded with USSR and Chinese interests. However, the other main exporter, Australia, had to register 7 per cent less shipments as higher exports to China and Western Europe were not large enough to compensate for the Japanese cutbacks. Both Brazil and Australia increased their efforts to diversify away from the European and Japanese markets, which can only show satisfactory results in the long run. Aggressive marketing policy pursued by the Indian state agency responsible for iron ore marketing succeeded in pushing up Indian sales to a total of 31 million tons (+6 per cent). Exports were mainly destined for Romania, South Korea and Japan. However, moves to penetrate the Western European markets were not successful. Canadian exports declined, on the other hand, by almost 10 per cent to 29 million tons; lower shipments were reported by all main importing countries. Together these four main exporting countries supplied about three-quarters of the seaborne movements. In Africa, mine closures and production problems resulted in reduced exports, but South Africa managed to keep up its 1985 level of about 11 million tons.

With both the EEC and Japanese steel mills cutting back production, iron ore producers were forced to concede price cuts. Negotiations proved to be a rather protracted affair and cuts varied from producer to producer but most price changes were around 4 to 5 per cent. In real terms, importers made even larger savings as prices are normally fixed in dollars, whose value depreciated against currencies of most importers. Because of this and although mine production costs have been reduced during recent years, a large number of mining companies had difficulties in achieving a positive result. It was therefore not surprising that 1986 saw continued cutbacks in production capacity, with closures taking place primarily in North America and Western Europe. With the near completion of the Carajas project (whose reserves are calculated at 18 billion tons), an era of more than ten years of worldwide planning and construction of new iron ore mines will come to an end.

These trade developments have led to increasing movements to developing countries with size restrictions in many of their steel ports. Since there has also been a transfer of combination carriers out of ore in order to take advantage of the short-term swings in oil freight rates, it is not surprising that the size breakdown of vessels employed in iron ore trades changed during the year. For the first time for many years, less cargo was shipped by vessels above 80 000 dwt, although shipments were still dominated by this size category. Vessels in the 40 to 80 000 dwt range are estimated to have increased their carryings from about 19 per cent in 1985 to approximately 21 per cent in 1986, which contributed to a reduction in that sector's tonnage surplus. However, it cannot be expected that this trend will continue during the years to come. Developing steel producing countries are making serious efforts to improve their terminal facilities in order to benefit from the economies of scale of larger vessels and certain developed market economy countries are employing, or are trying to employ, vessels above 300 000 dwt. With the opening of the Ponta da Meideira iron ore terminal to serve the Carajas project, an increased use of such vessels in the trades to Japan and Europe can be expected. During 1987 five vessels in excess of 300 000 dwt will come into service.

Shipping arrangements, however, showed little change. The majority of iron ore exports to Japan was executed by long-term charter, whereas European steelmakers organised most of their shipments on a medium-term or voyage charter basis. Such shipping arrangements were to a large extent based on sales contracts guaranteeing long-term offtakes of specific quantities by importers. As a large proportion of the shipments is done on a contract-of-affreightment basis, with rates considered as matters of commercial secrecy, very little can be said about the profitability of iron ore shipping except for owners which operated on the spot market. For this market segment, the financial returns were disastrous, as ocean freight rates for spot chartering were the lowest for more than seven years.

Details of iron ore movements in 1985 compared with those of 1984 are described in Table IV of the Statistical Annex. Overall shipments, transport performance and shipping distance since 1976 are shown in the following graph.

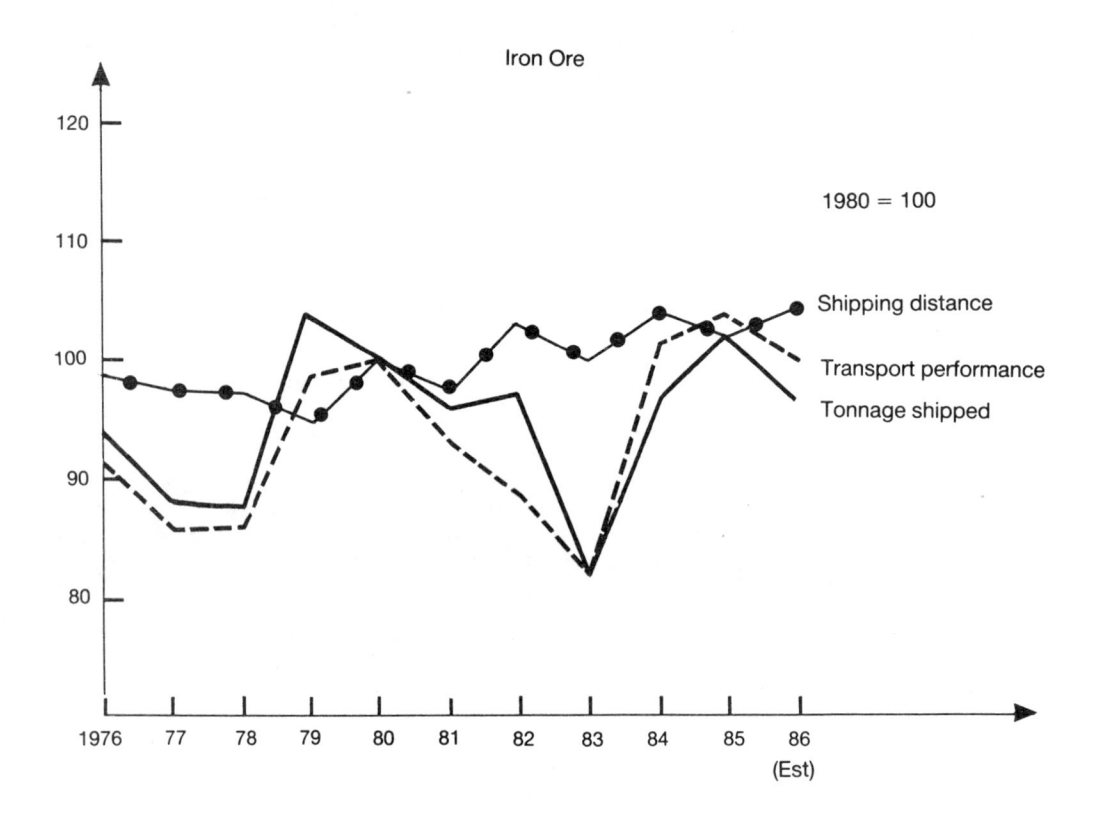

Iron Ore

1980 = 100

● Shipping distance
--- Transport performance
— Tonnage shipped

1976 77 78 79 80 81 82 83 84 85 86
(Est)

There are no firm indications that world steel consumption and hence seaborne trade in iron ore will increase in 1987. During the last decade, seaborne iron ore shipments fluctuated at around 300 million tons with the bulk of the quantities going to developed market economy countries. This will probably also be the 1987 scenario. However, with the emergence of steelmakers in developing countries, a shift in trade pattern can be expected in the long term. Domestic production will keep imports into Africa and Latin America at a low level but significantly higher imports are to be expected into countries such as South Korea, Taiwan and China as well as certain Eastern European countries. To what extent this will influence demand for bulk shipping services is rather difficult to assess at this stage, but it seems certain that such developments will not generate additional transportation demand but may, it is hoped, partly compensate for declining demand from industrialised countries.

Coal

The 1986 coal shipping scene was characterised by too many ships, rock-bottom freight rates, but only marginally less cargoes. After two years of significant growth, international seaborne coal trade had a disappointing setback in 1986. It only reached some 268 million tons, some 4 million tons or 1 per cent less than the record 1985 volume. This would have been even worse since overall coal trade slumped by 7.5 per cent, but long term agreements forced many major importers to maintain shipments at an agreed high level. Energy coal shipments accounted for about 48 per cent of the total coal trade, almost the same as during 1985. Overall, coal represented 13 per cent of the volume of total dry cargo shipments in 1986 and, due to the long-haul character of most trade movements, 19 per cent in terms of tonne-miles.

On the export side, the major trend noted in 1986 was a continuing increase in Australian coal exports in spite of an overall worldwide decline in traded quantities. Following the trend established in the past couple of years, record export tonnage of 48.7 million tons of coking coal and 43.3 million tons of steam coal were recorded in 1986, 4.7 per cent more than a year earlier. The underlying factor determining this surge was the policy of diversification away from Japan, with Europe, South Korea, Taiwan and other Asian trade areas becoming more important. Low production costs combined with high coal quality made Australia a strong competitor, particularly in the Pacific Rim but also, because of low transportation costs in Europe. Canada too performed well and shipped almost exactly the same as in 1985, in spite of two notable weaknesses: more than 80 per cent of their shipments are coking coal which is facing rather difficult markets and almost all of their steam coal is marketed in countries involving somewhat longer transport distances, whose freight rates have to be added to long rail haulage costs. Through aggressive marketing and the proximity to its markets, Poland almost maintained its market share and supplied 36 million tons to East and West European countries.

Although South Africa has the world's lowest cost mining operations and a specially designed low-cost transportation system that moves coal relatively short distances to the ports, it could not repeat its 1985 export performance and shipped about 11 per cent less. This was largely due to restrictive actions taken by a number of European countries, although South Africa was able to compensate for some of these reductions by exporting to the Pacific area. The other loser in the export market was the United States. US exports of both steam and coking coal moved up and down during the first half of the 1980s, and in 1986 they showed a decline of almost 20 million tons. Oversupply and low prices on international markets, together with uncompetitive f.o.b. prices for US steam coal were primarily responsible for this decline. In addition US exporters have to cope with a number of marketing drawbacks which were especially felt in the 1986 market environment, such as the high sulphur content of many of the low-priced East Coast coals and relatively long inland distances from mines to ports. In addition to these traditional exporters, there were a number of smaller exporting countries which tried to capture an increasing market share. Colombia is still in the early phases of production, but it quite significantly increased its exports, benefiting from favourable mining conditions, good-quality coal and the proximity of mines to its ports and to both European and Asian markets. China too made substantial investments in its coal production and exporting capability and for the first time shipped a certain amount to Europe. However, the quality was rather poor and the cargoes had to be disposed of at very low prices.

With regard to the demand side, 1986 was characterised by a decline in the established EEC and Japanese markets and almost sustained demand in certain developing countries. In view of the critical state of the steel industries in Japan and the EEC, most steel mills in Japan and, to a lesser extent, in Europe, reduced their purchases of coking coal and cut back contractual deliveries in order to prevent an excessive rise in stocks. However, countries with an increasing steel production, such as South Korea and Taiwan, as well as certain other smaller Asian countries, increased their imports of coking coal. On the steam coal side, the developing countries of the Far East maintained high import levels whereas Japan and Europe took slightly less than in the previous year. Trade flows (except from South Africa) remained broadly unchanged. The primary factor influencing steam coal demand is the price of oil and when oil prices plummeted in early 1986, suppliers had to make substantial price concessions in order to keep up the high level of steam coal imports. South Africa and Australia were the leaders in this, reducing their prices below the 1985 average by 32 and 15 per cent respectively. The United States and Canada followed with 7 and 9 per cent. As a whole, European buyers benefited from these developments by a price reduction of about 10 per cent.

Coal shipments by bulk and combined carriers over 40 000 dwt totalled more than 200 million tons, equivalent to almost 75 per cent in terms of tonnage and to about 85 per cent in terms of tonne-miles of total seaborne trade in this commodity. The long-distance trades from North America, South Africa and Australia to Europe and Japan continued to use a very large proportion of bulk vessels in the above 100 000 dwt size range, whereas most trades from European countries showed a significantly lower participation of such ships. Nevertheless, with infrastructure improvements in both exporting and importing ports, even these short-haul trades continued to change to bigger ships, since the volumes involved were large and substantial cost savings could be made by economies of scale. Due to the different buying and trading pattern of the steam coal trade, more handy-sized and Panamax vessels were used to transport steam coal than in the coking coal trades, for which the use of very large bulkers is much higher. Compared with 1985, the average trading distance showed little change and stood at 5 470 miles per voyage.

Efforts to improve and expand port throughput continued, although at a slower pace, in a large number of countries especially in the Far East. No further substantial coal port developments are to be expected in Europe since existing capacity in coal handling is already excessive. On the other hand, serious consideration is being given in South Africa to expanding the throughput capacity of Richards Bay from the present 45 million tons to about 70 million tons per year. Port infrastructure measures and projects in both Europe and the Far East are mainly concerned with improvement and expansion of transshipment facilities.

The pattern of seaborne movements by origin and destination in 1985 is shown in Table V of the Statistical Annex. Since 1976 total coal shipments, transport performance and shipping distance developed as follows:

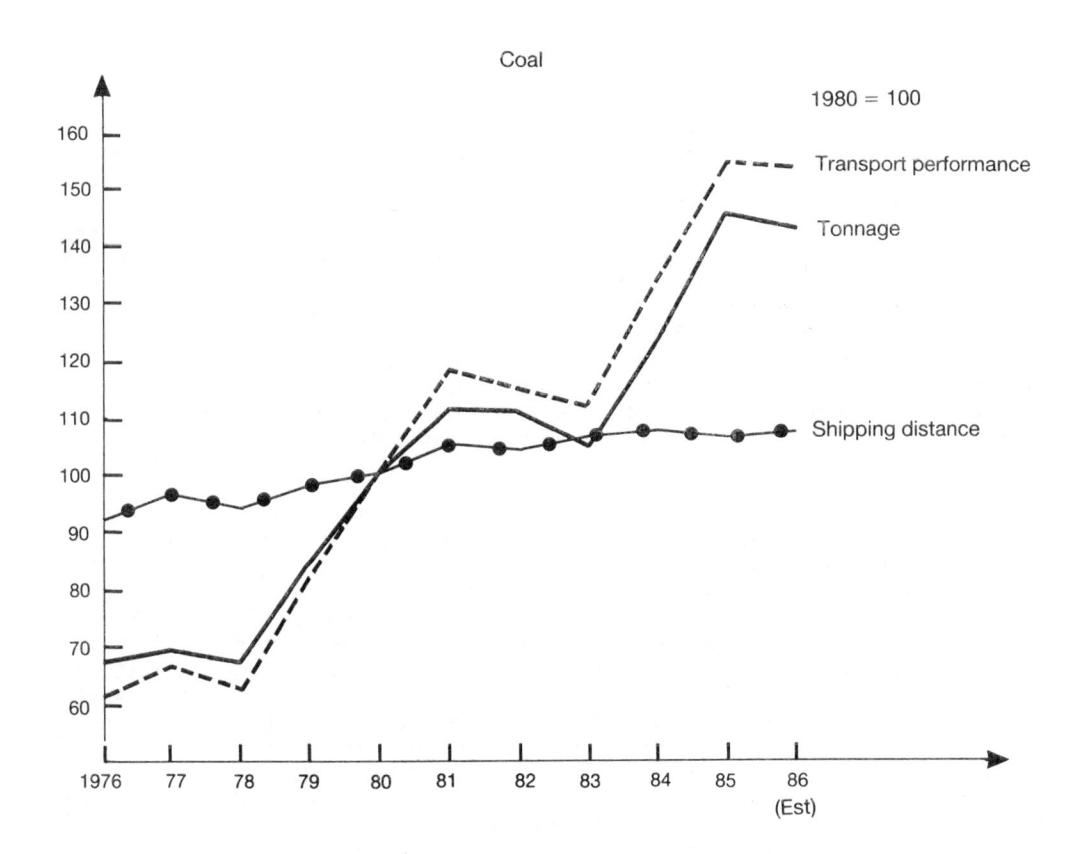

The primary factor influencing the 1987 seaborne coal trade is the price of oil since no demand stimulus can be expected from the world steel industry. Assuming that OPEC's target oil price of $18 is a realistic expectation for 1987, the cost advantage for steam coal will widen again and in view of a more than adequate supply situation at low prices, this should lead to higher steam coal shipments which will balance the expected decline in coking coal trading. Overall seaborne coal shipments could well be around 270 million tons. Due to action taken by certain European governments to limit and/or prohibit imports of South African steam coal, some additional tonnage will be required since it can be expected that Australia will take up much of the shortfall from South Africa. In view of the overall tonnage situation as well as the depressed prospects for other bulk commodities, in particular for grain, any additional demand will not push up freight rates to profitable levels.

Grain

A record world output in cereals, cereal stocks reaching unprecedented levels, a further substantial decline in international seaborne trade accompanied by freight levels at extremely low levels; those were the main features for grain in 1986. A decline in seaborne trade for two successive years brought it down to 160 million tons, the lowest level since 1978. This reflects the good harvests of cereals in a large number of main importing countries, particularly the USSR, as well as the inability of a number of developing countries to purchase the quantities they needed, because of their serious economic problems including low prices of many of their primary export commodities and credit restrictions. For dry bulk shipping in general and for owners of the smaller bulk carriers particularly used for grain, most of which are operated on the spot market, the 1986 trade slump had disastrous financial consequences since it was a main contribution to freight rates falling to levels at which owners were lucky to cover operating costs.

World cereal production for 1986 stood at 1 858 million tons, about 16 million tons larger than in 1985, which was itself a record. A higher output was realised in almost all producing regions of the world as well as in a number of the main importing countries. Production in developing countries increased by some 2 per cent to 946 million tons, mainly as a result of better harvests in the major producing countries of Asia, notably in China, India and Pakistan. Elsewhere, in Africa and South Central America the aggregate production of cereals exceeded slightly the good 1985 outturn. By contrast, output in the OECD area fell by about 4 per cent, mainly as a result of events in the USA as a consequence of the deliberate policy of a cutback of 7 per cent in the cereal area harvested. In Eastern Europe, larger outturns were realised in a number of countries but notably in the USSR where total production is estimated to have been 210 million tons, about 18 million tons more than in 1985 and 30 million more than the average for the previous five years. Of the aggregate world production, coarse grain accounted for 46 per cent, rice for 26 per cent and wheat for 28 per cent.

For the third consecutive year, cereal production was in excess of consumption, so that stocks reached a new record of 448 million tons, equal to some 26 per cent of world consumption. Most of this increase occurred in the United States and Canada and consisted of coarse grain.

Total world wheat production reached a new record of 526 million tons in spite of a production decline in the largest wheat producing country, the United States, whose 14 per cent decline was more than offset by gains elsewhere. Approximately half of the total increase of 21 million tons was due to higher output in Asia where several major producing countries harvested record or near-record crops. A sharp increase in wheat output also took place in the USSR (plus 7 million tons). On the other hand, the EEC's wheat crop showed little change from 1985 at a little over 80 million tons, although the EEC wheat area increased slightly. Of the other big exporters, Australia produced almost a million tons more, and the Canadian yield was about 7.5 million more. However, the Argentinian harvest was on a par with the previous year's 9 million tons.

Output of coarse grain was 3 million tons short of the 1985 harvest. Indeed many of the main producers lost ground. The United States' crop was down by 9 per cent to 251 million tons resulting from an increased participation in the 1986 acreage reduction programmes. A similar decline was experienced by the EEC, while more minor losses also happened in a number of other OECD countries. By contrast, crops in China, India and South America increased. A very sizeable improvement over the 1985 harvest has also been reported for the USSR where output rose sharply by 10 million tons to a new record of 112 million. The application of intensive technology contributed largely to the favourable outcome of the 1986 USSR harvest.

As a result of good harvests in a number of importing countries and continuing financial constraints on the grain purchases of many developing countries, total seaborne grain trades contracted to about 160 million tons, made up almost equally of wheat and coarse grains. Grain prices on international markets fell as a result of the oversupply situation and exporters competed extensively to maintain market shares but neither low prices nor any other buying incentives could prevent a trade decline.

Among the wheat importing countries, a substantially lower amount was taken by the USSR (13 as compared to 17 million tons in 1985), whereas aggregate imports by developing countries remained almost the same as in 1985. After the crop failures of the early eighties, good harvests in several African countries led to a decline in imports into that area for the second year in a row. With the exception of Pakistan, all countries in Asia took more than in 1985. Higher wheat imports were also reported for Central America but by contrast imports into South America fell.

Import movements of coarse grain showed different trends to those for wheat, although here also total traded quantities declined. The most notable difference was that imports into developing countries resumed their upward trend after having declined in 1985, in particular to South and Central America. As in the case of wheat, the USSR took significantly less coarse grain bringing down the total USSR share of imports from 26 per cent in 1984 to 19 per cent in 1985 and 16 per cent in 1986. The USSR, although still remaining the largest single importing country, reduced shipments from all suppliers, particularly the United States, and in a number of cases failed to take the quantities to which they were committed under long-term grain agreements signed with several important exporting countries. However, the second largest importing country, China, raised its imports to meet the general trend in consumption although its overall harvest also increased.

To promote their exports of cereals in a contrasting market, both the United States and the EEC expanded their export support programmes which put other exporters, notably Australia, Canada and Argentina, into a difficult competitive position. Despite the strong price competition, Australia managed to increase cereal shipments in 1985/86 by about 5 per cent, although it is not expected that this increase will be maintained next year. Canada managed to stabilise its shipments at around its 1985 level of 18.5 million tons, whereas Argentina had to accept the lower shipments that resulted from price competition. Apart from the major exporting countries, a number of other countries harvested good crops and had larger exportable quantities available. However, most of them had difficulties in marketing as they could scarcely meet the terms of sales offered by major exporters.

The decline in overall shipments was associated with a slightly greater decrease in transport performance. Expressed in tonne-miles, the total seaborne grain trade declined from 1 004 billion tonne-miles in 1985 to 875 billion in 1986, with an average shipping distance down from 5 560 to 5 470 miles. Higher short-haul shipments from the EEC to the USSR and less long-haul trade from Argentina to the Far East were largely responsible for this decrease. As in the past, bulk vessels in the 40 to 80 000 dwt size range dominated the trade and accounted for more than 50 per cent of the total while a large proportion -- around 40 per cent -- was still carried by vessels under 40 000 dwt. Nevertheless, 1986 saw again a confirmation of the long-term trend away from the under 40 000 dwt category to the 40/80 000 dwt bulkers, the latter being particularly used in the long-haul trades from North America and Argentina to Europe and Japan. The volume shipped by vessels of over 100 000 dwt remained small -- around 5 per cent -- due to the rather difficult characteristics of the cargo, including hygiene requirements, draft limitations in port and problems related to loading, unloading and storing.

Owing to the highly volatile character of the grain trade, it is not surprising that grain shippers tend to arrange shipments on the basis of voyage or trip chartering. This continued to be the case during 1986. Although it is not possible to say how much grain was transported under trip charter terms, it is not unreasonable to assume that at least 60 per cent of all grain cargoes were transported under short-term arrangements and as a result the sheer size of short-term grain charter arrangements made them again the main determinants of spot fixtures levels for other bulk commodities.

Seaborne grain movements during 1985 compared with those of the two preceding years are shown in Table VI of the Statistical Annex. Total shipments, transport performance and shipping distance since 1976 are shown in the following graph.

Grain

1980 = 100

Shipping distance

Tonnage
Transport performance

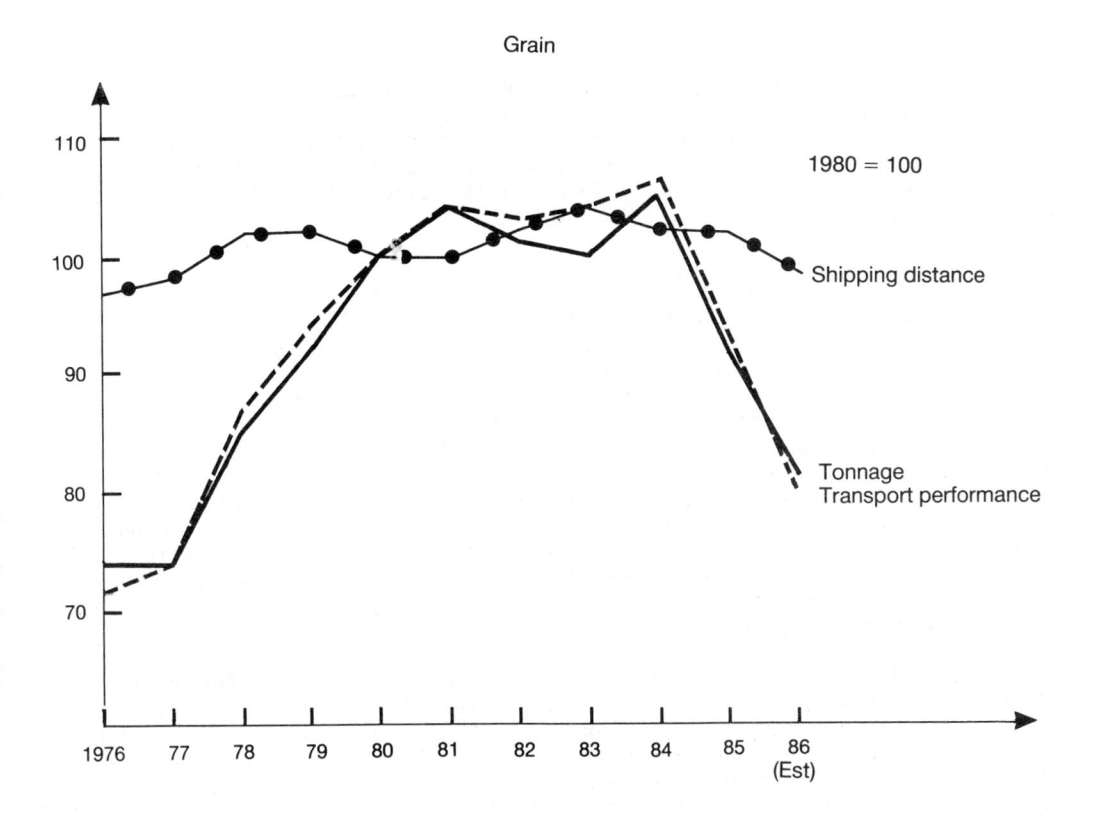

1976 77 78 79 80 81 82 83 84 85 86 (Est)

Prospects for 1987 grain shipments are not too bright as a further fall of up to 5 per cent in volume terms seems to be very likely. The 1987 market developments will probably be marked by: good harvests in importing and exporting countries; ample supply to meet import demand; intensive competition for markets; and a further downward pressure on prices for grain. The impact of these developments in the grain shipping market will be very considerable since total dry cargo demand for shipping services could decline and freight rates could remain at their present unprofitable levels. However, over a five-year period, the outlook is slightly more encouraging as a modest growth can be expected. By the end of that time, shipments could have come back to a level of around 190 million tons. The main import demand will originate from developing countries while little change is expected in the average import requirements of China, Eastern Europe and the USSR or in the trade shares of major exporters.

Bauxite/Alumina

With the continued moderate economic recovery in industrialised countries, an end to running stocks of primary aluminium products and slightly lower alumina prices, seaborne movements in bauxite and alumina stabilised at their 1985 level of around 40 million tons. Bauxite accounted for 70 per cent of this total. Overall, bauxite and alumina contributed 2 per cent of total dry cargo movements in terms of volume and for almost 4 per cent in terms of transport demand.

The world's top two bauxite producers, Australia and Guinea, continued to supply the vast majority of raw materials for aluminium-producing countries in North America, Europe (mainly Germany, France and Italy) and Asia. Other supplies originated from Caribbean, South American and West African producers. Alumina production (derived chemically from bauxite) reached some 11.9 million tons, the same as in 1985. Higher outputs were achieved in almost all producing countries except in the United States where there was a decline in production of 400 000 tons. As in the case of bauxite, Australia was the world's largest alumina exporter. Approximately 65 per cent of the total traded quantities of 12 million tons originated from that country and went predominantly to North America and Europe. However, whereas the bauxite trade is directed exclusively to traditional markets, i.e. North America, Europe and the Far East, trade in alumina is much more widespread as more than 50 per cent of aluminum-producing facilities running on alumina are located away from alumina-producing areas.

Shipments by bulk vessels over 40 000 dwt accounted for more than 50 per cent of the total seaborne trade. Vessels in this size range were primarily used for the longer hauls from Australia to the United States and Europe while smaller ships were generally preferred in the trades from Africa and the Americas. The sizeable intra-European trades in alumina predominantly employed handy-sized bulkers in the 20 000 dwt range. The average haul-length was 4 150 miles, reflecting little or almost no change in trade pattern. Unlike other bulk commodities, few shipments of alumina (which require dust-free vessels) were arranged on the open market. The highly integrated industry structure and major aluminium producers have incorporated the transportation of aluminium raw materials into their overall operation, using their own specialised vessels.

Table VII of the Statistical Annex shows movements of bauxite and alumina in 1985 by origin and destination. The development of the bauxite/alumina trade since 1976 is given below in the form of a graph.

Bauxite / Alumina

1980 = 100

Shipping distance

Transport performance
Tonnage

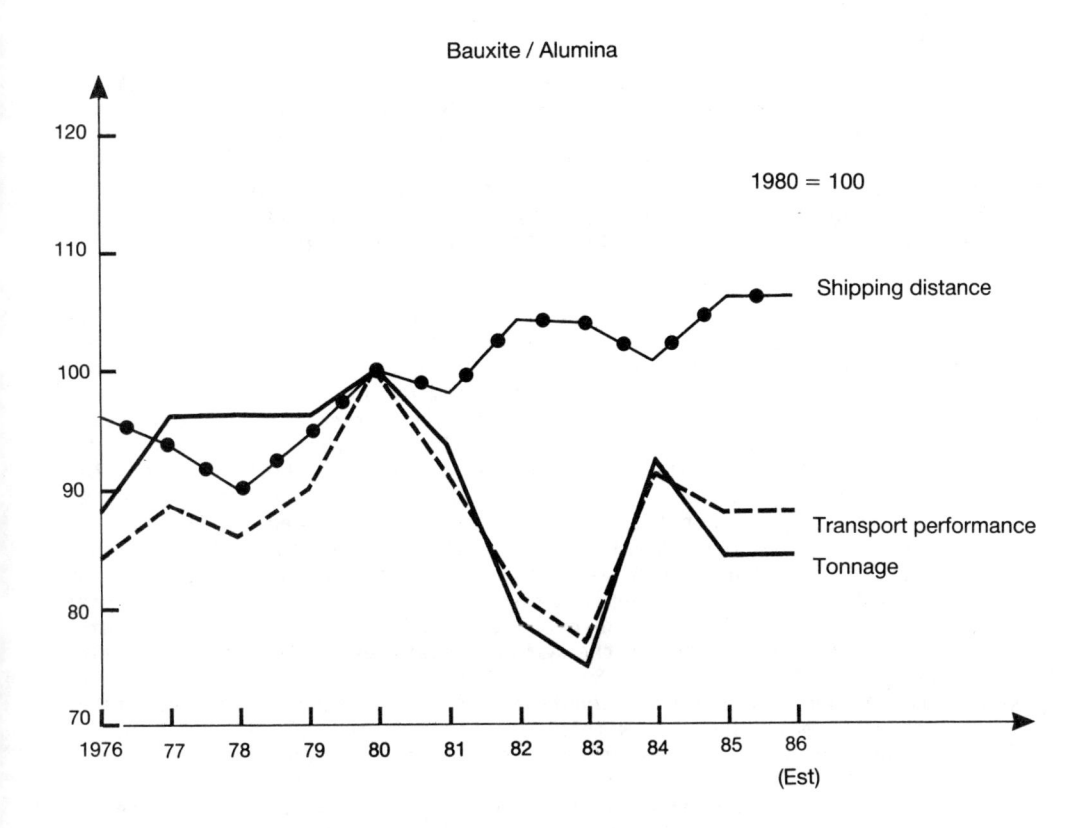

The 1987 prospects for the aluminium industry and hence for seaborne movement of bauxite and alumina are relatively favourable. During the last months of 1986, the development of demand was rather satisfactory and a large number of available indicators point towards increased aluminium consumption. However such an increase will only generate a modest increase in bauxite transportation whereas trade in alumina is expected to be more pronounced. Overall, it seems quite possible that seaborne trade in bauxite and alumina will again be in the area of 44 million tons, with an average voyage distance rising from 4 150 to about 4 500 miles.

Phosphate Rock

With an oversupply in the world's fertilizer market, international seaborne trade in phosphate rock showed no sign of improvement from the already depressed 1985 market and amounted to an estimated total of about 40 million tons, a decline of almost 7 per cent. These quantities were equivalent to some 25 per cent of world phosphate rock demand which was itself about 18 per cent less than world production capacity. Overall, in 1986 phosphate rock accounted for slightly less than 2 per cent of total dry cargo shipments.

Almost all rock-producing countries were affected by this decline in trade but the two leading world exporters, Morocco and the United States, which together accounted for about 60 per cent of the traded total, were particularly touched. Moroccan shipments were down by more than ten per cent because of significantly lower shipments to Germany and Belgium and the near-absence of sales to China, one of its largest single markets. US exports were marked by an almost catastrophic fall in shipments to India. This was largely the result of overbuying in the last two years, together with a further shift in Indian trading deals which sought to avoid payment in hard currencies and encouraged countertrade. Jordan, on the other hand, managed to increase its sales, in particular to its Asian markets. Many of these additional sales involved countertrade deals such as the trade agreement between Jordan and Indonesia whereby Jordan will supply phosphate rock in exchange for rubber, coffee, tea, textiles, plywood and cooking oil. In addition Jordan enjoys significant freight advantages in the Asian markets over other main suppliers like the United States. Tunisia, Syria and Iraq successfully expanded their market shares in Western European countries at the expense of Morocco, albeit on a relatively small scale. Within Oceania, Nauru Island and Christmas Island continued to serve the domestically-oriented fertilizer industry.

Of the total cargoes moved by sea, 50 per cent came to West Europe with France, Belgium and Spain taking more than half of this. Next ranked Asia, followed by Eastern Europe, Oceania and Latin America. Imports to all markets were lower in 1986 than in 1985 but the rate of decline was spread very unevenly.

With few long-distance trades, it is not surprising that the vast majority of the trade was carried by vessels under 40 000 dwt. Only the United States and Morocco recorded shipments of any significance by bulk vessels over 40 000 dwt but even in these trades, the trend towards using larger vessels slowed down. Approximately a third of the total was shipped by bulkers in the 20-40 000 dwt range while quite a large amount of cargo was carried by small vessels ranging from 3 000 to 5 000 dwt. In particular, these vessels were used in trades from the Near East, North and West Africa to Asian destinations. Given the stable trading pattern, the average trading distance showed little change and stood at 3 600 miles. As in previous years, only a very few shipments were arranged on the spot market since longer-term contracts of about one year tended to be the norm.

Table VII of the Statistical Annex shows movements of phosphate rock by origin and destination from 1983 to 1985, while the graph below describes phosphate rock shipments, transport performance and shipping distance since 1976.

Phosphate

1980 = 100

Shipping distance

Transport performance
Tonnage

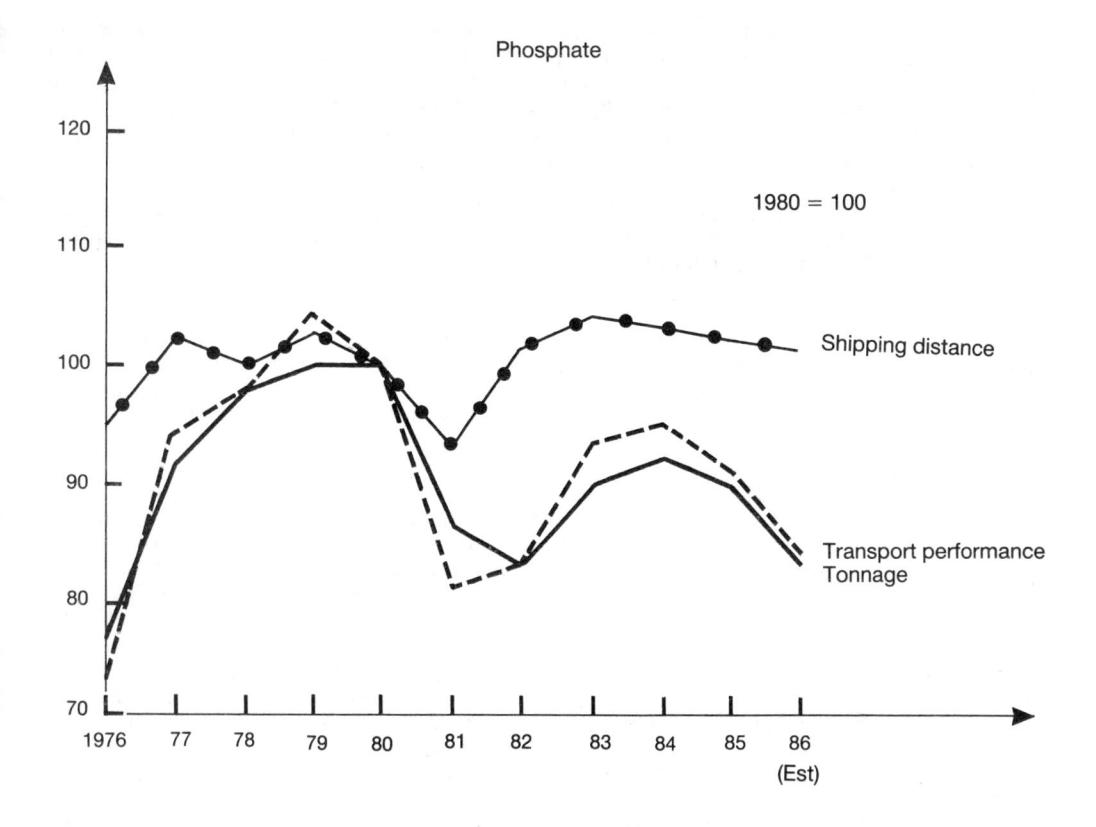

1976 77 78 79 80 81 82 83 84 85 86
(Est)

For 1987 there are no indications that seaborne trading in phosphate rock is going to increase, given the high fertilizer stocks kept in a number of importing countries. 1987 natural phosphate shipments will probably be again at about 40 million tons. Even in the long term, there are no real indications that rock trading will increase significantly because of the growing requirements of the vertically-integrated producers in North African countries.

Other Bulk Commodities

In addition to the five major bulk commodities, there is a substantial seaborne trade in so-called minor bulk commodities comprising a very wide range of cargoes including manganese ores, gypsum, salt, petroleum coke, sulphur, limestone, scrap iron, cement, non-ferrous ores, tapioca, etc. 1986 seaborne trade data are not yet available for any of these commodities.

Table XI of the Statistical Annex shows the volumes shipped in some major trades of these commodities for the years 1984 and 1985, representing about half of the total shipments of all the commodities listed. Shipments of these minor bulk commodities declined by almost 4 per cent, whereas major bulk trades increased by 4 per cent during the same period, mainly due to reductions in demand for cement by Middle East countries.

Shipments of sugar (for 1985 trade data see Table IX of the Statistical Annex) are estimated to have declined to about 25 million tons in 1986 (minus 5 per cent). Increased production in most regions, particularly in industrialised countries, accounted for a large portion of this decline. The world's largest importer, the USSR, remained at its 1985 level of around 5 million tons, of which more than two-thirds originated from Cuba. The rest was purchased from Australia, Brazil and Thailand. For 1987 a further overall decline in sugar shipments has to be expected as a result of a sharp reduction of more than 40 per cent which is planned for US imports of raw sugar.

Although most of the major European countries imported less softwood in 1985 than in 1984, total softwood movements increased by about 2 per cent, due to a significantly higher intake by the world's major importer, the United States (+10 per cent). More than half of the traded quantities originated in Canada. Other major suppliers remained Sweden, the USSR and Finland. Taken together, these four countries accounted for about 83 per cent of the overall trade, almost the same as in 1984.

The seaborne transport of steel products, cars and wood products is not covered by Table XI of the Statistical Annex although the quantities shipped are larger than any of the commodities mentioned. The reason for this exclusion is the difficulty in determining the shipped quantities as well as the large number of commodities falling under steel and wood products, which makes exact monitoring almost impossible. Nevertheless preliminary indications suggest that seaborne trade in these commodities developed along the following lines:

-- steel products: total 1986 seaborne trade in steel products declined significantly and experienced a considerable change in the volume of the various steel trade flows. There was a rather remarkable reduction in exports to the United States whereas the EEC and Japan had very strong increases in imports. In the latter country, the increase came essentially from non-OECD countries. In addition, Japan and West European steel exporters not only experienced falling exports to the USA but also a considerable decline in their exports to the non-OECD areas. As a result, OECD net exports of steel products to the rest of the world fell in 1986 by about 30 per cent to their lowest level since 1973.

-- wood products: world wood product trades again attracted increased bulk carrier activities. Higher shipments were particularly noted in the North America/North Europe trade but there were also brighter prospects in the Pacific trades to Asia, with increased shipments to Japan, South Korea and China.

-- automobiles: the 1986 car carrier market was again very active and achieved rather satisfactory rates at profitable levels. However profits largely depended on the carriers' ability to fill their vessels with cargoes on their return trips from Europe and the United States to Japan and South Korea. The fact that the trade remained fairly buoyant throughout the last few years led during 1985/86 to the entry of a number of new owners and with the number of vessels entering a largely protected trade, with long-term contracts, overcapacity, lay-up and accelerated scrapping seems only too possible within the next few years.

The total tonnage of all bulk commodities covered in Tables IV to XI of the Statistical Annex was 974 million tons in 1985 as compared to 952 million tons in 1984 and accounted for approximately 46 per cent of total 1985 dry cargo shipments. Table III(b) of the Statistical Annex describes the pattern of world seaborne trade carried by bulk carriers in 1985.

GENERAL CARGO

In all major liner trade routes, earnings declined in 1986. The depreciation of the dollar against almost all other currencies and increased competition resulting from overcapacity (3), particularly in the container shipping market, were the main reasons for this unsatisfactory development. In addition, non-commercial rating policies by a number of state trading shipping lines and flag discriminatory measures exercised by some sixty developing countries (see Chapter VI) contributed to the difficulties confronting liner trades worldwide.

Significantly lower liner imports were reported from countries dependent on the export of primary commodities as their export prices generally declined and their overall debt situation worsened. The benefits which accrued to oil-importing countries did not balance out these lower shipments and oil-producing countries reduced their liner commodity imports because they also had less money available.

The reduction in bunker prices and the slowdown of inflation contributed to a welcome reduction in transportation costs but were of little benefit to operators who were forced to pass most of such cost savings onto the shipper, due to the very competitive environment.

The world's main individual trade-routes reflected these general developments but also showed the following specific trends:

-- <u>Europe-North America</u>: the 1986 market scenario was again characterised by an oversupplied market, depressed freight rates and intense competition for the slightly higher cargoes available. Developments were especially influenced by liner companies which had not previously served this trade. In addition to the extremely low freight earnings, overall financial results were strongly affected by the lower value of the dollar, which also led to marginally lower westbound cargoes. However, this decline was more than compensated by higher US shipments towards European destinations, although westbound shipments greatly exceeded eastbound trade. During the next two years, trade movements are projected to increase in both directions but will not be sufficient to absorb overcapacity. On the contrary, the supply of shipping tonnage is expected to grow at a significantly higher rate than demand so that, by the end of 1988, a total overcapacity of about 35 per cent can be expected.

-- Far East-North America West Coast: despite rate increases and other measures decided upon at a series of meetings of the Trans-Pacific Rate Agreements and their associated conferences in early 1986, profitability in the transpacific market could not be restored as the fundamental problem of overcapacity continued to confront carriers. In addition, the decision of one of the largest and most aggressive participants in the market to quit two of the most important agreements added to the difficulties facing the trade. As during recent years, eastbound exports from Japan and the newly industrialised countries in the Far East, which account for almost one-fifth of total long-haul sea container traffic, far outstripped westbound movement, although the overall cargo volume level was reduced. Although measures have been taken to try to change this situation, it is almost certain that this trade imbalance will continue for the foreseeable future. Given the rapid rise that has been predicted for transpacific container capacity, the trade seems set for a period of continuing instability. By the end of 1988, the eastbound trade will probably show an overcapacity of about 50 per cent while the weaker westbound trade will be marked by an excess of more than 60 per cent.

-- Europe-Far East: westbound cargoes again showed an increasing tendency. Both Japan and the newly industrialised countries successfully tried to compensate for the losses they suffered in the export trades to the United States by higher shipments to European markets. A number of liner conferences and rating agreements succeeded in increasing tariffs but, overall, freight rates remained under pressure as shippers feared that rising transport costs were effectively pricing them out of the export market, even allowing for the depreciation of the dollar. European shipments to the smaller countries of the Far East -- notably Indonesia -- declined although liner exports to China showed an increasing trend. In this trade too, rates were not sufficient to compensate for higher transportation costs. Given the high value of the Yen, the westbound trade imbalance is likely to diminish and the routes will become more evenly utilised. While it is expected that overcapacity will continue, it ought not to exceed 10 per cent by the end of 1988.

-- ASEAN trades in the Pacific: container capacity in the Asean trades increased by 25 per cent during 1984/85, pushing the surplus to approximately 20 per cent, i.e. about one million TEU. Most of this additional capacity was due to new Far East shipping companies from Taiwan, South Korea and Hong Kong. Smaller countries in the Pacific experienced significant trade deficits with Japan but balanced these through substantial surpluses with the United States. Overall, the volume of trade available in 1986 was not much higher than during 1985 so that unremunerative rates were often the order of the day. Rates were especially threatened by non-conference lines. For the first time COSC (China Overseas Shipping Corporation) appeared as a major cross-trader and undercut conference rates by as much as 30 per cent.

-- Europe-South America (East and West Coast): eastbound cargoes from South America to Europe declined quite considerably, mainly due to lower coffee shipments which in certain cases hardly reached 50 per cent of the amount moved in 1985. Shipments to South America differed according to destinations. Imports to the oil-producing countries of the area declined as a result of lower oil prices. Given the difficult overall economic situation in Latin American countries, no substantial increases in cargo flows are expected and overcapacity is likely to increase by 20-25 per cent by the end of 1988.

-- Europe-Australia/New Zealand: measures to stabilise the overall economic situation in Australia and New Zealand, notably by the devaluation of the Australian currency, led to a sharp fall in southbound cargoes. On the other hand, the northbound trade showed slightly higher movements but not enough to balance the southbound decline. For the immediate future, no substantial growth in trade movements is to be expected, although an increasing number of outsiders are expected to reroute their surplus capacity to these trades, which could increase the surplus on the southbound leg to about 25-30 per cent.

-- Europe-Middle East: shipments towards the Middle East were about 30 per cent below those in 1985 and caused the withdrawal of a number of liner companies from these trades. Others opted for rationalisation or transhipment-based services as a better way to serve the area but, overall, the capacity reductions were not sufficient to employ the tonnage that was left at a profitable level. Despite an assault in 1986 by outsider wayport operators, shipowners on the Europe/Far East-Europe routes still controlled the main part of the trade. The 1987 outlook is brighter as rates started to harden towards the end of 1986 after months of downward movement. However, mainly as a result of some new round-the-world services, capacity will increase again in 1987, which could lead to more than 40 per cent overcapacity by the end of 1988.

-- Europe-North Africa: overcapacity, declining cargo volumes and low freight rates also characterised these trades. In addition they were affected by a number of administrative measures taken by some countries in the area relating to the transfer of freight earnings, payments related to the storage of containers, etc. The trade to Algeria, for example, was hampered by the introduction of a 10 per cent freight tax which, in addition to its effects on earnings, led to a certain discrimination among the companies serving Algeria, because some carriers benefited from exemptions derived from double taxation agreements which their countries had signed with Algeria. Oversupply will remain considerable, although certain adjustments in container capacity are expected.

-- Europe-East Africa: as during 1985, low cargo volumes and intensive competition marked the trades from and to the countries in this area. Soviet cross-trading activity was particularly noticeable and these lines acquired around 12 per cent of both the northbound and southbound trades. However the overall cost situation did not deteriorate from 1985. The outlook for this trade is rather encouraging as a number of existing infrastructure problems are expected to be solved in the near future, leading to shorter round voyages and thus a reduction in costs. Overcapacity is estimated to have reached around 15-20 per cent and will probably remain at this level throughout 1987.

-- <u>Europe-West Africa</u>: good coffee and cocoa harvests and hence higher northbound shipments led to a halt in the declining trend in overall cargo volumes over recent years. Overall the two directions were almost in balance and conference and non-conference shipping lines had nearly equal shares in the trades. There were different reactions of the non-conference lines to the increasing competition: recent entrants increased their activities while lines which had been in the trade over a long period withdrew or cut back their services. As in the East African trade, overcapacity is estimated at about 15-20 per cent.

To combat the hostile conditions which have persisted in the sector, liner companies have been taking steps to achieve greater efficiency and consequent reductions in costs. These included greater co-operation with other shipping companies through joint ventures and rationalised ship assignment, reduced levels of crewing, more cross-trading and expansion into the new area of intermodal services with transport companies offering comprehensive packages. However, in spite of this, overall financial returns in 1986 were calamitous, because of the large number of new container ships which came into service. This led to a worldwide surplus of as much as 30 per cent of available container capacity which triggered off fierce competition among all carriers. This huge rise in the available space with less cargo available to each operator led inevitably to low load-factors and hence to unprofitable operations, even where the rates were maintained. Unfortunately, there is little hope that this situation is going to change during the next few years, as no dramatic increase in trade movements can be expected which could absorb the existing surplus, let alone the additional tonnage which will come onto the market in the near future.

By the end of 1988 the container-carrying fleet of vessels above 399 TEU will amount to some 2 100 vessels with a combined capacity of 2.2 million TEU. This is an increase of 10.7 per cent in terms of vessels and almost 16 per cent in terms of TEU over the corresponding end-1985 position. West European and North American operators will control 54 per cent of this capacity (compared to 58 per cent at the end of 1985), while Far Eastern operators will control nearly 27 per cent against 23 per cent three years earlier.

Given the expected trade and capacity levels, it seems almost inevitable that a certain number of liner companies will go into liquidation. Financial disasters, however, do not provide other than very short-term solutions as the vessels owned by the bankrupt companies continue to exist. The obvious main task of the international shipping community is to get rid of a large number of container vessels, even although these are almost all relatively modern, so that trades can revert to a more balanced supply/demand situation. Measures to alleviate the existing surplus situation have to come primarily from the private sector and experience over the last few years in the bulk shipping sector has shown that intensified scrapping, if possible encouraged via subsidies by national governments, is almost the only method to achieve this. In addition, every effort should be made to avoid a further widening of the demand/supply situation. In particular, credits should only be granted for newbuildings where there is a clear evidence of ability to repay and a very substantial proportion of the equity in shipping deals is provided by the owner himself.

OIL

Production

World production of crude oil and natural gas liquids recovered strongly in 1986 from the depressed level of 1985, increasing 5.1 per cent from 2 730 million tons to 2 869 million tons. Output was strongly influenced by the changed policy of OPEC producers who pursued a vigorous policy of price cutting to increase world market shares in the December 1985/August 1986 period. In particular the members of the Gulf Corporation Council (Saudi Arabia, Kuwait, Abu Dhabi and Qatar) aggressively regained market shares which had been eroded by the combination of depressed oil consumption and increased oil production outside the OPEC area in recent years, both resulting from high oil prices. From a low point of 15 mbd in mid 1985, OPEC output reached a peak of 21 mbd in August 1986 prior to introduction of new restraints. From September 1986 OPEC countries again limited output and managed to achieve some recovery in prices which had been halved in the early months of the year. For the year as a whole, OPEC production rose 16 per cent to 950 million tons. This is reflected in an increase in the OPEC share of world oil production from 29.6 per cent in 1985 to 32.5 per cent in 1986.

T.2.C

WORLD CRUDE OIL (+NGL) PRODUCTION IN 1985 AND 1986
(Million tons)

	1985	1986	% Change
North America	576.6	561.4	-2.6
Caribbean	258.5	257.6	-0.3
Other Latin America	77.7	77.7	0.0
W. Europe	190.7	186.4	+2.9
E. Europe	615.6	633.8	+3.0
Africa	242.7	236.4	-2.7
Middle East	493.2	618.7	+25.4
Far East	274.5	297.4	+8.3
Total	2 729.5	2 869.4	+5.1

Within OPEC, Saudi Arabia, Kuwait and Abu Dhabi achieved dramatic production increases of 57 per cent, 49 per cent and 22 per cent respectively. Iranian production fell 15 per cent reflecting bomb damage on oil terminals and the tankers using them. The terminal at Sirri Island in the lower Gulf was badly damaged and Larak Island in the Strait of Hormuz was used as a main terminal. Iraq was able to increase exports by 23 per cent as new pipelines came on stream. Production among other OPEC members developed less dramatically with Venezuela increasing production 1.3 per cent, Nigeria reducing production by 1.6 per cent, Libyan production little changed and Algerian production down by 9 per cent. Outside OPEC lower oil prices began to have an effect on production levels. In the US, production which had been increasing steadily in recent years dropped by 3.3 per cent, reducing the US share in world production from 17.8 per cent in 1985 to 16.4 per cent in 1986. There was a further smaller increase in North Sea production, however, with the result that production overall in Western Europe increased by 2.9 per cent. While UK production was little changed Norwegian production increased by 10.6 per cent and sharp production increases were achieved by some of the smaller European producers (Denmark, France, Italy and the Netherlands).

With a high degree of success in overcoming technical problems in the industry the USSR was able to increase production by 3 per cent to 613 million tons. Since this rise was somewhat less than that for the world as a whole, the USSR share in world oil production fell from 21.5 per cent to 21 per cent in 1986. China, too, increased production significantly with 3.8 per cent gain to 130 million tons.

Elsewhere in the Far East, Indonesia, Australia and Malaysia increased production by 12 per cent, 22 per cent and 17 per cent respectively. India achieved a less dramatic increase of 3.7 per cent to 31 million tons.

Consumption

Oil consumption in the OECD countries ended several years of decline and stagnation with an increase in 1986 of about 3 per cent. This increase is to a large extent due to a continuing and consistent upward trend in demand for transport fuel, motor gasoline, diesel oil and aviation kerosene, all of which achieved consumption increases in the 2.5/4.5 per cent range with the increase fairly evenly distributed between North America, Europe and the Pacific area. Light fuel oil and naphtha demand also increased reflecting the economic recovery but heavy fuel oil demand increased only in North America as medium term technology changes in electricity generation and industry continued to result in a phase-out of heavy fuel oil use in Europe and Japan. Some parts of the increase in apparent consumption of light heating oil in Europe, notably in Germany, resulted from a major increase in consumer stocks when prices were at their lowest in the first half of 1986. In the second half of 1986 deliveries to consumers were reduced somewhat as they began to draw on the stocks built in the first half of the year. At the end of 1986 stocks on land in OECD countries stood at 445 million tons, an increase of about 20 million tons on the corresponding figure at the beginning of 1986.

1.2.D

OIL DELIVERIES TO INLAND CONSUMPTION AND MARINE BUNKERS 1985/86
(million tons)

	North America 1985	1986	%	Europe 1985	1986	%	Pacific 1985	1986	%	OECD Total 1985	1985	%
LPG/Naphtha	64.9	61.7	-4.9	46.6	47.9	2.8	34.5	36.0	4.3	146.0	145.6	-0.4
Aviation Fuel	62.9	66.5	5.7	21.6	22.6	4.6	4.5	4.8	6.1	89.1	93.9	5.3
Motor Gasoline	314.5	321.5	2.2	104.2	109.3	4.9	40.0	40.8	2.0	458.7	471.7	2.8
Gas/Diesel Oil	153.6	151.7	-1.2	201.4	208.3	3.4	47.2	49.1	4.0	402.1	409.0	1.7
Heavy Fuel Oil	73.8	83.7	13.4	117.7	117.0	-0.5	52.4	47.4	-9.5	244.0	248.2	1.4
Other Products	73.3	73.8	0.7	35.9	38.6	7.5	34.2	35.0	2.3	143.3	147.4	2.9
Total	743.3	760.8	2.4	527.4	544.0	3.1	225.5	226.5	0.5	1496.3	1531.3	2.3

With OECD oil consumption increasing and production in the area overall falling, there was a strong increase in import demand from the OECD countries. Stockbuilding contributed further to this and net imports of the OECD increased from 779 million tons in 1985 to 865 million tons in 1986. This reflected a 21.2 per cent increase in North America, an increase of 9.5 per cent in Europe, and an increase of only 1.3 per cent in Japan.

1.2.E

OECD -- IMPORTS OF CRUDE OIL AND PRODUCTS IN 1985 AND 1986
(million metric tons)

	Europe	N.America	(of which USA)	Pacific	(of which Japan)	Total
1985	621.8	273.0	254.6	219.6	208.4	1114.3
1986	675.8	330.7	308.0	222.7	211.1	1234.3
Change in Volume	54.0	57.7	53.4	3.1	2.7	120.0
% Change	8.7%	21.1%	21.0%	1.4%	1.3%	10.8%

Seaborne Trade

With imports into N. America and Europe rising faster than overall imports, ton miles covered increased more than imports. For all seaborne trade, Fearnley's Review 1986 estimates this increase at 16 per cent.

T.2.F

OECD - IMPORTS BY SOURCE, 1985 AND 1986
(million metric tons)

a) Crude Oil and Products

Importing Region	Europe		N. America		Pacific		OECD Total	
Source	1985	1986	1985	1986	1985	1986	1985	1986
Europe	203.2	213.6	31.4	39.3	0.3	1.1	234.9	254.0
N. America	8.1	8.0	41.1	42.8	6.8	7.5	56.0	58.3
Other W. Hem:	42.1	34.7	106.8	112.2	7.7	10.4	156.6	157.3
Africa	136.4	131.8	41.3	51.0	0.9	0.7	178.6	183.5
Middle East	144.7	191.4	18.6	52.3	140.7	139.8	304.0	383.5
Far East	3.5	2.2	26.8	26.7	55.9	58.8	86.1	87.7
Others	83.8	99.3	7.0	6.4	7.3	4.4	98.2	110.0
Total	621.8	681.0	273.0	330.7	219.6	222.7	1114.4	1234.3

b) Crude Oil

Importing Region	Europe		N. America		Pacific		OECD Total	
Source	1985	1986	1985	1986	1985	1986	1985	1986
Europe	101.5	98.8	21.8	29.7	0.0	0.5	123.3	129.1
N. America	0.4	0.5	32.0	35.3	0.0	0.1	32.4	35.9
Other W. Hem:	31.9	28.0	77.4	78.6	7.5	10.0	116.7	116.6
Africa	123.7	120.7	36.0	41.6	0.5	0.1	160.3	162.4
Middle East	129.4	174.4	16.9	50.7	125.0	118.8	271.4	344.0
Far East	3.0	1.7	23.3	23.0	38.6	41.5	64.9	66.2
Others	38.9	47.8	3.5	3.6	3.9	1.6	46.1	52.8
Total	428.8	471.9	210.9	262.5	175.5	172.6	815.1	907.0

c) Products

Importing Region	Europe		N. America		Pacific		OECD Total	
Source	1985	1986	1985	1986	1985	1986	1985	1986
Europe	101.7	114.7	9.6	9.6	0.3	0.6	111.6	124.9
N. America	7.7	7.5	9.1	7.5	6.7	7.4	23.5	22.3
Other W. Hem:	10.2	6.7	29.4	33.6	0.2	0.5	39.7	40.7
Africa	12.7	11.1	5.3	9.4	0.4	0.6	18.4	21.1
Middle East	15.3	16.9	1.7	1.6	15.7	21.0	32.6	39.5
Far East	0.5	0.5	3.5	3.7	17.3	17.3	21.2	21.5
Others	4.9	49.2	3.5	2.8	3.5	2.6	52.1	57.3
Total	193.0	206.6	62.1	68.2	44.1	50.0	299.1	327.3

Whereas world production of crude oil was about 6 per cent higher last year than in 1985, the tonnage traded by sea was up by 8 per cent, partly owing to the decline in US production and the need for higher imports. Reflecting also the rise in Middle East output, the average length of haul rose almost 10 per cent. As a result, the total volume of trade in crude oil was 18 per cent higher, having risen from 4 007 to 4 730 billion tonne-miles. This was the highest figure recorded since 1982. Continuing the recovery of the previous four years, seaborne trade in products rose 10 per cent to 1 270 billion tonne-miles -- the highest ever recorded.

In view of the increased shipping requirements, the tonnage of crude oil carriers in lay-up fell from 36 million in 1985 to 13 million dwt, but with the persistent surplus of VLCCs the average of the year's single-voyage freight rates for VLCCs and ULCCs differed little from that of 1985 and provided no relief for owners of that type of tonnage. The average for medium-sized crude carriers rose sharply, on the other hand, by 14 per cent over 1985, while that for small crude/products tankers jumped by 16 per cent.

The size of the vessels used for transportation of crude oil in the various trades continued to differ but it can be assumed that the different size groups share of the overall seaborne shipments were as follows: below 60 000 dwt, 10 per cent; 60 to 100 000 dwt, 21 per cent; 100 to 200 000 dwt, 34 per cent; and vessels above 200 000 dwt, 35 per cent. Vessels above 200 000 dwt accounted for more than 50 per cent of the total ton-mile volume, approximately 5 per cent higher than a year earlier due to an increase in the trading of such vessels in the long-haul trades from the Middle East.

Tables XII(a) and (b) of the Statistical Annex analyse by origin and destination, world interregional oil movements for 1985 in terms of tonnage and transport performance. The overall development of interregional oil transport by sea since 1976 is given in the following graph.

Oil

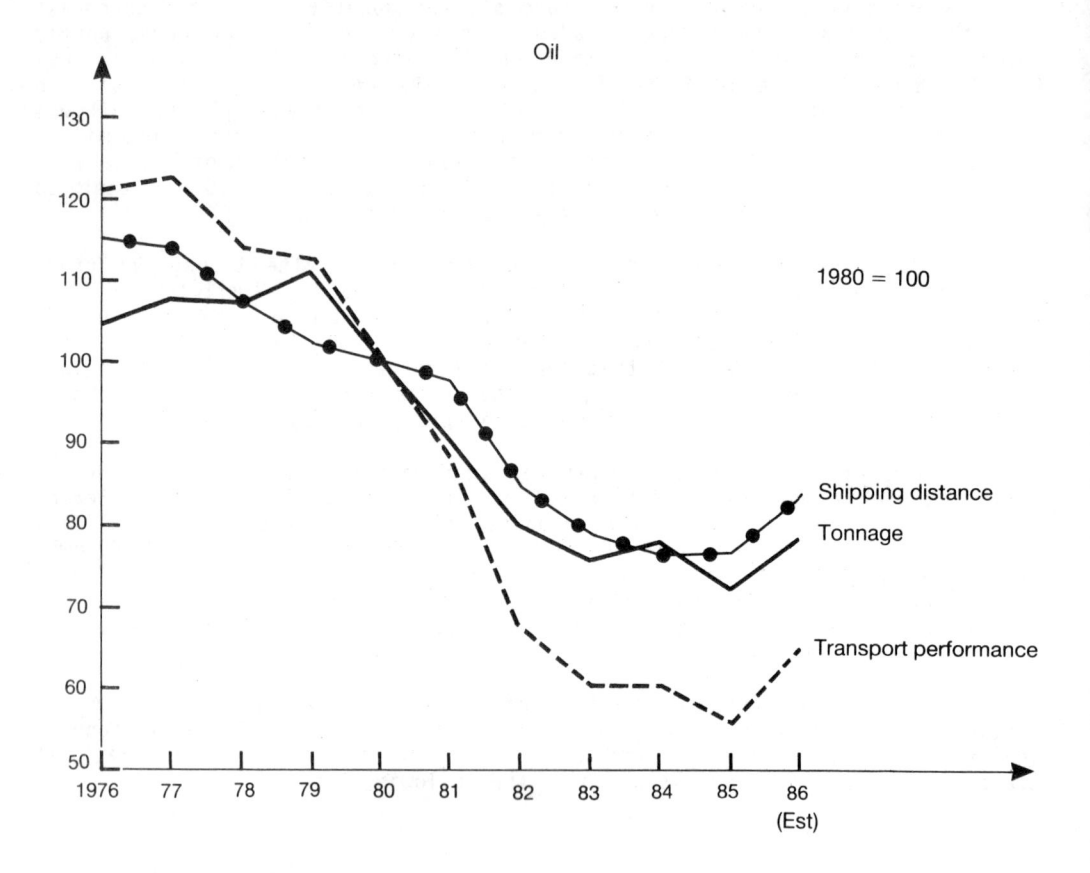

1980 = 100

Shipping distance
Tonnage
Transport performance

1976 77 78 79 80 81 82 83 84 85 86 (Est)

The depressed market conditions which prevailed throughout 1986 are very likely to continue for most of 1987. Despite an expected increase in oil demand as well as a higher OPEC production during the second half of the year, there is little reason to assume that market conditions are going to improve during the months to come, especially as pipelines, particularly in the Gulf, will be reducing seaborne transportation requirements. The only way to achieve any sustainable improvement in the tanker market has to be seen in accelerated scrapping at a high tonnage level accompanied by a restraint in ordering of new vessels. However, looking at the end-1986 orderbook for tankers, fears have to be expressed that a new speculative building boom in the tanker market is looming on the horizon.

NOTES AND REFERENCES

(1) "Economic Outlook No. 41", OECD, Paris, June 1987.

(2) "Review 1986", Fearnley's, Oslo, 1987.

(3) The data concerning overcapacity originate from a large variety of sources, notably from information received from Hapag-Lloyd, Shipping Policy and Planning Division.

Chapter III

THE SUPPLY OF SHIPPING SERVICES

GENERAL

A substantial decline in the world fleet

Between mid-1985 and mid-1986, the world fleet of merchant vessels in excess of 100 gross tons (gt) declined, according to Lloyd's Register of Shipping, by 11.4 million gt, from 416.3 to 404.9 million gt. (1) This is the most substantial reduction ever recorded except during major wars, and this 2.7 per cent fall brings the fleet to a level nearly 5 per cent below the peak value which was recorded in 1982. For the first time this has also been associated with a smaller number of vessels, which in mid-1986 were more than a thousand fewer than twelve months before. This significant cutback brings the world fleet in tonnage terms back to the level it had reached in 1978 and can be seen as marking a significant step towards correcting the gross imbalance between supply and demand which has been the constant theme of world shipping since the beginning of the decade. Nevertheless there is still a subsantial way to go before a healthy balance is attained in all sectors, and events in the second half of 1986 did not bode well for a continued reduction in several sectors.

The major contributor to the reduction was a further elimination of a large part of the world tanker fleet which, during 1985 and the first months of 1986, maintained a level of scrapping which had never previously been reached; as a result, during the period under consideration, more than 7 per cent of gt was removed from the fleet. There were also very substantial reductions in the combination carrier fleet, as well as in conventional general cargo shipping. In addition, the dry bulk carrier fleet virtually ceased to expand, after the vigorous growth which had characterised the previous five years during which it had increased by 35 per cent. The only sector which continued to expand significantly was the fully-containerised fleet, which was still receiving the very large capacity vessels which had been ordered for the round-the-world services. Although the number still on order are much fewer than they were, this sector is still expected to go on growing, in spite of the lack of a similar increase in demand.

When considered from the point of view of carrying capacity, which for dry and liquid bulk shipping can be best indicated in terms of deadweight tons (dwt), the world fleet was reduced from 673.7 million dwt in mid-1985 to 647.6 in mid-1986, a reduction in one year of 4.0 per cent, substantially more than the reduction in gt because of the large number of very large tankers and combination carriers that were scrapped during the period, which have a dwt/gt ratio very much higher than smaller tankers, bulk carriers and general cargo ships. By the end of 1986 the tanker and combination carrier fleets were, in deadweight terms, down to 266.4 million compared to their peak level of 380.2 million nine years earlier. (2) Unfortunately, however, the short-term movements in the tanker freight market during 1986 led to a burst of new orders for tankers and a major slowdown in demolition which suggests that the tanker fleet will start to increase again, although the level of dry bulk carrier scrapping and the small numbers of new orders should see a continuing contraction in the bulk carrier fleet.

The long-term evolution of the main constituents of the world fleet since 1960 is set out in Table XIV of the Statistical Annex. The following table shows the way the various sections developed since the beginning of the seventies in five-year periods up to 1980, and for each year during the present decade.

Annual average percentage change (of total grt)

MID-YEAR to MID-YEAR	WORLD FLEET	OIL TANKERS	DRY BULK CARRIERS(*)	OTHER SHIP TYPES
1970-1986	3.7	2.6	6.8	2.7
1970-1975	8.5	11.8	12.9	2.4
1975-1980	4.2	3.1	5.1	4.9
1980-1981	0.2	-1.9	3.2	0.5
1981-1982	0.9	-2.8	5.5	1.9
1982-1983	-0.5	-5.7	4.3	1.7
1983-1984	-0.9	-6.2	3.2	1.4
1984-1985	-0.6	-6.1	4.4	0.7
1985-1986	-2.7	-7.2	-0.8	-0.2

(*)Including combination carriers

SOURCE: Lloyd's Register of Shipping; Statistical Tables

The prospects for the next two years are clouded by the basic uncertainty over the level of demand for oil transportation which seems likely to delay scrapping decisions and, if there are renewed short-term rises in market levels, to encourage speculative ordering. However, the lack of such pressures on the bulk side should lead to continued contraction which could lead to a more healthy supply/demand situation by the end of 1988. On the general cargo side, the bringing into full operation of the very large container ships, many of which are facing an uncertain future from the point of view of their ultimate ownership, seems inevitably to be leading to a continued period of heavy overcapacity.

THE WORLD MERCHANT FLEET BY TYPES

General

The substantial differences in the way the principal categories of shipping have evolved between mid-1985 and mid-1986 are set out in Table T.3.A. It also shows the pronounced dissimilarities which exist in the participation of the five main economic groupings of the world in the individual vessel types. The constitution of the individual fleets of OECD Member countries, as well as those of non-Member countries with more than 400 000 gt under their flags, are shown in more detail in Table XV(b) of the Statistical Annex.

It is instructive to compare Table T.3.A with the comparable table in the 1985 annual report, and with that five years earlier. The most significant changes in the short-term have been the rapid expansion of the container fleet, as the full impact of the very large container ships has been registered, the addition of a number of new ships to the passenger fleet with the growing importance of the short-sea and cruise market, the near-stagnation in the dry bulk and gas carrier sectors and, as mentioned above, the substantial fall in tankers, combination carriers and general cargo ships. The changes in the participation of the main economic groupings, however, have shown much more substantial changes, particularly in the position of the developing market-economy countries who have achieved their target that they set themselves at the end of the seventies, of 20 per cent of world tonnage by the end of the decade, with three years to spare. Their participation in the tanker, combination carrier and dry bulk sector has been particularly notable. Of the dry bulk carrier fleet, they now hold 24 per cent, compared to 13 per cent only five years ago. The OECD has continued its rapid decline and now has less than 40 per cent of world tonnage under its flags, compared to 51 per cent in the middle of 1981. This has been the result of both scrapping and flagging-out, although the traditional open registry countries have benefited less than a number of countries or dependent territories which have been providing facilities which are very similar to those offered by the "big four". The USSR and Eastern Europe have not expanded their fleets significantly but, because of the overall reduction, their shares have shown a moderate rise.

Tankers and combination carriers

The world fleet of oil tankers in excess of 100 gt continued its rapid decline, falling, according to Lloyd's Register, from 138.4 million gt in mid-1985 to 128.4 million in mid-1986 (from 268.4 to 247.5 million dwt). In effect, this reduction of nearly 8 per cent in carrying capacity is the most substantial so far recorded and the pure tanker fleet was at that time less than three-quarters of that which it had been at the beginning of the decade. The decline coincided with the first notable rise in demand since the late seventies with an increase in tonne-mileage of more than 16 per cent during 1986, with the result that the overall theoretical surplus capacity, according

T.3.A.

WORLD FLEET BY TYPE OF VESSEL AND REGIONAL DISTRIBUTION, MID-1986

			Percentage of type registered in:				
TYPE OF VESSEL	TOTAL TONNAGE MILLION GRT	PER CENT INCREASE/DECREASE MID-1985 MID-1986	OECD COUNTRIES (5)	OPEN REGISTRY COUNTRIES (6)	USSR/ EASTERN EUROPE (7)	DEVELOPING MARKET- ECONOMY COUNTRIES	REST OF THE WORLD (8)
Oil tankers	128.43	-7.2	41.2	36.3	4.0	16.2	2.4
Combination carriers	21.27	-10.4	31.8	36.1	3.6	26.9	1.6
Ore and dry bulk carriers	111.64	+1.3	36.1	29.2	6.1	24.3	4.3
General cargo ships (1)	73.24	-3.4	32.6	19.1	15.4	23.9	9.0
Container ships (2)	19.61	+6.8	59.3	12.7	4.1	18.3	5.6
Liquefied gas carriers	9.83	-1.3	57.1	20.0	2.0	17.7	3.1
Chemical carriers	3.56	+4.1	34.8	44.1	0.3	20.3	0.5
Ferries and passenger vessels	8.81	+5.8	66.7	12.1	9.1	9.7	2.4
Other cargo ships (3)	5.03	+10.1	47.2	38.8	0.5	13.4	0.1
Fishing and fish handling vessels	13.37	+1.4	26.3	1.2	57.0	12.6	2.9
Other non-trading types (4)	10.12	-0.9	49.2	11.4	14.4	20.2	4.9
All types	404.91	-2.7	39.3	27.5	8.6	20.4	4.3

1. Single and multideck: including passenger/cargo ships.
2. Fully cellular and lighter carriers.
3. Vehicle and livestock carriers and sundry tankers.
4. Including supply ships, tugs, dredgers, icebreakers, research ships and other miscellaneous types.
5. Including Great Lakes and United States Reserve Fleets.
6. Cyprus, Lebanon, Liberia, Panama, Bahamas, Oman and Vanuatu.
7. Albania, Bulgaria, Czechoslovakia, Germany (Democratic Republic), Hungary, Poland, Romania and USSR.
8. Bermuda, Cuba, China (PR), Faroe Islands, Falkland Islands, Gibraltar, Israel, Korea (North), Monaco, South Africa, Vietnam.

SOURCE: Lloyd's Register of Shipping: Statistical Tables.

to John I. Jacobs (3), fell during the first half of the year from 109 million dwt to 82 million although it had risen again by the end of the year to 90 million. Since a large part of this theoretical reserve is related to slow steaming from a design speed which is very unlikely to be technically attainable and includes excess port time and part-cargo incidence which appears to have become almost unavoidable, the actual surplus at mid-year was very much lower than this and at specific times and places actual shortages developed. This gave significant profits to the owner, who happened to be in a position to take advantage of them, but they were on the whole short-lived and the owner of an 85 000 tonner who, according to Galbraiths, was able to make a profit of $15 000 per day on the voyage market in August was, by February 1987, scarcely covering his running costs.

In 1986 as a whole the world tanker fleet in excess of 10 000 dwt was reduced, according to Fearnleys (2), by only 6 million dwt, virtually all during the first half of the year, compared to 25 million during the previous year. Table T.3.B shows that this limited reduction was entirely located in the VLCC/ULCC category, with product carrier and small/medium-sized crude carriers increasing in tonnage for the first time since the short-lived upturn for small and middle-range vessels in 1981/82 at the time of the ill-fated Sanko deal. During 1986 only 27 tankers and combination carriers over 200 000 dwt were sold for scrap, of which nine had been declared constructive total losses after missile attacks in the Gulf, compared to 71 ships during 1985. Indeed, Jacobs only recorded three such vessels actually broken up during the second half of the year.

This slowdown in scrapping was associated with a rapid rise in new orders during the second half of the year. Whereas in January-June only 1.8 million dwt had been fixed, one of the lowest levels this decade, in the following six months no less than 7.8 million dwt were ordered, including 12 VLCCs. The sale and purchase market was also extremely buoyant and second-hand values for ULCCs, which have been scarcely saleable for several years, doubled during the course of the year. Whether this activity will continue significantly during 1987 will depend essentially on whether OPEC's production quotas and raised crude prices will be maintained. If so, there seems a considerable danger that many of the orders placed during 1986, even at the price levels then prevailing, may be delivered onto a market which will not be able to offer them profitable employment.

The product trades were also affected by the price falls, as consumers increased their demands and ensured that all available storage was topped up at the low levels which, correctly, it was expected would not last for a very long time. However, the increase in new orders was not as vigorous as for the larger size categories and the volume at the end of 1986 was not significantly higher than at the end of either of the two previous years. This is a sector in which there has been a steady process of modernisation and Jacobs estimate that about 40 per cent of the tanker fleet capable of carrying products was built within the last five years. This has been partly due to the stringent requirements placed by IMO regulations which many older vessels were unable to meet without excessive expenditure, but has also reflected the changed character of product carriers for servicing the producer-based export refineries with large parcels of relatively unsophisticated products. These have now almost reached their maximum, after extensive cancellation of the more visionary projects, and a number of refinery projects in the Far East and South America may lead to a reduction again in the long-haul product trade.

T.3.B

THE GROWTH OF THE WET AND DRY BULK CARRIER FLEETS

1981-1987

In thousand dwt

SIZE GROUPS IN DWT		IN SERVICE AT 1ST JANUARY:							ON ORDER: 1ST JAN. 1987
		1981	1982	1983	1984	1985	1986	1987	
OIL TANKERS	10-40 000	29 863	30 103	30 404	29 743	28 303	27 557	28 092	1 642
	40-150 000	90 485	93 851	88 779	84 723	81 485	78 623	78 867	7 306
	150 000 +	204 358	196 204	181 740	155 813	154 724	133 160	126 025	6 147
	Total	324 706	320 158	300 923	280 280	264 512	239 340	232 984	15 095
COMBINATION CARRIERS	10-60 000	1 775	1 631	1 353	1 456	1 626	1 592	1 588	200
	60-100 000	9 272	8 733	8 390	8 366	7 908	7 082	6 368	122
	100 000 +	36 219	34 886	33 402	32 378	31 544	26 905	25 477	1 470
	Total	47 266	45 250	43 145	42 200	41 078	35 579	33 433	1 792
DRY BULK CARRIERS	10-60 000	101 242	105 116	109 328	112 190	117 047	121 383	116 233	3 654
	60-100 000	22 725	26 141	31 294	35 199	37 912	38 464	37 573	2 758
	100 000 +	18 091	23 456	28 608	30 698	32 818	37 632	42 225	5 294
	Total	142 058	154 713	169 231	178 087	187 777	197 479	196 031	11 706

NOTE: A more detailed breakdown by size at mid-1986 is given in Table XVI(b) of the Statistical Annex.

SOURCE: 'World Bulk Fleet', Fearnleys, Oslo 1981-1987.

This will, however, depend very much on the import policies to be pursued in the United States and Japan and the evolution of the international spot market.

At the beginning of 1987, the outlook for the world tanker fleet seems probably more optimistic than at the start of 1986. A smaller fleet and a higher demand level has reduced the surplus during parts of the year to near equilibrium. However, the virtual stoppage of demolition and the disturbing level of new orders, many of them for companies which do not have a tradition of cautious management, gives cause for concern, and the violent instability of rates during 1986 make any type of prediction of a stable market virtually impossible. All that can be hoped for is that the sources of finance for new buildings will insist on high equity participation by owners and that tonnage which becomes uneconomic will be scrapped rather than returned to lay-up where it can continue to overhang the market.

The combination carrier fleet has continued to decline, as can be seen from the middle section of Table T.3.B, although rather more slowly than in recent years. This was partly a reflection of the improvement in the oil market, which led to a very pronounced switch of these ships from dry cargo to oil, which Fearnleys estimated to have taken up 60 per cent of the cargo transported (compared to 40 per cent in the previous year) with a maximum in September of 77 per cent (according to Jacobs). The latter source indicates that the switch was most marked for the smaller ships (under 140 000 dwt) mainly because the larger vessels are in many cases committed to long-term contracts in iron ore. The prospects for employment in oil during the early months of 1987, however, became less attractive and since most combination carriers are at the upper end of the size bracket for dry cargo, their utilisation is largely restricted to iron ore and coal, both of which commodities appear likely to contract during the year. Accordingly, it seems quite probable that the fairly high level of scrapping of the last two years will be maintained and even increased. In spite of the lack-lustre nature of the dry cargo market, eight combination carriers, with a total tonnage of 1.2 million dwt were formally designated pure dry cargo ships, a trend which has continued for several years.

The lack of attractive prospects for combination carriers and the substantial extra cost involved in newbuildings over similar sized tankers or dry bulk carriers has led to a continued contraction in the order book for such ships. At the end of 1986 there were only 12 vessels on order, with a total deadweight of 1.8 million, the lowest that Fearnleys has recorded, at least since 1975. Only two small vessels were ordered during the year and the only interest seems to be directed to the PROBO (products/bulk/oil) carriers of around 40/50 000 dwt with, at the other end of the scale, four 300 000 dwt vessels intended for operation on the Brazilian Carajas iron ore project. Overall, flexibility has proved, except in very particular cases, not to justify the extra capital and operating costs of the combination carrier.

Dry bulk carriers

After a year in which the dry bulk carrier fleet increased more than in any year for a decade, it was remarkable that the dry bulk fleet at the beginning of 1987 was 1.5 million dwt less than a year earlier. This was in spite of the addition of 200 new vessels with a total tonnage of 11.6 million, the last of the flood of orders for those vessels placed during 1983 and 1984.

Although there was a continuing flow of new orders during 1986, at much the same level as the previous year, the world order book at the beginning of 1987 stood at 11.7 million dwt, lower than at any time during the current decade. Of these, 7.6 million are scheduled for delivery during 1987, with only 4 million booked for later years.

The reason for this remarkable turnaround was the astonishing amount of dry bulk tonnage which was disposed of for demolition during the year. According to Fearnleys, no less than 14 million dwt were scrapped or lost during the year, almost twice the amount recorded for 1985, which was itself a record. Of the tonnage sold for breaking up (i.e. excluding losses and ships broken up but sold in the previous year), more than three-quarters were the smaller bulk carriers of less than 60 000 dwt, although they constitute just over half of the existing fleet. This is not surprising, since the average size of bulk carriers has been increasing rapidly over recent years and only 9 per cent of dry bulk tonnage over 60 000 dwt is more than fifteen years old compared to 18 per cent for those below that level. Indeed, of the 39 dry bulk carriers which went for demolition in the last two months of 1986, only three ships were over 60 000 dwt and all but one were built before 1972 (4). In view of the volume of such ships which are still in service, which were constructed in the days of very cheap bunkers and lack the extensive technological developments in cargo handling and machinery which have been introduced over recent years, there seems little doubt that, if the dry bulk market continues at its present unprofitable level, the rate of dry bulk scrapping will probably continue. Certainly, the first two months of 1987 have shown no slowdown in the process.

The trend towards very large bulk carriers which was noted in last year's report has continued, although at a slightly lower rate. Of the new orders placed during the year, 67 per cent (equivalent to 3.8 million dwt) were for vessels in excess of 100 000 dwt and twelve extra vessels were in the over-150 000 dwt range, which are virtually limited to employment in the iron ore trades. It is not easy to see how such vessels will find employment other than by replacing the categories immediately below, which are currently operating to ports which are capable of accepting larger vessels, a domino effect which can only be corrected by additional scrapping at the lower end of the fleet, as is currently occurring.

The standstill in the dry bulk fleet is to be commended after the unjustifiable growth of the last few years. However, there seems no doubt that even if the fleet is reduced during 1987 and 1988, there will still be a substantial volume of excess supply, in view of the very limited prospects for expansion in the main bulk commodities, as described in the previous chapter. Even the most optimistic forecasters still envisage a surplus of 25 million dwt by the end of 1988 and, unless the present high scrapping rate of 1986 can be maintained and the level of new ordering remains at or below the current level, the present malaise could well continue until the end of the decade.

Liquified natural gas, petroleum gas and chemical carriers

Between mid-1985 and mid-1986, the world fleet of liquified gas carriers declined, according to Lloyd's Register, from 9.96 million grt (15.04 million m^3) to 9.83 million (14.75 million m^3), with a reduction of six units. Within this figure, LNG carriers were reduced by 1 vessel and 125 000 m^3. During 1986 as a whole, three of the standard 125 000 m^3 vessels which have been in layup for a number of years were sold for scrap and four others are scheduled for sale in the near future. This reflects the final conclusion that there appear to be no prospects for any of the laid-up fleet which has not already been earmarked for specific projects, and the fifteen remaining vessels, with a total capacity of 1.6 million m^3 which were in layup at the end of the year are unlikely to trade again. This conclusion has been reinforced by the decision that the Australia-Japan operation from the North-West Shelf will be operated entirely with new ships, for which the first three orders were placed in Japan during the year. Eventually, seven vessels will be involved in this trade and will come into operation progressively between 1989 and 1993. The year also saw the start of the Indonesia-South Korea trade using two existing vessels; and the resumption of Algerian gas sales to Europe led to the reactivation of part of the Algerian gas fleet. However, overall, the prospects for LNG during the next few years gives little cheer to the owners of existing uncommitted ships, or to the world shipbuilding industry.

The prospects for liquid petroleum gas carriers seem scarcely brighter. The levels of demand during 1986 were very irregular because of the violent movements in oil prices and associated LPG production. This resulted in almost all the fleet being maintained in operation, with only three small vessels in layup at the end of the year. The unpredictability of future demand has meant that only two new orders for vessels were placed during the year and the entire order book only contains twelve ships with a total capacity of 0.16 million m^3. The major cause of long-term uneasiness is the Japanese attempts to diversify their sources of supply by switching from the Gulf to South East Asia, with a consequent halving of the haul-length. A recent survey (5) suggests a rise in Japanese imports between 1986 and 1990 of some 20 per cent but virtually all the increase will come from Indonesia as well as part of existing demand.

The chemical carrier fleet also experienced a year of instability since there is a very substantial overlap between the markets of these ships and those of both clean-product carriers and LPG ships. Twenty-three pure chemical carriers were added to the fleet during 1986 with a total dwt of 0.55 million but the outlook is such that at the end of the year only 11 ships, in total less than 200 000 dwt, were on order, all but one for delivery during the coming year. The problems of refinery capacity reduction mentioned earlier affect both product and chemical carriers and the entry into force of the exacting requirements imposed by Annex II of Marpol, which will occur on 1st April 1987, has imposed considerable extra costs on shipowners.

General cargo and unit-load ships

The pressure which the conventional general cargo ship has endured from, at one end the fully-containerised and other unit-load vessels, and at the other from the bulk, part-bulk and bulk/container carriers, was maintained throughout 1986. Between mid-1985 and mid-1986 the general cargo fleet declined, according to Lloyd's Register, from 75.8 million gt to 73.2 million, the largest drop in a single year so far recorded, over a period during which unit-load ships added 1.25 million gt, a growth of 6.8 per cent. However, this reduction has been mainly caused by a sustained level of scrapping of old uneconomic ships amounting, according to Fearnleys, in 1985 and 1986 together, to some 9 million dwt of non-bulk dry cargo shipping, of which unit-load vessels contributed only a very small element. Fairplay's assessment (6) was that more than 2 million dwt of dry cargo shipping other than container ships were completed worldwide during 1986 and 1.7 million dwt of new orders were placed compared to 2.2 million dwt of container ships completed and 1.3 million ordered, although part of the general cargo element will not enter international trade.

One category which has contributed recently to the reduction in general cargo shipping has been the refrigerated cargo sector. A reasonably profitable market in the early eighties led to a spate of ordering and a capacity increase between 1982 and 1984 of 44 million ft^3, equivalent to more than 20 per cent of the total fleet capacity. As a result, competition became intense and rates fell dramatically, contributing among other things to the bankruptcy of the Salen group at the end of 1984. This activity was particularly concentrated in Japan, using both Japanese and open registry flags. There was a very large volume of scrapping during 1984 and 1985 but this only just exceeded new deliveries and as a result there was no substantial improvement in the market. According to a recent study (7) the reefer industry was in surplus in mid-1986 by some 6 per cent capacity, a less unsatisfactory situation than for most shipping sectors, and a continued scrapping level during 1986 and '87 equivalent to that of the two previous years, combined with the drastic cuts which have already taken place in the level of ordering could bring this sector at least into a healthy financial condition over the next eighteen months. However, it should be recalled that reefer ships themselves only carry three-quarters of the refrigerated cargo travelling by sea, the remainder being in refrigerated containers in container and ro/ro vessels and hence the extent of overcapacity in the container fleet impinges directly upon this sector.

The unit-load fleet itself has continued its rapid expansion, although not quite as fast as in 1985. In terms of gt, according to Lloyd's Register, it increased between mid-1985 and mid-1986 from 18.4 to 19.6 million tons, plus 6.8 per cent. In terms of container capacity during 1986 as a whole, the fleet, including ro/ro shipping, increased from 1 366 to 1 457 thousand TEU, a very similar rate of growth of 6.6 per cent, compared to 12.1 per cent in 1985 (8). However, there is still estimated to be 216 000 TEU capacity on order, including more than fifty ships with capacities in excess of 2 000 containers, although a substantial part of these are for delivery in 1988 and 1989. The failure of the United States Lines round-the-world service has placed a major question-mark against the future use of the very large container carrier, although other operators, from both Europe and the Far East appear to be optimistic of the long-term profitability of this type of operation. However, in the short-term as indicated in the previous chapter, the advent of the third-generation container ships has placed particularly heavy pressure on the transatlantic and transpacific trades, with falling load factors and severe imbalances in the two directions.

T.3.C.

THE DEVELOPMENT OF THE SHARES OF MAJOR NATIONAL GROUPS IN THE WORLD FLEET

TOTAL FLEET AS AT:

	MID-1975		MID-1983		MID-1984		MID-1985		MID-1986	
	MILLION GRT	PER CENT OF WORLD TONNAGE	MILLION GRT	PER CENT OF WORLD TONNAGE	MILLION GRT	PER CENT OF WORLD TONNAGE	MILLION GRT	PER CENT OF WORLD TONNAGE	MILLION GRT	PER CENT OF WORLD TONNAGE
OECD Countries (1)	198.7	58.1	198.7	47.0	188.9	45.1	178.2	42.8	159.0	39.3
Open Registry Countries (2)	83.0	24.3	107.0	25.3	109.8	26.2	111.6	26.8	111.2	27.5
USSR/Eastern Europe (3)	25.4	7.4	33.7	8.0	33.5	8.0	34.2	8.2	34.9	8.6
Developing Market-Economy Countries	29.0	8.5	70.2	16.6	73.1	17.5	77.1	18.5	82.4	20.4
Rest of the World (4)	6.0	1.7	13.0	3.1	13.4	3.2	15.2	3.7	17.4	4.3
World total	342.1	100.0	422.6	100.0	418.7	100.0	416.3	100.0	404.9	100.0

1. Including Great Lakes Fleets.

2. Bahamas, Cyprus, Lebanon, Liberia, Oman, Panama and Vanuatu.

3. Albania, Bulgaria, Czechoslovakia, Germany (Democratic Republic), Hungary, Poland, Romania and USSR.

4. Bermuda, Cuba, China (PR), Faroe Islands, Falkland Islands, Gibraltar, Israel, North Korea, Monaco, South Africa, Vietnam.

SOURCE: Lloyd's Register of Shipping.

THE WORLD MERCHANT FLEET BY FLAGS

General

Table XV(a) of the Statistical Annex sets out how the tonnage in the world fleet was distributed in mid-1986 among the principal maritime countries of the world, both OECD and non-OECD, in terms of both gt and dwt, showing how the various national fleets had expanded or contracted during the twelve months since mid-1985. The table also breaks down the world oil tanker fleet in the same way (including oil/chemical tankers but excluding chemical carriers, gas carriers and tankers used for the carriage of liquids other than crude oil or oil products). Table XV(b) shows how these fleets were constituted by main vessel category. This information is summarised in Table T.3.C so that it can be seen how the five principal economic groupings of countries which operate ship registers have evolved year-by-year since mid-1983 with the addition of the situation in mid-1975 to reflect the longer-term trend. Table T.3.A earlier in the chapter shows how these five blocs participated in the various main categories as at mid-1986.

The most striking element which appears from the tables is the continued very rapid decline in the part of the world fleet under OECD flags, both in absolute terms and in the percentage share of the total. At the start of the seventies, more than two-thirds of world tonnage was under the flags of Member countries but it has now fallen below 40 per cent. The open-registry fleets, while having virtually maintained their total tonnage, increased their share of the world fleet and the socialist countries of Eastern Europe continued their very modest growth. The developing market economy countries, on the other hand, have continued to expand at a high rate equivalent to an annual growth of more than 7 per cent, and their addition of 5.3 million gt is the second-highest single annual rise that they have recorded, in a year when the world fleet contracted substantially. In so doing, they have achieved the target that they set themselves at the end of the seventies, of having 20 per cent of the world fleet under their flag by the end of the Third Development Decade, with more than three years to spare. Indeed, at the present growth rate, the developing countries should have a quarter of the world fleet by 1990. The "Rest of the World" group grew even faster, mainly due to the continued expansion of the Chinese People's Republic fleet, and the very rapid growth in Bermuda and Gibraltar, the latter adding more than a million gt to its register during the year.

The fleets of the OECD countries

The decline in the fleets operating under the flags of OECD Member countries between mid-1985 and mid-1986 was by far the greatest recorded in a single year. In total no less than 19.1 million gt (37.2 million dwt) were removed from their fleets, equivalent to an overall reduction of 10.8 per cent in gross and 13.0 per cent in deadweight tonnage. All the major fleets of the OECD recorded very drastic cuts except for the United States and Australia which, respectively, increased its container fleet by the last of the USL vessels, and added to its tanker and bulk carrier fleets by a small number of large units, together with Belgium and the Netherlands, which managed to maintain the existing level of their fleets.

T.3.D

INCREASES AND DECREASES IN NATIONAL FLEETS
BETWEEN MID-1985 AND MID-1986

Fleets with more than 250 000 grt change

	MID-1985	MID-1986	CHANGE 1985-1986	
	'000 GRT	'000 GRT	'000 GRT	PER CENT
OECD Members				
United States	19 517.6	19 900.8	+383.2	+2.0
Australia	2 088.3	2 368.5	+280.2	+13.4
Turkey	3 684.4	3 423.7	-260.7	-7.1
Denmark	4 942.2	4 651.2	-291.0	-5.9
Portugal	1 436.9	1 114.4	-322.5	-22.4
Finland	1 974.0	1 469.9	-504.1	-25.5
Germany	6 177.0	5 565.2	-611.8	-9.9
Sweden	3 161.9	2 516.6	-645.3	-20.4
Spain	6 256.2	5 422.0	-834.2	-13.7
Italy	8 843.2	7 896.6	-946.6	-10.7
Japan	39 940.1	38 487.8	-1 452.3	-4.6
France	8 237.4	5 936.3	-2 301.1	-27.9
Greece	31 031.5	28 390.8	-2 640.7	-8.5
United Kingdom	14 343.5	11 567.1	-2 776.4	-19.4
Norway	15 338.6	9 294.6	-6 044.0	-39.4
Other Countries				
Cyprus	8 196.1	10 616.8	+2 420.7	+29.5
Philippines	4 594.0	6 922.5	+2 328.5	+50.7
Bahamas	3 907.3	5 985.0	+2 077.7	+53.2
Hong Kong	6 858.1	8 179.7	+1 321.6	+19.3
Gibraltar	583.3	1 612.9	+1 029.6	+176.5
China (P.R.)	10 568.2	11 567.0	+998.8	+9.5
Cayman Islands	413.8	1 389.9	+976.1	+235.9
Panama	40 674.2	41 305.0	+630.8	+1.6
Iran	2 380.1	2 911.4	+531.3	+22.3
St. Vincent	235.2	509.9	+274.7	+116.8
Argentina	2 457.3	2 117.1	-340.3	-15.8
Algeria	1 347.4	881.7	-465.7	-34.6
Liberia	58 179.7	52 649.4	-5 530.3	-9.5

SOURCE: Lloyd's Register: Statistical Tables

The top section of Table T.3.D sets out the individual Member countries which expanded or contracted their fleets during the period under consideration by more than a quarter of a million gross tons, and includes no less than thirteen countries with a reduction of between 4 and 40 per cent. The overall cutbacks in the OECD fleet were particularly concentrated in tankers (-11.9 million gt), dry bulk carriers (-3.2 million), combination carriers (-2.2 million), general cargo ships (-1.4 million) and chemical carriers (-0.4 million). Even the container ship fleet showed no overall expansion. The decline in the dry bulk carrier fleet is particularly regrettable, being the only sector where a substantial volume of new tonnage was added, but a very large amount of this was added to the newer open registers and the newly industralised countries of the Far East, whereas the European countries divested themselves either by sale or scrapping of many of their existing less economic vessels.

The reactions to the flight from OECD flags have been varied. In several countries extensive plans have been introduced to seek to assist the national mercantile marine. In France, a two-year restructuring programme involving public finance was introduced, together with reductions in social charges, funding for redundancies, changes in work patterns, with associated cuts in operating costs and the sizes of crews, and introduction of an offshore register in Kerguelan. Greece, after a fleet reduction between mid-'85 and mid-'86 of 4 million dwt, lost a further 2.4 million dwt of tankers and bulk carriers during the second half of the year, resulting in the Greek government bringing in measures to increase the permitted use of foreign ratings to 40 per cent and reduce the crew complements to bring them into line with other European scales. The measures appeared to have encouraged certain owners to repatriate their ships but the overall impact is not yet clear. Spain also introduced an extensive programme of fleet renewal, including scrapping subsidies, with the aim of bringing the Spanish fleet into a condition in which it can compete with other EEC fleets by the time that, under the new Community shipping policy, the special advantages available in several EC countries have been phased out by the end of 1992. In Norway, where the most dramatic reductions have taken place, there is now more Norwegian tonnage under foreign flag than under national flag. During 1986 as a whole there was a net reduction of 6.2 million dwt to bring the fleet to only 10.7 million dwt (compared to over 30 million in mid-1984) and the addition of 4 million to the foreign flag fleet raised this to 13.6 million. Faced with this development which stemmed partly from earlier measures to make flagging-out easier, the Norwegian government introduced early in 1987 plans for the establishment of a Norwegian international shipping register to come into operation in mid-1987.

In several other countries, the reduction has been reinforced by labour troubles and exchange problems. In Denmark, where certain investment concessions were withdrawn at the beginning of the year, total foreign earnings in 1986 fell by 16 per cent, mainly due to the dollar decline, and in Japan, where the fleet was reduced by the largest amount in any year since the war, with a cut in its tanker and bulk fleet during 1986 of 11 per cent in dwt terms, several of the major shipping companies recorded very substantial losses. In Germany, after a major seafarers' strike in April which resulted in an agreement for extra time off, equivalent to an estimated 10 per cent increase in wage costs, the speed of flagging-out increased substantially and at the end of the year German-flag tonnage (3.3 million gt) was for the first time below the German-owned foreign-flag tonnage of 4.1 million gt, 25 per cent more than at the beginning of the year. The German-flag fleet is now back to the level it had attained in 1971 and is largely limited to tanker and liner shipping with virtually all its bulk carriers operating under foreign flags, although in many cases retaining their place in the German register.

Table T.3.E summarises the extent of the participation of the various OECD flag fleets in their national import and export trades, as well as in the international seaborne trade of the OECD area as a whole over the years 1983-1985. For seven countries, comparable data is also provided for the general cargo movements separately, which can be taken as an approximate indication of the national participation in their own liner trades, which are not generally available broken down by flag of carrier. Tables XIII(a)-(d) of the Statistical Annex give the summaries of results for total imports and exports by partner country within the OECD and by region for the rest of the world, covering the year 1985. They also set out the flag shares of the principal flags in total trade and, where available, general cargo trade for each respondent country. Tape records are available from the OECD, for an appropriate fee, giving the complete flag data for each partner/partner or region for each respondent country, as well as, in many cases, comparable data for oil, dry bulk and general cargo separately. These tapes now cover the five years 1981-1985. The reduction in the sizes of the OECD national fleets has led to a decline in their participation in their national trades, particularly in Japan, Finland, Germany, Belgium, Denmark and the United Kingdom, although often to a lesser extent than in the tonnage of their fleet. Norway, on the other hand, in spite of the drastic decline in her shipping, has largely maintained the share of her national trade, mainly because of her oil exports.

The fleets under open registry flags and the development of offshore registers

The tonnage operating under the flags of the formally designated open-registry states (i.e. Liberia, Panama, Cyprus, Bahamas, Lebanon and Vanuatu) declined between mid-1985 and mid-1986 from 111.6 million gt to 111.2 million (203.0 million dwt to 200.3 million). This reduction is rather surprising in view of the widespread "flagging-out" that has been reported from a considerable number of OECD flags but it appears to be principally due to the immense quantity of tankers and bulk carriers which were scrapped from the fleets under these flags during 1985, which amounted to 4 million gt for Liberia and 3.9 million gt for the other open registers. The competition between the four largest fleets became more pronounced during the year with Liberia, which cut its dues in the middle of the year, being followed by Panama which reduced its registration fees by 30 per cent and introduced a short-term registration for vessels being taken to scrapyards. Cyprus also made its register easier to enter, and the Bahamas introduced the possibility of dual registration, to assist shipowners wishing to maintain the liens associated with mortgage arrangements in their original country while being able to avail themselves of the benefits of the open-registry flag.

Pressure on the larger registers has also come from a proliferation of new more-or-less open registries, which have benefited from the international recognition, with the adoption of the United Nations Convention on Conditions for the Registration of Ships, that there does not need to be an economic link between flag and vessel, provided that the administrative and judicial responsibility is accepted. As a result, several countries have made registration

T.3.E

SHARES OF VARIOUS OECD FLAGS IN OECD INTERNATIONAL SEABORNE TRADE

per cent of total tonnage

FLAG OF REGISTER	SHARE OF NATIONAL TRADE						SHARE OF OECD TRADE(1)					
	IMPORTS			EXPORTS			IMPORTS			EXPORTS		
	1983	1984	1985	1983	1984	1985	1983	1984	1985	1983	1984	1985
Belgium(O/D)	9.0	8.2	7.1	6.2	5.6	5.2	0.9	0.7	0.9	1.1	0.6	1.2
(Non-bulk only)	(11.6)	(9.6)	(8.9)	(14.1)	(13.5)	(11.9)	..	..	..	..	..	..
Denmark	..	13.1	7.7	20.7	17.4	11.7	1.2	0.8	1.1	1.4	1.1	1.3
France	24.2	21.0	..	21.2	21.7	..	3.1	2.6	..	2.0	1.9	..
Germany	13.5	13.2	12.9	18.5	20.1	20.4	3.5	3.1	3.5	5.0	4.3	4.4
Italy	24.7	..	..	8.2	8.5	8.7	3.1	..	..	1.9	1.9	..
Netherlands	2.3	2.1	2.4	(9.0)	(8.3)	(9.0)	1.4	1.2	1.4	2.3	..	2.1
(Non-bulk only)	(7.2)	(6.8)	(8.2)	23.5	24.0	22.9	..	..	..	..	..	..
United Kingdom	25.4	22.2	23.1	(28.3)	(30.2)	(30.2)	7.2	6.4	6.9	7.6	6.4	7.4
(Non-bulk only)(2)	(30.5)	(30.9)	(31.3)	46.5	46.7	41.9	..	..	..	..	..	..
Finland	48.4	50.6	46.0	(47.3)	(46.6)	(43.5)	1.7	1.8	1.8	1.8	2.1	2.0
(Non-bulk only)	(30.6)	(31.5)	(34.5)	43.3	41.4	..	..	..	..	..	..	..
Greece	48.5	58.4	..	64.3	61.3	65.5	6.3	4.8	5.2	7.8	4.8	6.1
Norway	31.7	29.6	30.1	14.4	14.4	8.9	4.8	4.3	5.3	4.2	3.0	3.5
Spain	46.0	49.3	43.8	28.5	28.5	27.7	2.8	2.8	2.6	1.7	1.1	1.3
Sweden	16.5	17.7	19.6	22.6	22.7	20.8	1.5	1.4	1.7	2.0	1.9	2.2
Japan	44.5	43.4	43.1	12.8	11.8	11.0	14.5	14.6	16.5	11.5	9.9	12.7
Canada	51.6	49.8	44.3	(5.2)	(6.3)	(8.5)	2.1	1.6	2.4	2.9	1.4	3.6
(Non-bulk only)	(2.7)	(2.2)	(8.9)	3.8	3.7	4.3	..	..	..	..	..	..
United States	8.0	5.2	4.7	(22.9)	(20.0)	(20.4)	2.6	1.3	2.3	2.4	1.4	2.5
(Liner only)	(26.6)	(23.0)	(21.5)				..	..	..	..	..	..

1. In the total imports or exports of Belgium, Canada, Finland, France (1983 and 1984), Germany, Greece (1983), Italy (1983), Japan, Netherlands, Spain, Sweden, United Kingdom, United States and Australia.

2. As defined in the "United Kingdom Business Monitor MA8 1978" page 13. London 1979.

NOTE: .. Data not available. Japanese data does not separate Belgian, Finnish, Spanish or Canadian tonnage. Italian data does not separate Finnish or Canadian tonnage.

SOURCE: Seaborne Trade Statistics Exercise: data provided by National Delegations.

under their flag by non-nationals very much easier, which has led to rapid growth in the fleets, inter alia, of Malta, Honduras, St. Vincent and Gibraltar and the Cayman Islands. Unfortunately the clients for these new registers have tended to be small operators with over-age ships, which has led to some question of their capacity to maintain and supervise the standards of the vessels under their flags in relation to those established under the various IMO Conventions. This led to certain UK dependent territories, including the Cayman Islands, making considerable changes in their control and supervisory procedures.

These developments have taken place at a time when a number of OECD countries have taken steps towards the introduction of "offshore" registers. In June, France established the Kerguelen register which is open to non-oil bulk vessels which are enabled to use the French flag but employ up to 75 per cent of non-French seamen. The status of this has been challenged by the unions, and the oil-tanker companies have also accused the government of discrimination. In the United Kingdom, there has been a very extensive transfer of shipping to the Isle of Man, which is expected to have some 5 million dwt on its register by the middle of 1987. The attractiveness of the Isle of Man has been the proposed introduction of regulations for ship management, low personnel and corporate taxation, the absence of an annual registration fee and, most notably, its acceptance by the International Transport Workers' Federation as not being a flag of convenience, although operating from the Isle of Man enables social costs and manning scales to be reduced from UK levels. Spain is considering the possibility of a Canary Islands register, and the Aland Islands have also been suggested as a Finnish offshore register location. Within the OECD, Luxembourg is examining the possibility of a register, possibly from 1988, and Yugoslavia has amended its legislation to facilitate foreign shipowners operating under the Yugoslav flag, provided they employ Yugoslav personnel. The potentially most significant development is the proposal currently before the Norwegian Parliament for a Norwegian international register which will enable shipowners to hire foreign nationals on local pay scales and provide tax exemption for foreign investors while maintaining the very high standards which already exist for Norwegian-flag vessels. A considerable number of Norwegian and other Scandinavian shipowners now operating under other flags are reported to be interested in repatriation to the new Register.

The "offshore register" is not a new invention. They have been in existence, for example, in Bermuda and the Netherlands Antilles for very many years. They are based on the concept of the maintenance of administrative control and the supervision of internationally-accepted standards while providing flexibility from the point of view of taxation, corporate organisation, and the absence of constricting labour agreements. The present fervour appears to be partly the result of the continuous pressures of ship operators to reduce costs in an economic climate of oversupply which prevents any reasonably sustained profitability, partly the growing concern of governments that the fleets under their control are approaching the minimum level needed for strategic or security purposes and partly a defensive reaction to the proliferation of open and half-open registers, and the introduction of offshore registers elsewhere. It is, however, a matter of some concern in this atmosphere of competition between registers, whether it will, in fact, be possible to maintain the general standards that have been established. At the same time, they make no contribution to the underlying problem of overcapacity which has generated them, and indeed may even exacerbate it. The other risk

T.3.F.

SHARES OF OPEN REGISTRY AND USSR FLEETS IN OECD INTERNATIONAL SEABORNE TRADE

per cent of tonnage

	OPEN REGISTRY SHARE IN TRADES(1)						USSR SHARE IN ALL TRADES						USSR SHARE IN TRADES WITH EASTERN EUROPE					
	IMPORTS			EXPORTS			IMPORTS			EXPORTS			IMPORTS			EXPORTS		
	1983	1984	1985	1983	1984	1985	1983	1984	1985	1983	1984	1985	1983	1984	1985	1983	1984	1985
Belgium(O/D)	13.7	14.7	12.9	11.7	13.5	13.8	7.4	6.3	5.2	6.1	4.7	5.7	60.7	53.5	48.7	66.7	69.7	62.5
(Non-bulk only)	(4.3)	(6.3)	(7.0)	(9.1)	(9.8)	(11.4)	(3.7)	(3.9)	(2.5)	(2.4)	(2.1)	(3.2)	(67.6)	(54.0)	(54.2)	(38.2)	(50.5)	(54.4)
France	22.8	19.9		15.4	14.2		5.0	4.0		9.9	8.5		57.6	53.9		71.6	59.7	
Germany	23.4	24.4	24.8	13.0	15.4	13.3	4.8	5.4	6.2	9.9	9.4	10.0	44.6	47.1	53.9	68.8	76.3	54.5
Italy	19.3	..	..	17.2	..	..	5.8	..	..	6.3	..	..	44.5	..	..	87.7	..	..
Netherlands	26.5	29.2	32.7	16.1	17.3	17.2	6.7	6.3	5.0	2.6	1.9	2.9	67.6	61.0	58.4	60.2	60.8	55.0
(Non-bulk only)	(17.4)	(17.2)	(14.9)	(13.9)	(14.1)	(12.6)	(1.1)	(1.2)	(1.3)	(1.9)	(2.0)	(2.0)	(51.8)	(47.0)	(48.4)	(60.3)	(52.4)	(54.7)
United Kingdom	13.5	15.4	17.1	17.4	18.2	18.9	3.6	3.4	2.4	0.7	0.9	1.2	51.1	37.4	33.3	32.1	35.5	33.8
(Non-bulk only)(2)	(7.0)	(7.2)	(7.5)	(7.6)	(8.0)	(8.0)	(1.0)	(1.1)	(1.2)	(2.6)	(2.4)	(2.9)	(17.5)	(16.6)	(19.7)	(52.4)	(54.4)	(52.3)
Finland	3.3	1.4	3.5	2.0	3.1	3.5	22.0	21.0	20.4	2.0	3.9	2.9	34.2	33.8	35.7	30.0	39.9	16.4
(Non-bulk only)	(3.9)	(1.7)	(0.5)	(1.5)	(2.2)	(2.9)	(17.5)	(13.3)	(14.2)	(2.3)	(2.9)	(2.8)	(36.5)	(36.1)	(44.2)	(26.6)	(33.5)	(16.2)
Greece	13.2	..	..	22.1	24.5	..	15.4	8.2	..	5.5	4.6	..	..	..	..	..	..	..
Spain	21.7	19.0	21.8	23.1	25.6	27.4	2.7	2.6	2.2	3.2	3.2	4.7	57.0	41.1	58.6	72.0	68.7	80.8
Sweden	8.4	6.5	9.2	6.4	7.0	6.4	9.8	8.5	7.3	1.7	2.2	3.1	..	..	..	..	..	..
Japan	32.0	31.1	30.9	39.7	40.2	40.8	1.2	0.9	0.9	4.1	3.9	4.0	..	..	..	..	..	..
Canada	17.6	19.0	21.0	26.1	29.2	32.5	0.2	0.4	0.5	4.5	4.5	3.4	27.8	18.0	30.2	53.3	49.6	47.9
(Non-bulk only)	(14.6)	(21.7)	(23.2)	(21.9)	(22.5)	(23.5)	(2.1)	(3.3)	(2.5)	(2.0)	(2.4)	(1.8)	(52.1)	(23.9)	(22.0)	(73.6)	(65.5)	(41.2)
United States	47.0	43.1	44.5	33.7	33.9	35.9	0.2	0.2	0.2	0.7	0.8	0.6	18.3	11.9	15.2	17.4	12.9	10.6
(Liner only)	(14.6)	(12.5)	(13.9)	(18.5)	(16.3)	(15.6)	(0.0)	(0.0)	(0.0)	(0.1)	(0.0)	(0.0)	(2.8)	(0.0)	(0.0)	(12.2)	(0.0)	(0.0)
Australia	35.7	25.0	19.6	22.2	20.4	16.1	1.2	1.0	1.4	0.6	0.7	1.0	4.7	39.3	60.0	40.5	40.9	38.9
(Non-bulk only)	(13.5)	(12.8)	(7.2)	(26.0)	(25.9)	(17.8)	(3.5)	(3.5)	(3.5)	(2.3)	(4.4)	(5.0)	(13.2)	(39.3)	(60.0)	(78.0)	(80.8)	(80.7)
All OECD reporting countries	26.8	26.8	28.3	23.1	23.4	23.4	3.4	2.7	2.3	2.5	2.3	2.1	45.0	39.9	37.5	45.3	30.2	30.1

1. Liberia, Panama, Cyprus (except for Italy and Japan), Singapore (except for Italy).

2. Defined as in Table T.3.E.

NOTE: .. Data not available. Figures in brackets are not taken into account in the overall total.

SOURCE: Seaborne Trade Statistics: data provided by National Delegations.

is that their existence may give encouragement to countries which are not in a position to establish such registers to counter the advantages they provide, either by subsidy or by protectionist measures in favour of the national fleet.

The left-hand section of Table T.3.F sets out the participation of the three largest open registers (together with Singapore, although this is not, as a rule, still classified as an open register; data on Bahamas is not separately available) in the external seaborne trade of OECD Member countries. For most European countries there has been a progressive rise in the open registry share. Outside Europe, however, while their importance in the Canadian trades has been maintained, there are signs of a reduction for Japan and the United States, together with a massive drop in Australia, mainly as a result of the effect of union activity in Australian ports which has discouraged operators from sending open registry ships to Australia.

The fleets of the East European countries

By comparison with the considerable changes which took place in the other areas of the world fleet, the fleets under the flags of the East European countries followed a relatively uneventful path, with a very modest growth between mid-1985 and mid-1986 of 0.7 million gt, an increase of just over 2 per cent. None of the countries recorded reductions in tonnage terms, although Romania, after the rapid growth of recent years, only added 200 000 gt to its fleet, equivalent to 6.7 per cent, with four additional dry bulk carriers to its large existing fleet. Poland also expanded its dry bulk fleet to assist with its campaign to increase its coal exports.

The Soviet Union itself only expanded its fleet by 0.9 per cent in terms of gt and, in fact, in dwt terms, it actually declined. This was due to an extensive pruning of its tanker fleet, with a large scrapping programme of ships in the 35/45 000 dwt range built in the late sixties. The USSR has also continued to pursue its programme of modernisation of fully and partly containerised vessels to replace older units in its fleet operating on international trades, and during 1986 took delivery of 23 new vessels in these categories with a total of 270 000 dwt as well as a further addition to its barge carrier fleet, intended for use on the Arctic coastal trades. During 1985 and early 1986 there were no indications of any substantial increases in the quantity of Soviet-flag vessels operating on international liner trades and during the second half of 1986 it is estimated that just over 200 vessels with a total of 2 million dwt were so employed, 10 per cent less than during the period 1984-85. There has been no indication that the USSR intends to participate in the very large container ship sector. However, Soviet lines have benefited from the sudden withdrawal of the USL round-the-world services, particularly in the Mediterranean and Middle East sector.

The right-hand section of Table T.3.F sets out the participation of ships operating under the Soviet flag in the international trades of OECD countries overall and in their seaborne trades with the East European countries for the period 1983-85. There have been extensive changes from year to year in the participation of the USSR fleet in the bilateral trades with OECD countries, but overall there appear to be signs of a decline in their share of the OECD export trades to Eastern Europe, certainly in 1985 (except for Spain), and in the import trades (except for Spain and Germany), although in many cases the amounts involved are fairly limited. In the seaborne trade of the OECD as a whole, the involvement of the USSR fleet has remained relatively constant at about 3 to 3 1/2 per cent of imports and 2 to 2 1/2 per cent of exports, but during 1985 and 1986, in a number of trades, the USSR penetration has been somewhat reduced. However it is too early to say whether this is a continuing trend.

The fleets of the developing countries

The addition of 5.3 million grt between mid-1985 and mid-1986 to the fleets of the developing market-economy countries, which brought them past the Third Development Decade target was heavily biased in favour of a fairly small group of countries. Table XV(a) of the Statistical Annex and the lower section of Table T.3.D show very clearly that five countries, two of them dependent territories with virtual open-register status, received 5.4 million, while the remainder effectively balanced out on gains and losses. In Latin America, moderate growth in Brazil and Chile, both restricted by balance of payments problems, was cancelled out by a substantial cutback in Argentina, which removed a large quantity of its oldest tankers and general cargo ships. The only African countries to have made any appreciable growth were Egypt, which made additions to its dry bulk and general cargo fleet, and Nigeria, which expanded both its liner and its oil carrier capacity.

The oil producing countries of OPEC have been severely affected by the steady erosion of their oil revenues, and their tanker fleets have continued to shrink. Only Iran and Kuwait have increased their oil carrier tonnage under their flags. In the case of Iran, this has been forced upon it because of the need to establish shuttle services and floating storage so that crude exports from the mouth of the Gulf could be maintained. Kuwait has been operating shuttle services too, to Khor Fakkan, but is also continuing the expansion of its fleet of large product carriers as part of its downstream integration programme, although it has put back the scheduling of the latter vessels to be ordered, in view of the instability of the 1986 oil market. In contrast, the UAE and Algeria have made drastic reductions in their fleets, with Algeria having now virtually withdrawn from the oil shipping scene and limiting its activities to LNG transportation. The Gulf states have also been badly affected by the fall in imports as a result of lower oil revenues and liner companies of Saudi Arabia and Kuwait have been subjected to low load factors and excessive competition, with the result that the United Arab Shipping Co. (UASC), the largest company in the region, has recorded severe losses for 1984 and 1985 and estimates 1986 results to be even worse. As a result, at the end of 1986 only one company in the area, Norasia, had any general cargo or container ships on order.

South and South-East Asia, with the newly-industrialised countries of the Far East, continue to be the only substantial areas of growth for the developing countries, although here also the economic stresses of world shipping have led to major disturbances. Hong Kong, which has now apparently weathered the restructuring of the Tung and Wah Kwong groups, continued to increase the tonnage under its flag, partly by repatriation from other flags, which contributed to the reduction in the size of the Singapore fleet, but globally the financial upheavals are estimated to have resulted in an overall reduction of Hong Kong owned and managed fleet by some 10 per cent during 1986, mainly in tankers and bulk carriers. (9) The South Korean shipping industry is undergoing a major rationalisation programme, which involved extensive debt rescheduling, the second in four years and the companies have been instructed to dispose of more than 1 1/2 million gt over the next two years. A regulation has also been introduced requiring the use of Korean flag ships for imports unless their freight rates are more than 10 per cent higher than the foreign-flag competitor. (10) The Korean container fleet has grown considerably, partly as a result of defaults for new buildings ordered from Korean yards, which the shipyard group has had to operate itself, contributing to the existing overcapacity in the Europe/Far East and Europe/Australia trades, in competition with the two large Taiwanese operators which have both continued to expand their container fleets. At the end of 1986, ten of the third generation container ships were still on order for these two companies. The other remarkable development in the area has been the continuing rapid expansion of the Philippine dry bulk carrier fleet. During 1986, according to Fearnleys, 50 ships with a total of 3 million dwt were added, making the Philippines the sixth-largest dry bulk fleet in the world, after the UK, Greece, Japan, Liberia and Panama. As a country with no major dry bulk imports or exports, these ships are being operated in third country trades, and their connection with the Philippines is essentially a question of manning.

SIZE AND AGE OF SHIPS

Tables XVI(a) and (b) and XVII of the Statistical Annex give a detailed breakdown, by both gt and dwt, of the distribution of the world fleet by categories of size and age, according to Lloyd's Register, as at the middle of 1986. This is also given separately for oil tankers, dry bulk carriers, general cargo ships and other vessels. Since these mid-year figures take into account the massive volume of scrapping of tankers during 1985, the average size of the entire tanker fleet fell by nearly 6 per cent and tonnage over 100 000 grt now makes up only 43 per cent of that fleet, compared to 49 per cent only three years earlier. In contrast, the pure bulk carrier fleet (i.e. excluding combination carriers) has increased its average size by more than 10 per cent during the same period, and in 1986 as a whole (2) bulk carriers over 150 000 dwt (approximately equivalent to 100 000 grt) added more than three million tons, to constitute 8 per cent of the fleet (against 6 per cent a year earlier). The limited volume of new orders for bulk carriers in 1986 was principally at this end of the scale with 67 per cent of the total being for vessels over 100 000 dwt. More disturbingly, a similar trend was notable for tankers, with more than 3 million dwt of VLCCs being ordered during the second half of the year. (3) Table T.3.G indicates the pattern that has been followed for the average size of the principal categories of ships in service and on order at the beginning of each of the last four years and shows clearly the decline in the size of tankers and the rise for existing dry bulk ships, together with the increasing size for new orders.

Tables XVIII(a)-(c) of the Statistical Annex set out the age structure of the total fleets of OECD Member countries and the largest non-Member countries, as well as their oil tanker and dry bulk carrier shipping. In general, the age structure of the OECD fleet as a whole is not dissimilar to that of the world fleet, although as the tables clearly indicate, the variations among individual countries is very considerable. Overall the "under five years" group still constitutes 19 per cent of the world fleet (20 per cent of OECD) but the next bracket has fallen from 26 to 22 per cent during the twelve

T.3.G

AVERAGE SIZE OF SHIPS IN SERVICE AND ON ORDER

1984-1987

in dwt

	EXISTING FLEET AS AT 1ST JANUARY:				VESSELS ON ORDER AS AT 1ST JANUARY:			
	1984	1985	1986	1987	1984	1985	1986	1987
Tankers over 10 000 dwt	100 700	100 000	95 500	92 700	51 700	57 600	66 400	78 400
Combination carriers	118 900	116 200	120 400	118 100	86 200	122 500	154 300	156 700
Dry bulk Carriers	37 800	38 500	39 600	40 700	40 000	48 600	59 500	60 700
Other cargo-carrying ships	8 400	8 500	8 500	8 500	12 000	11 700	11 000	11 300
All cargo ships	26 900	26 500	25 800	25 600	31 000	33 900	35 700	39 800

SOURCE: "Review 1986" Fearnleys, Oslo, January 1987.

months between mid-1985 and mid-1986, while the 10/15 year group now makes up exactly a third of world tonnage.

Among the main OECD fleets, Belgium remains substantially the youngest at 6.9 years, followed by Australia (7.9). Japan, Sweden, Germany and the Netherlands have all much the same average age, between 8.5 and 8.8 years, followed by Denmark (9.2), Norway (9.7), France (10.3) and Finland (10.6). The considerable reductions in the Greek, Norwegian and British fleets have been more concentrated in the older vessels and all three have reduced their average age, although Greece is still among the highest at 12.8, being only exceeded by Turkey (14.3), Italy (14.4), the United States (16.0) and Canada (18.0), the two last being particularly influenced by the high average age of the Great Lakes and US Reserve fleets. Spain, although younger than any of these (11.3 years), has introduced a major programme for the rejuvenation of its fleet.

Outside the OECD the variation is as wide with, at one end, Hong Kong and Kuwait, both of whose fleets are just over 8 years old on average, and at the other Malta at 18.1 years. However, this is exceeded by one of the more recent additions to the open registries, the Cayman Islands, which appears to have achieved its record growth partly by accepting large quantities of over-age tanker tonnage from other flags, with the result that its fleet has an average age of 18.9 years. By comparison, the four largest open-registries are very much younger, with Panama now the lowest at 10.6 years, followed by Liberia (10.9), Bahamas (11.3) and Cyprus (14.7). The Panamian decline has been particularly pronounced, due to a combination of a large volume of scrapping of old tonnage, the acquisition of a major part of the new dry bulk carriers which have been delivered over the past years and a transfer of a significant number of smaller elderly ships to the newcomer flags, particularly those located in the Caribbean.

The table below shows how the world fleet as a whole has aged over the last five years. The low level of deliveries, combined with the scrapping of relatively young tankers, has resulted in a progressive overall rise in the fleet as a whole, particularly located in the tanker fleet, whereas the dry bulk fleet has remained at the same level. It may be noted that between mid-'85 and mid-'86 the average age of the pure bulk carrier fleet declined from 10.0 to 9.8 years but was balanced out by the combination carrier fleet which rose from 11.6 to 11.9 years, the same as that of the tanker fleet. Similarly, within the "other vessels" category, the container and lighter carrier fleet, which makes up 28 per cent of the group, reduced its average age from 9.3 to 8.9 years as a result of the influx of the "third-generation" very large container ships.

Years of age (in terms of grt)

	WORLD FLEET	OIL TANKERS	DRY BULK CARRIERS(*)	GENERAL CARGO SHIPS	OTHER VESSELS
1981	10.6	9.7	9.7	13.7	10.9
1982	11.1	10.1	10.3	14.2	11.3
1983	11.3	10.3	10.5	14.3	11.6
1984	11.4	10.7	10.5	14.2	11.6
1985	11.5	11.3	10.2	13.9	11.8
1986	11.7	11.9	10.2	13.4	12.3

(*) Including combination carriers.

NOTE: Age calculated by assuming that all tonnage within each five-year bracket given by Lloyd's had the age of the mid-point of that bracket and that tonnage "30 years and over" was aged 35 years.

SOURCE : Lloyd's Register of Shipping.

TONNAGE LAID UP, LOST AND SCRAPPED

The volatility in the tanker market during 1986 led to a very substantial reduction in the volume of tonnage in layup worldwide. The gradual decline during 1985, mainly associated with scrap sales, turned into a flood as a large number of ships were reactivated to take advantage of the rapid rises in voyage rates associated with the decline in crude prices and the resulting increased volumes being transported. As a result the 39 million dwt of tankers and combination carriers in formal layup at the start of the year had fallen by the end to 15 million. (4) All indications would suggest that the ships remaining in layup constitute a bloc of tankers which are unlikely to be reactivated unless there is a sustained and significant rise in market levels, which at present appears improbable. Most will eventually go to the scrapyards. By comparison, in spite of the lack of prospects for dry bulk carriers throughout the year, the number of such ships in layup has remained very low, at around 3 million tons. It appears, on the whole, that over the last two years dry bulk owners have preferred to take the deliberate decision of scrapping their tonnage rather than holding it in layup on the chance of improvement in the market.

The decline in tankers laid-up was reinforced during the second half of the year by a substantial increase in the volume of tonnage used for short-term storage. There has been a fairly stable quantity of shipping used worldwide as semi-permanent floating storage, estimated by Jacobs to have been around 7 million dwt throughout the year, somewhat less than in the latter part of 1985. However, during the late spring and autumn there was a vigorous upswing of ships being utilised for short-term storage as companies filled their land-based capacities with low-priced crude oil, with the result that in October 1985, 13 1/2 million dwt were so employed, the highest level so far recorded. The great majority of this was utilised in the Gulf/Red Sea and South-East Asia, although there was also a significant amount in both West

Africa and North-West Europe. This level was maintained into the early months of 1987, but with the crude oil price rise, seems likely to decline during the year.

Table XIX of the Statistical Annex sets out the tonnage which Lloyd's Register has recorded as lost or scrapped during the three years 1983-1985. The total figure for losses in 1985 was very much lower than in the previous year although at 1.65 million gt it was still among the highest recorded. However, the total includes 0.62 million lost as a result of hostilities, almost entirely in the Iran/Iraq war. Excluding this element, the volume of total losses due to normal marine hazards was the lowest for more than a decade. According to the Institute of London Underwriters, the 1986 figures were even better than 1985 with 1.21 grt of shipping being recorded as either actual or total losses. In terms of numbers of ships, indeed, the loss record in 1986 was better than that recorded in any year since the late sixties. There seems no doubt that the campaign for improvement of safety standards which IMO has been pursuing over many years, reinforced by the various port state control inspection programmes, has led to a progressive improvement and a reduction in serious casualties, particularly when it is recalled that the total loss figures include constructive total losses which have increased with the decline in the ratio between second-hand values and cost of repairs. The ILU figures exclude war losses and are hence more informative here than the total Lloyd's figures but the continued virulence of the Gulf war led to a rise in casualties due to hostilities in 1986. Eighty-two attacks on tankers and combination carriers took place during 1986 (3), nearly three times as many as in 1985 and at least 17 ships with a total of almost 3 million dwt were sunk or sufficiently seriously damaged to lead to their subsequent scrapping. This continued drain on both shipping and seafarers from attacks on ships flying neutral flags has led to surprisingly little political action by the governments of the flag states and there does not appear to be any immediate prospect of any countermeasures against the states involved.

After the record level of scrapping which was recorded for 1985, developments in the tanker freight market led to a near cessation of tanker scrap sales during most of 1986. According to Fearnleys, only 12.3 million dwt of tankers were disposed of during the year (compared to 27.8 million in the previous year) of which only 3 million were sold during the second half of the year, two-thirds as a result of damage sustained in the Gulf hostilities. This violent reduction was partly compensated by a record level of dry bulk carriers sold for scrap estimated by H. Houlders (11) at 15.1 million dwt, compared to 9.1 million in the previous year which itself waw more than 60 per cent above the previous record level. The greater part of these were in the below 40 000 dwt range, where the main pressure from new deliveries had been exerted and where the vast majority of elderly bulkers are located. The ships scrapped had an average age of 18.7 years. There was a slight hesitation with the modest upturn of bulk rates in the autumn and the penury of vessels available led to a sharp rise in scrap prices, which early in 1987 reached $155 per lightweight ton in the Far East, 45 per cent higher than at the end of the third quarter of 1985. The sales of bulk carriers resumed in the early months of 1987, with 1.6 million dwt sold during January and February, and the poor prospects for the dry bulk trades in the coming year seem likely to encourage this trend which may be expected to be accompanied by a resumption in tanker scrapping if the reduced quotas for crude production are maintained.

The wide differences in the prices paid for vessels for demolition and the amount on offer at particular times make the economics of operating facilities for ship demolition extremely risky, which was compounded in Taiwan by a major explosion in the middle of the year, leading to a detailed re-examination and enforcement of the gas-freeing regulations on the island. This sort of problem has led to the bankruptcy of several small ship breakers, particularly in Pakistan, and the enthusiasm for developing new facilities in South East Asia seems to have diminished considerably. Although the Liberian scheme finally came into operation during the year on a limited scale, new plans in West Africa and the Caribbean appear to be hanging fire and, objectively, unless very special local demand situations exist, the economic justification for introducing new facilities, at a time when it is apparent that existing capacity is more than ample, looks very problematic.

PERSONNEL

Tables XX(a) and (b) of the Statistical Annex contain such information as is available on the seagoing personnel who man the merchant fleets of Member countries, accompanied by a breakdown of the main categories of officers and ratings together with an indication of their distribution between nationals of the flag state and non-nationals from other Member and non-Member countries. The data contained in these tables has been derived from surveys using different criteria, as well as different limiting size-ranges, a matter of importance for the smaller and more numerous ships of certain national fleets and, as a result, are not by any means fully comparable. However, they give some clear indications of general trends and of how the personnel of individual fleets have evolved over recent years.

The rapid decline in the fleets operating under the flags of almost all OECD Member countries has inevitably resulted in a substantial shrinking of the seagoing personnel employed in them. During the two years between the end of 1983 and 1985 the number of seafarers in the United Kingdom declined by 30 per cent, in France by 24 per cent, in Denmark by 17 per cent, in Finland, the Netherlands and Spain by 15 per cent, and Norway by 6 per cent. Of the principal shipping countries, Germany and Belgium appear to be the only countries which did not record a significant decline in their personnel up to 1985, but both had severe reductions during 1986 of 12 and 6 per cent respectively. Japan, for whom data has not been available for the years between 1982 and 1985, has probably suffered the most radical reduction with more than 40 per cent less effectives reported between the two years, but this appears to involve a change in the method of evaluation and the figures may not be comparable. The trend appears to have quickened in 1986 with 19 per cent reductions recorded for France and Norway, 12 per cent in Denmark and 7 per cent in the United Kingdom, Japan and Finland, although Spain appears to have stabilised its seagoing personnel as part of its Fleet Revival Plan.

The contraction of the fleets and the need to maximise economies of operation has led to increased demands to permit the use of non-nationals aboard the ships under OECD flags. This is only legally possible in a limited number of countries, and one of the reasons for the increased interest in offshore registries, particularly the French use of Kerguelen, the Norwegian International Register and the fleets in UK dependent territories, has been the possibility of using non-nationals at pay scales competitive with those in operation on ships under open registry flags. Greece, in its efforts to encourage repatriation of Greek shipping, has increased the permitted percentage of foreign ratings on Greek-flag ships to 40 per cent of the total and now allows free choice of such non-domiciled seamen, a move strongly opposed by the Greek seafarers' unions.

Of those OECD countries which permit a substantial element of non-nationals for which data has been provided, it appears that where cutbacks have taken place, these have fallen hardest on the non-national elements. In the United Kingdom, between 1983 and 1985, the non-national element fell by 52 per cent compared to the overall 30 per cent; in the Netherlands the comparable figures were 22 per cent and 15 per cent; in Denmark 29 per cent and 17 per cent; and in Germany (1983-1986) 19 per cent and 12 per cent. Only in Norway and Sweden have the ratios between nationals and non-nationals remained fairly constant, but in the case of Norway, the situation is likely to be severely affected by the new International Register.

NOTES AND REFERENCES

(1) These figures include the Great Lakes fleets of Canada and the United States as well as the United States Reserve fleet, estimated at 2.6 million gt. During the twelve months between mid-1985 and mid-1986 the Lakes fleets declined substantially, by 330 792 gt, almost 10 per cent and at the end of the period there were 1 821 347 gt (238 ships) under the Canadian flag and 1 507 794 gt (173 ships) under the United States flag. These fleets are both ageing steadily and less than a quarter of the tonnage is under 10 years old.

(2) "World Bulk Fleet", Fearnleys, Oslo, February 1987.

(3) "World Tanker Fleet Review", John I. Jacobs PLC, January-June, July-December 1986.

(4) "Shipping Statistics and Economics", Institute of Shipping Economics and Logistics, Bremen, February 1987.

(5) Lloyd's List, 26th February 1987.

(6) "World Ships on Order", Nos. 85-89, Fairplay, London 1986/1987.

(7) "The Present Situation of the Refrigerated Cargo and Reefers", JMRI, Tokyo, August 1986.

(8) "Shipping Statistics and Economics", Drewry Shipping Consultants Ltd., London, January 1987.

(9) Hong Kong Shipowners' Association, January 1987.

(10) Lloyd's List, 20th February 1987.

(11) H. Houlders Chartering Ltd., London, January 1987.

Chapter IV

THE FREIGHT MARKETS

GENERAL

Projections did not foresee a significant upswing in the general economic climate at the start of the second half of the 1980s. Similarly, prospects for a better performance of the freight markets in the dry and liquid bulk sectors were characterised by pessimism. In 1986, as in the previous years, the economic slump in shipping persisted and it was another turbulent year for bulk trades, despite certain peaks but, once again, freight rates suffered significantly.

Voyage charters for the carriage of the major dry bulk commodities were down by almost 5 per cent and period chartering arrangements dropped even more. The tanker sector experienced a switch by charterers from time charters to single voyage shipping arrangements. The demand for spot VL/ULCCs got off to a slow start, but gradually increased during the second quarter and they continued their upward trend for the balance of the year. Rates for this type of carrier were very volatile during the second half. The interest in medium-sized carriers, especially for 120/130 000 and 80 000 tonners, rose during the first half and fell during the last six months. In January, time chartering in the tanker market was low, but as the year progressed interest picked up gradually, particularly in six-month fixtures.

A record amount of obsolete tonnage was demolished, but the delivery and ordering of newbuildings were still too high to make any significant change to the overall surplus capacity situation during 1986. The world fleet only declined by 2 per cent or 11.8 million dwt. This development failed to trigger permanent improvement of the freight markets. The tanker fleet and combined carriers were both down by 3 per cent, dry bulk carriers by 1 per cent and others by 0.5 per cent.

During 1986, oil trading was the only bulk commodity to experience growth, estimated to be about 8 per cent, while the dry bulk trades endured significant lows. Notably, grain shipments suffered the most with a 12 per cent decrease, iron ore with 5 per cent and coal with 1.5 per cent. Towards the middle of the year, the tanker sector enjoyed short-lived improvements in its freight rates, while it was not until September/October that the rates for the dry cargo market experienced an upturn, only to go down again in December.

As the year progressed, both dry and liquid bulk cargo owners faced severe disappointments. In the dry bulk sector, they saw very little encouragement in their revenue as market freight rates fell more than could ever have been imagined. They were especially low during July. Hopes were revived during the "traditional" September/October upturn, particularly in the coal sector, but quickly faded as rates slumped again in October and continued to do so until the end of the year. In the tanker sector, rates more or less stagnated until July but by the end of August they had risen sharply. Most of them reached a level double the one recorded during the previous year and continued to increase until September, at which time tanker owners' hopes evaporated. OPEC then decided to reintroduce oil production quotas and, although output increased slightly for most OPEC members in mid-October, the uncertainty resulting from that decision caused rates to go up very little until the end of the year. Although OPEC's efforts did not bring about improvement during 1986, it is expected that any positive repercussions may be felt later in the decade. Despite the fact that relatively low oil prices seem to be here to stay, at least for the next 2 to 3 years, their improvement alone cannot trigger an upturn in the present depressed freight market situation. Other factors, such as increased scrapping and lower newbuilding orders, must also be part of the revival package.

This chapter discusses, as well as illustrates by graphs and tables, the various interactions in freight markets during 1986, with specific emphasis on the major bulk commodities: grain, iron ore, coal, oil and oil products. The liner freight market and bunker prices are also examined.

DRY BULK FREIGHT MARKET

<u>General</u>

At the end of 1985, a genuine recovery of the dry bulk freight market for 1986 was not expected to occur. This projection did hold true as freight rates for dry cargo movements during the year were slightly lower than in 1985, with some short-lived fluctuations. There were nonetheless some positive signs, such as the continuing pace of demolition and the rise in the number of combination carriers employed in the oil trades, which have caused a reduction in the tonnage surplus, and which could have subsequently generated more favourable freight rates. Unfortunately this was not the case.

Shipowners/charterers had difficulty maintaining their optimism. In June and July, rates fell even further. August saw a slight increase which continued until November, at which time the rates dropped again, particularly for grain shipments moving between the United States Gulf and Japan, to finish the year at a record low.

Graph 4.A shows the monthly trends in the dry bulk rates for the year 1986. The first illustrates the spot market rates in US dollars for coal shipments moving on the Hampton Roads/Richards Bay/Japan routes and also for grain on US Gulf-ARA. Again in 1986, the rate movement patterns for these two seemingly unrelated commodities were closely linked. Around September, the rates peaked almost simultaneously and towards the middle of October, the two trades experienced the same rate level, around $7.00. The second graph shows the Biffex Futures Index (Baltic International Freight Futures Exchanges) by

Graph 4.A

MONTHLY TRENDS IN DRY BULK RATES (1986)

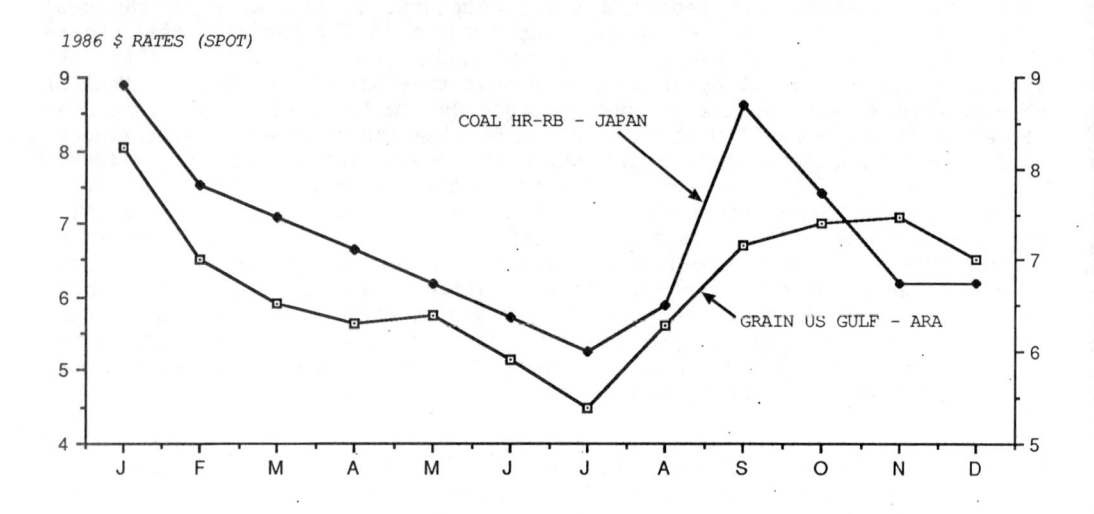

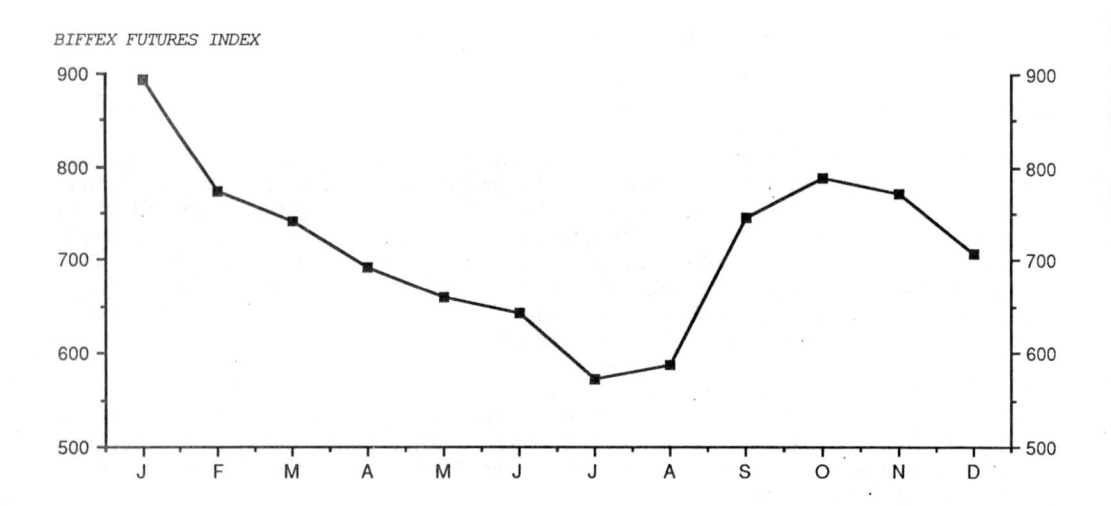

1986 $ RATES (SPOT)

BIFFEX FUTURES INDEX

Sources: Fearnleys, Drewry Shipping Consultants Ltd.

month. Contrary to the previous year where the Index reached its annual peak in April, 1986 witnessed a constant drop from 893.3 in January to 572.5 in July. Following a substantial increase during the next three months, it experienced another annual low of 707.2 at the end of the year.

Dry bulk voyage and trip market

The first half of Table XXI of the Statistical Annex sets out the development for the last eleven years of the main dry bulk cargo freight indices on quarterly and annual averages bases. The first section of Table XXII shows monthly variations for the last three years including yearly averages. These indices are based on tramp voyage rates of 28 trade routes and includes tankers in the grain trade. Graph 4.B illustrates the movement in the dry cargo voyage and period charter monthly rate indices for the years 1985-1986 and also shows the annual averages fluctuations for the last six years (1981-1986).

The annual average of the voyage charter for 1986 amounted to approximately 158, a decline of 4.8 per cent from the previous year, which in turn represents a decrease greater by 2.2 per cent than for the years 1984-1985. The rates were especially low during July and August, when the monthly Shipping News International index recorded 150.8 and 148.1 points respectively. Although the rates picked up slightly between September and November as they usually do in the autumn, they remained extremely low all year.

Table 4.A shows, in US dollars, the highest and lowest average price per ton of dry bulk cargo in a number of representative trades for the years 1984-1986. For all three commodities examined (grain, coal and iron ore), the overall downward trend in rates continued in 1986. For grain movements, the decline in rates was less than during the previous year. Rates for a 55 000 dwt shipment on the US Gulf-Continent routes varied from a high of $8.25 to a low of $4.50 or a 45.4 per cent fall. For the carriage of 50 000 dwt of grain between the US Gulf and Japan, rates dropped by 45.1 per cent from $13.50 to $7.40 per ton. In the coal sector, for a 55 000 dwt shipment between Hampton Roads and Japan, rates decreased from $9.00 to $6.00 per ton, representing a 33.3 per cent drop. Lastly, 120 000 dwt of iron ore between Brazil and the Continent decreased by 40 per cent from $4.50 to a record low of $2.70 per ton.

Table 4.B shows a breakdown of the various types of charters and contracts in cargo tons for the tonnage fixed for dry cargo during the first and second half of the years 1984-1986. The first part sets out in million cargo tons voyage charters fixed for the major dry bulk commodities. Grain shipments were rather stable with a total of 25.5 million cargo tons (1985: 24.8) during the first half of the year and 25.4 million in the second half (1985: 27), representing respectively a 2.5 per cent increase and a 6 per cent decrease with the 1985 shipments.

Coal movements were higher in 1986 than during the previous year, with 18.6 million cargo tons fixed in the first half (1985: 17) and 17.2 million tons in the second half (1985, 16.4), which amounted to a 7.2 per cent increase for 1986. Iron ore was the most affected by the weak market situation. During the first half of the year, 21.8 million cargo tons were fixed (1985, 24.2) and only 15.8 million (1985, 17.8) in the second half, representing a significant drop of 10.5 per cent during 1986.

T.4.A

PRICE PER TON OF DRY BULK CARGO

(1984-1986)

in US dollars

		1984	1985	1986
Grain				
US Gulf-Antwerp/Rotterdam/Amsterdam (55 000 dwt)	high low	10.75 7.75	11.60 5.65	8.25 4.50
-Japan (50 000 dwt)	high low	17.80 12.75	16.25 10.00	13.50 7.40
Coal				
Hampton Road/Richards Bay-Japan (120 000 dwt)	high low	11.25 9.50	10.95 8.60	9.00 6.00
Hampton Roads-Continent (60 000 dwt)	high low	6.90 6.45	6.75 4.20	5.25 3.25
Iron Ore				
Brazil-Continent (120 000 dwt)	high low	5.60 5.50	6.05 3.65	4.50 2.70

SOURCE: Lloyd's List

T.4.B

TONNAGE FIXED ON THE DRY CARGO VOYAGE AND PERIOD MARKETS

(1984-1986)

	1984 1st HALF	1984 2nd HALF	1985 1st HALF	1985 2nd HALF	1986 1st HALF	1986 2nd HALF
VOYAGE CHARTERS (million cargo tons)						
Grain	28.8	30.6	24.8	27.0	25.5	25.4
Sugar	1.2	1.4	1.5	1.2	1.0	1.2
Iron ore	17.2	17.1	24.2	17.8	21.8	15.8
Other ores	0.8	0.5	0.8	0.8	0.8	0.5
Coal	10.6	12.9	17.0	16.4	18.6	17.2
Chemicals and fertilisers	2.7	4.5	2.9	2.9	1.6	1.4
Iron, Steel Products and Scrap	0.4	0.7	0.9	0.7	1.1	1.2
Miscellaneous	2.7	1.9	3.4	2.3	1.0	0.5
Total	64.6	69.6	75.5	69.1	71.4	63.2
CONSECUTIVES AND CONTRACTS OF AFFREIGHTMENT (million cargo tons)	25.2	35.7	4.0	8.2	6.0	1.0
TRIP CHARTERS (million dwt)	37.2	26.8	33.8	32.7	37.6	35.3
TIME CHARTERS (million dwt)						
Duration of 1 year or under	6.7	2.9	3.0	1.7	3.1	3.4
Over 1 year duration	1.5	1.6	1.7	1.9	0.6	2.1
Total	8.1	4.5	4.7	3.6	3.7	5.4
TIME CHARTERS (million dwt-years)						
Duration 1 year or under	4.7	2.1	1.2	1.0	1.1	1.1
Over 1 year duration	3.2	4.6	2.7	3.0	0.9	2.3
Total	7.9	6.7	3.9	4.0	2.0	3.4

SOURCE: "Shipping Statistics and Economics", Drewry Shipping Consultants Ltd.

Consecutives and contracts of affreightment (see Table 4.B) have gradually decreased to almost insignificant levels since 1984, when their popularity had peaked. In view of the overall economic situation and the resulting uncertainties in the international freight market sector in general, bulk shippers have given preference mostly to trip and voyage charters, to some extent to time charters of a duration of one year or less. For example, between 1985 and 1986, this type of shipping arrangement declined by 80 per cent.

The upper part of Graph 4.C sets out the amount of cargo tonnage fixed each month on voyage and trip charters for 1985-1986 and also includes the annual averages for the years 1981 to 1986. Voyage and trip charters combined totalled 207.5 million cargo tons, compared with 211.2 million tons in 1985, which represents a decrease of about 2 per cent.

Dry bulk period (time) market

As shown on Graph 4.B, the 1986 hire rates for period charters were generally lower than the voyage freight equivalents for most of the year. In comparison with 1985, when period charters exceeded voyage charters, there seemed to be a lack of interest in making mediumor long-term commitments and charterers opted more for voyage arrangements. The graph also shows the gradual drop for period charter rates from January through July. The usual autumn recovery of rates which occurred between September and October (respectively amounting to 153 and 166), comparable to the same period in 1985, was immediately followed by a gradual decline. Table XXIII of the Statistical Annex records the dry cargo time charter freight indices determined by the Shipping News International (SNI) and the General Council of British Shipping (GCBS) for the years 1984-1986.

In 1986, time charters maintained an overall trend similar to the previous year till December when the volume dropped to a low comparable to the one experienced in June 1984. The last two graphs of Graph 4.C illustrate respectively the volume in million dwt tons for time charters on a month-by-month basis for the years 1985-1986 and the left part shows the volume of shipments multiplied by the period of the charter, expressed in million dwt-years, for the last five years.

The fourth section of Table 4.B shows the tonnage fixed on time charters in million dwt tons during the first and second half of years 1984-1986. During the latter year, the volume remained about the same for the first as well as for the second half of the year, amounting to 3.1 and 3.4 million dwt tons respectively for charters of one year duration or under, which in total represent an increase of 38.3 per cent from 1985. During the first half of 1986, those over one year decreased by 1.1 million dwt tons, while the second half moved up by 0.1 million dwt tons compared with the respective periods in 1985. The last part of the same table and the bottom graph in 4.C provide an indication of ship utilisation on time charters measured in million dwt-years. The sharp drop recorded in 1985 was stabilised in 1986, especially for shipping contracts of one year duration or less. For the others, 1986 saw a decrease of 2.5 million dwt-years (43.8 per cent) from the previous year, which indicates a consistent overall shortening of the period of the time charters.

Graph 4.B

DRY CARGO VOYAGE AND PERIOD RATE INDICES (1985-1986)

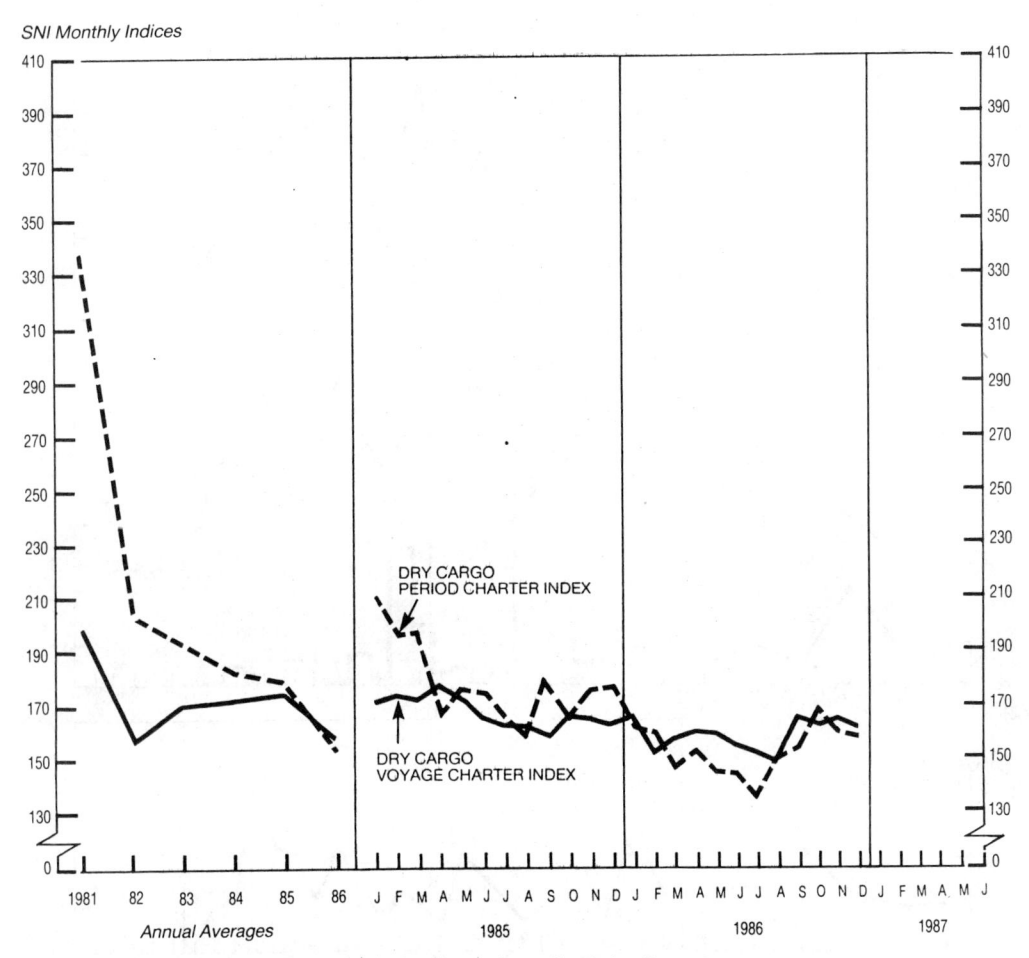

SNI Monthly Indices

Source: Shipping Statistics, Institute of Shipping Economics and Logistics, Bremen.

Graph 4.C
DRY CARGO CHARTERING (1981-1986)

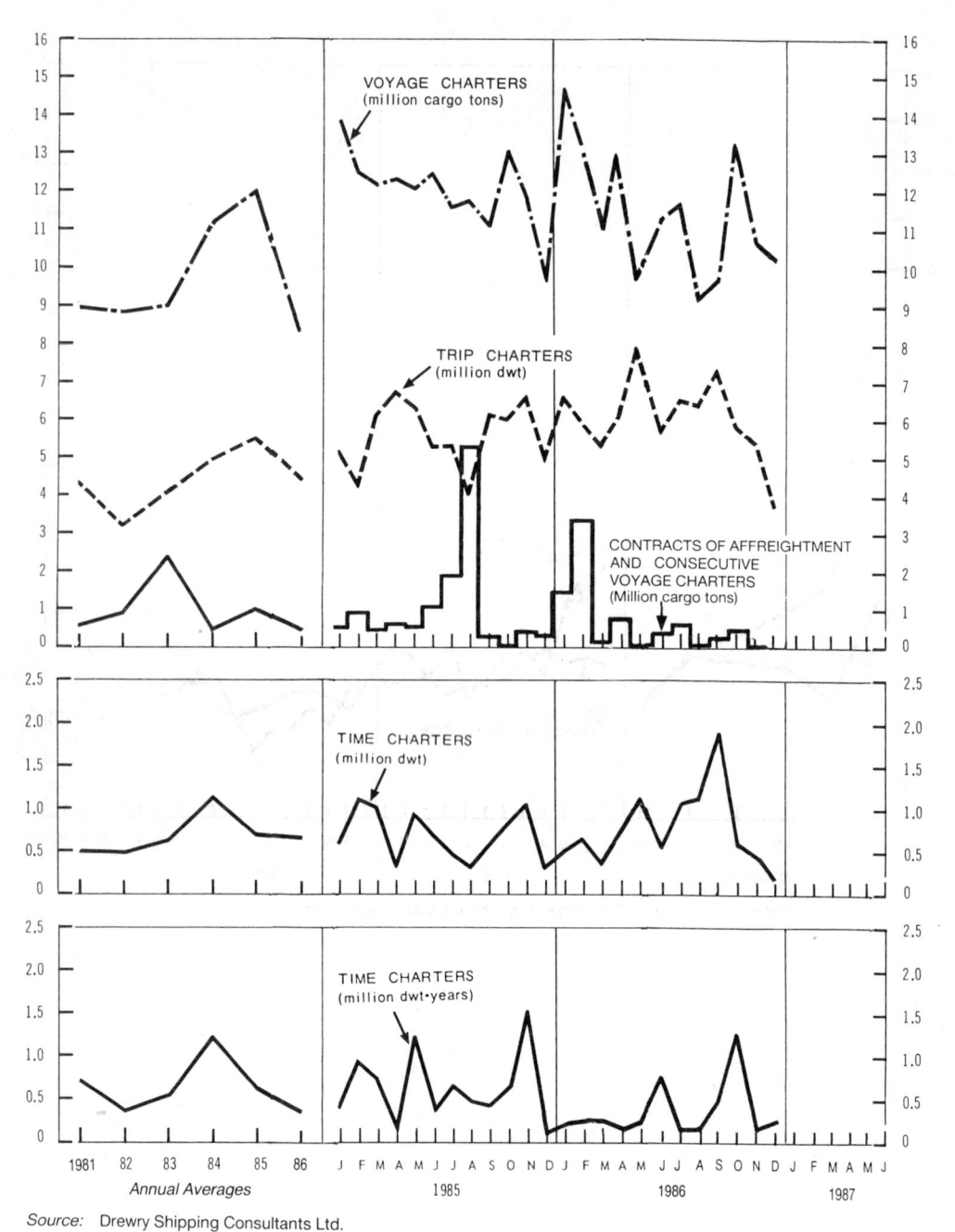

Source: Drewry Shipping Consultants Ltd.

Prospects for dry bulk rates

It is difficult to face forecasts for 1987 in a mood of optimism. Further scrapping of obsolete tonnage and a slower rate of orders and deliveries of newbuildings are expected during the year. There is still uncertainty as to whether these improvements in the overcapacity situation will provide more than temporary fluctuations in dry bulk freight rates.

TANKER FREIGHT MARKET

General

The international seaborne imports of crude oil and oil products are estimated to have increased by about 8 per cent in 1986, compared with 1985. Despite this improvement, the tanker market and freight rates have suffered as in previous years. As prices for spot charters on crude oil shipments continued downward, so did the tanker freight rates.

The following chart lists the major developments and events in oil markets and tanker freight rates from the beginning of the decade till the end of 1985. During that period, the oil market sector experienced, in particular, numerous peaks and valleys in prices per barrel, a significant reduction in demand for OPEC oil, and an increase in supply of non-OPEC crude from sources close to consumer markets, such as Mexico, North Sea and Alaska. It is worthy of note that during the last six years, crude oil and refined petroleum products sectors have not followed the same pattern. Between 1981 and 1983, the seaborne crude oil trade fell by about 20 per cent. The major factors for the depressed trade were the lower demand from industrialised countries and the significant reduction of oil production from OPEC member countries. The low trade volume persisted until late 1985. Refined petroleum products, on the other hand, experienced a growing demand especially from OECD Member countries. The next chart contains a month-by-month list of major events during 1986.

History of Major Developments and Events in Oil Markets and Tanker Freight Rates

(1980-1985)

1980

-- oil supply disruptions and Iranian crisis cause massive oil price escalation
-- volumes of tanker charter fixtures begin to fall

1981

-- OPEC crude oil prices peak
-- demand in developed countries falls
-- conservation measures and fuel switching sets oil consumption declines in motion
-- crude oil spot prices begin to fall gradually
-- expansion of oil output from non-OPEC suppliers

1982

-- substantial fall in charter rates
-- high oil prices are threatened
-- OPEC establishes oil production quotas, which are breached by many members
-- Saudi Arabia and Kuwait abandon production ceiling altogether
-- actual charter revenues begin to rise
-- non-OPEC suppliers refuse to practice output constraints
-- oil prices collapse

1983

-- OPEC cuts price of Arabian Light and retains production quotas
-- oil consumption in OECD countries shrinks

1984

-- higher levels of consumption in LDCs and OECD countries, particularly in US and Japan

1985

-- "netback" pricing policy introduced (crude price related to oil product prices)
-- non-OPEC (excluding centrally-planned economies oil production rises to about 60%
-- levels of consumption fall again
-- new peak in tanker scrappage

Month-by-Month Chart of Relevant Current Events in the Oil and Tanker Sectors in 1986

January

-- generally mild winter in Europe and US decreases oil demand
-- Iran's oil export capacity increased to 6MM barrels a day
-- Soviet oil production less than previous year
-- North Sea oil prices decline to $17 a barrel
-- OPEC production estimated in excess of 18MM barrels a day
-- total volume of spot and time chartering falls back
-- North Sea production rose by 11 per cent

Feburary

-- mining industries in France and the UK reduce coal prices to compete with low fuel oil prices
-- Venezuela adopts more flexible prices
-- Iran, Algeria and Libya call for a meeting between OPEC and non-OPEC producers

March

-- Mexico's crude oil exports drop by around 26 per cent
-- Meeting of Gulf Co-operation Council and OPEC's talks fail to reach agreement
-- Crude oil prices plunge further

April

-- Norwegian oil production is halted because of offshore catering workers dispute, causing rises in spot prices for North Sea
-- Wintershall of FRG cancels many new domestic and foreign exploration projects
-- Mexican budget cut of $1 billion, due to falling oil revenues

May

-- UK approves two new gas field developments in North Sea
-- Saudi Arabian netback crude prices are cut by $0.50-$1.15/bbl for May liftings
-- Plans for a $1.17 billion pipeline to carry Canadian natural gas to the US North East is abandoned
-- Thirteen VL/ULCCs are chartered in Arabian Gulf

June

-- Iran joins Saudi Arabia in selling crude oil to Japan at a discount
-- OPEC production soars
-- Iraq attacks Kharg oil terminal
-- OPEC agrees to meet at end of July on output quotas
-- China's imports of crude and product are increasing
-- Oil prices drop to about $10 a barrel
-- Volume of period chartering falls
-- Important increase in demand for VLCCs on spot market

July

-- OECD stocks are reported to be at their lowest level for over 10 years
-- Oil prices continue to drop
-- OPEC takes interim measure to boost oil prices

August

-- Decline in period chartering and increase in spot market
-- OPEC agrees on production quotas
-- Oil prices soar after Iraqi air attack at Sirri Island

September

-- Decline in period chartering
-- Spot prices strengthen following OPEC's new output policy

October

-- Spot prices continue to rise
-- Iraq attacks Iranian oil terminals
-- OPEC revenues are up by about 20 per cent

November

-- USSR is reported to have increased exploration and development activities
-- Many VLCCs are idle in the Gulf
-- Level of period chartering at its lowest

December

-- Oil prices soar when OPEC agrees to cut output by 5 to 10 per cent and sets prices at $18 a barrel
-- Forecasts predict lower oil demand in 1987
-- Volume of chartering rises in fear of possible oil price increases

Graph 4.D

MONTH BY MONTH CHART OF 1986 TANKER RATE INDICES

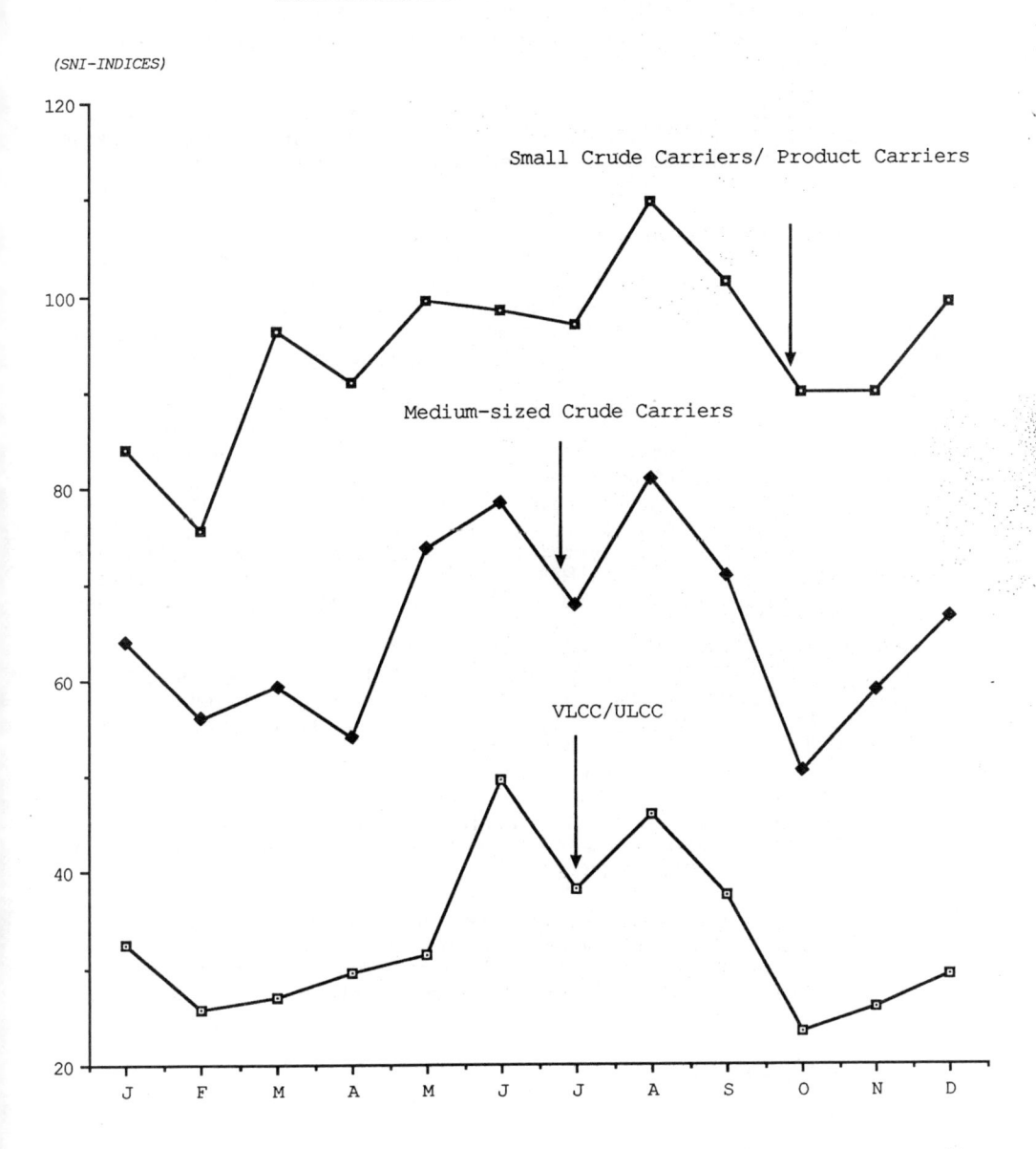

(SNI-INDICES)

Small Crude Carriers/ Product Carriers

Medium-sized Crude Carriers

VLCC/ULCC

Source: Shipping News International Ltd., Norway.

The uncertainty which shook various traders vis-à-vis the tanker market appeared as early as 1979. The amount of tonnage fixed on tanker period charters began to decrease and many charterers switched to single voyage shipping arrangements. The first half of the 1980s also witnessed a decline in the level of ordering of newbuildings and an increase in the volume of tanker tonnage being scrapped.

Graph 4.D shows the movement month-by-month in freight rates for small and medium-sized crude carriers as well as for VL/ULCCs during 1986, as recorded by the SNI index. Rates for the three types of tankers generally followed the same pattern in their increases and decreases throughout the year. On the whole, freight rates of the dirty tanker voyage market during the first quarter of 1986 did not maintain the upward trend witnessed in the latter months of 1985. During the early months of 1986, the Arabian Gulf produced, at about the same level, as in November and December 1985. Despite the stable output, the rates for VL/ULCC tonnage in the spot market nonetheless fell sharply between January and February, and increased rather insignificantly until May. This situation was due primarily to the important decline of laid-up tonnage in the Gulf (estimated at about 5 million dwt tons) and also to the increase in available tankers resulting from the higher operating speed of that category of ships. The available tonnage of VL/ULCCs rose from less than one million dwt tons in early January to about 4 million dwt by the middle of February. During that same period, the situation for small and medium-sized carriers was slightly more encouraging, particularly on short-haul shipments. From mid-March to the middle of June, the demand for VL/ULCCs rose, but it was only around May that the rates started moving upwards and soared until the end of June, reaching a level of about W49. At the same time, the spot market for medium-sized tonnage also witnessed an increase in its rates (up to about 60 per cent).

In early July, VL/ULCC rates once again fell sharply to approximately W38, as laid-up tonnage continued to decline and as ships, fixed during the upsurge in chartering activity in April, returned to the Gulf area. In the medium-sized tanker sector, rates had also fallen around the same period to about W68 from a high of around W79 in June.

Similarly, the clean products carrier sector was highly volatile as rates decreased between January and mid-February and rose again to their annual peak level by the middle of June.

Between July and August, rates picked up again for all types of carriers. As stocks were being accumulated before the winter season in the main consumer nations, tanker freight rates fell sharply from August to October. A record low was avoided as rates were reactivated towards the end of the year.

Tanker voyage (spot) market

a)   VLCCs and ULCCs

Table XXI of the Statistical Annex indicates the long-term development of tanker voyage charter freight indices based on quarterly and annual averages. Table XXIV provides the indices by month for the years 1984-1986 in Worldscale points as calculated by the German "Bundesministerium für Verkehr" and the journal "Shipping News International".

Table 4.C sets out the average tanker voyage rates on a number of major routes for the last 12 years and the monthly rates for 1986. The last column contains the average Mullion weekly dirty tanker index for the same period.

The generally mild winter in Europe and the United States compounded by the sharp drop in oil prices and the growing supply of Japanese tanker tonnage caused a softening of rates and a slowdown in fixture activity for all categories of tankers during January, particularly for VL/ULCCs. The negative impact was mainly felt by voyages to the Red Sea. The great uncertainty concerning the future of the crude oil market, which prevailed during February and March, restrained UL/VLCC activities considerably. There were less than a dozen fixtures originating from the Arabian Gulf during most of the first quarter. Rates in most trades nonetheless managed to rise slightly, notably for voyages to the West and Red Sea. In April, the situation improved to some degree, since there were numerous fixtures reported. May and June witnessed an important increase in demand for VLCCs. Freight rates climbed from W30 to around W55 for voyages to the Far East. Only a couple of ULCC fixtures were reported, but at almost the same rate as for VLCCs. During the second half of the year, VL/ULCC freight rates were very volatile. In early September, as OPEC imposed output constraints and crude oil prices continued to increase, rates for VL/ULCCs soared, but dropped again later in the month to reach a record low in October. Towards the end of the year, demand improved significantly which boosted the VL/ULCC market. Rates for Western destinations rose to W22.5, those for the East to mid-W30s and the rare cargoes to Red Sea were registered at W25.

b) Medium-sized and small tankers

Fixtures for medium-sized crude carriers of 150 000 dwts were practically non-existent throughout 1986. Only a few shipments were recorded, mainly in January, May and July. Freight rates for westward destinations of tankers of this size nonetheless increased during July and August. Generally, it was a slow and depressed year for the 150 000 tonners on almost all voyages. Conversely, fixtures for 120/130 000 dwt tankers were relatively frequent in January and remained active till the end of the year. The West African trade, which recorded rates between about W35 and mid-W60s, was consistently the most active compared to other crude tanker trades until October, at which time fixtures tapered off. Rates did not always follow suit with the frequency of fixtures in that trade. In January, for example, they slipped by some 5 to 7.5 Worldscale points to W35/37.5 levels for shipments to the States and the UK Continent. At the end of February, they increased to the W50 bracket and remained stable until June when they climbed to the mid-W60s. They began to slip again during July. An improved demand helped West African rates to rise from below W40 to W42.5/45 levels in November, especially for long haul shipments. Arabian Gulf shipments were second most active and rates climbed as high as W80 in May from the W40 level recorded during the previous month.

For the 100 000 dwt tanker category, demand remained limited throughout the year. Most activities were concentrated principally in West Africa and average freight rates were generally paid with some fluctuations. Fixtures occurred rather occasionally and were mainly limited to medium-haul shipments. In May, however, rates for the Mediterranean/UK Continent trading were boosted up from W50 to W100, but tapered off around September. Not many

T.4.C

TANKER VOYAGE RATES ON SELECTED MAJOR ROUTES
AND MULLION WEEKLY TANKER VOYAGE INDEX

Points of Worldscale

		Persian Gulf/UK Continent (via Cape)	Persian Gulf/Far East	Mediterranean/ UK Continent	Caribs/USAC Crude/Black Products	Caribs/USAC White Products	Mullion Weekly Dirty Tanker Index (average)
Average	1975	25	49	59	71	96	75
	1976	30	52	57	86	113	85
	1977	25	49	52	83	145	75
	1978	32	54	70	115	167	79
	1979	48	84	139	191	366	145
	1980	36	57	78	127	239	112
	1981	28	38	52	85	143	70
	1982	30	38	55	79	139	57
	1983	27	35	56	82	109	59
	1984	29	41	61	86	113	62
	1985	26	37	59	76	108	60
	1986	30	44	60	82	140	68
1986	January	33	37	51	76	115	66
	February	21	33	48	76	134	57
	March	21	39	64	90	162	61
	April	27	42	50	83	136	60
	May	30	50	79	81	143	64
	June	42	60	78	87	136	81
	July	35	54	57	82	159	74
	August	43	63	64	102	134	92
	September	32	53	69	82	139	80
	October	20	26	48	69	128	62
	November	22	32	48	73	139	60
	December	24	34	61	81	145	63
1987	January	31	38	68	117	176	77
	February	25	34	91	89	187	76
	March	25	33	75	70	159	64

NOTE: Since 1980, the base Worldscale schedule has been revised every six months, on 1st January and 1st July. 1976: +10%, 1977: +2%, 1978: +6%, 1979: +2%, Jan. 1980: +20%, July 1980: +25%, Jan. 1981: nil, July 1981: +13%, Jan. 1982: -7%, July 1982: -4%, Jan. 1983: -1%, July 1983: nil, Jan. 1984: +1%, July 1984: +4%, Jan. 1985: +2%, July 1985: -1%, Jan. 1986: +1%, July 1986: -6%.

SOURCE: "World Tanker Fleet Review", John I. Jacobs, London and "Petroleum Economist", London.

fixtures were recorded in the last quarter, but rates for the West African area jumped from W37.5 to W50/55.

Between January and April inclusively, demand for 80 000 dwt tankers was rather important; however, the high turnover did not prevent rates from slipping in most trading areas, mainly for short haul shipments. Improvements were recorded during May in the Mediterranean/UK Continent and West African trades, when rates increased significantly from W50 to W100 and W40 to W60 respectively. The North Sea experienced considerable trading and dominated most of the demand until the end of October. As of November, the Mediterranean and UK became the two main loading areas. Nevertheless, rates in the latter trade took a turn for the worse, while those in the former strengthened.

In the 60 000 dwt category, most business emanated from the North Sea throughout the year. Nonetheless, rates showed a decline in that trade. Towards the last quarter, demand in the Caribbeans gained momentum, causing freight rates to jump from W62 to W80.

Although demand for small crude carriers in the Caribbeans experienced a slow start, fixtures in the area quickly picked up and remained in focus throughout the year. February saw a significant upturn as rates jumped from W65 to W80 and W90. March produced yet another increase from W87.5 to W125. It was not until August that the depressed situation in the Western Hemisphere improved, causing rates to rise. During September and October, there was a general decline in all major trades, except for the Caribbean Sea. In November, the Mediterranean/States trade was finally revived and rates followed suit with an increase of 35 points from W75 to W110.

Tanker period (time) charter market

Graph 4.E illustrates the movements of the tanker chartering sector on a month-by-month basis for 1985 and 1986. In addition, the left section shows the averages recorded between 1981 and 1986. In January, the total volume of time chartering was down to 1.3 million dwt, representing a 50 per cent decrease from the 1985 year end level. Due to the chaotic market situation during the next three months, period chartering became gradually more active with most fixtures estimated for periods of about six months, in view of the uncertainty surrounding oil prices and the market situation in general. The 1986 annual high was reached in May when the volume of charters escalated to reach a total of 4.6 million dwt, of which 70 per cent were fixed for a period less than seven months. Most time charters during the first half of 1986 were for the medium-sized tankers due to a greater interest on the part of certain major oil companies for this category of ship. This revival was shortlived as the interest declined during the second half. Conversely, the VC/ULCC market was relatively slow during the same period, but the activity picked up in the second half of the year, and some of these ships were taken on charters for a duration of up to three years. It is worthy of note that the period chartering market remained highly volatile, with the interest up one month and down the next, with no clear seasonal pattern. In June, the volume of period chartering fell by 3.3 million dwt tons, in accordance with seasonal trends. No charters for periods in excess of twelve months were reported. Following a slight improvement in July, the interest diminished over the next two months, estimated to be due to the falling rates on the spot market which encouraged

Graph 4.E
TANKER CHARTERING (1981-1986)

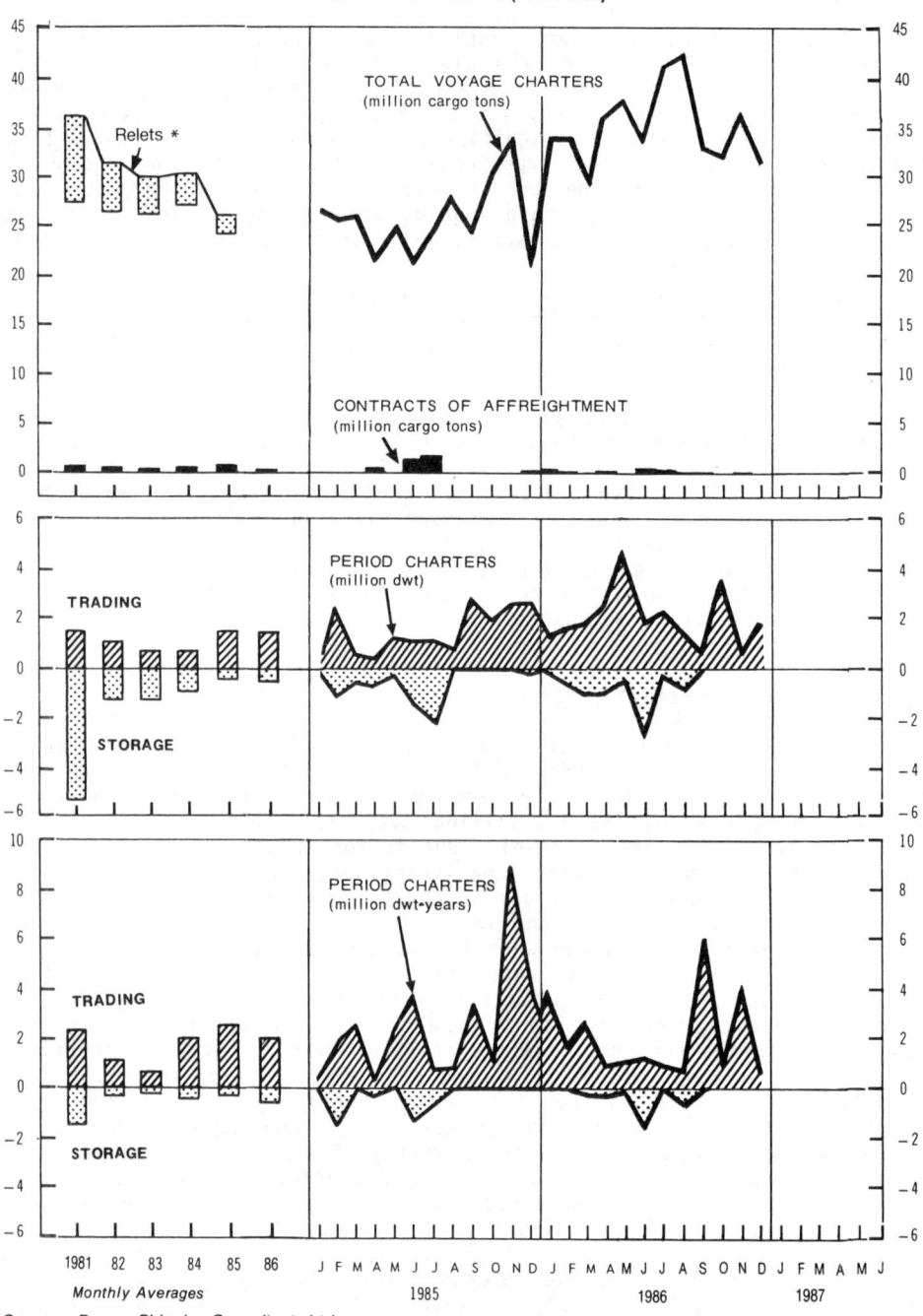

Source: Drewry Shipping Consultants Ltd.
* Relets have gradually decreased during the first half of the 1980s and this information is therefore no longer available.

charterers to wait in anticipation of further lower rates. During October, period chartering was up by about 450 per cent totalling 3.5 million dwt tons. Among the seven ships chartered, two VLCCs and one ULCC were reported to have been fixed for a period of three years. Volatility continued as the volume of time chartering dropped to its lowest level for over a year. It was estimated that this situation was attributable to the uncertainty created by requests from Saudi Arabia for a higher and stable oil price at $18 a barrel and for a bigger market share. As the year came to an end, period chartering had picked up slightly.

The new time charters for storage got off to a slow start, since the effects from the little interest shown for this type of charter during the second half of 1985 were still being felt. They gradually rose between February and April. Following a slight decrease during May, these charters subsequently reached a record high totalling 2.6 million dwt tons not seen since autumn 1984. The uncertainty, which had chronically prevailed among the oil traders since the early 1980s, reached rock bottom during the second half of the year when storage charters were virtually non-existent, as none had been reported between September and December inclusively. Similarly, very few contracts of affreightment were issued during 1986.

Prospects for tankers

In January 1987, OPEC decided to continue its oil production output quotas during the first few months of 1987 until its next meeting (when the quotas set in 1986 will be re-examined). In March 1987, the oil price was just under $16 per barrel on the spot market and it is expected that during the second half of the year it will stabilise at around the $18 per barrel mark aimed for by OPEC. Most likely OPEC will not find sufficient unity to agree on greater output quota limitations to allow prices to be restored even further, but there are other factors to be taken into account when estimating future oil prices and tanker freight rates, in particular the ongoing Iran/Iraq conflict. These two countries' production quota increase for 1987 amounts to 78 and 31 per cent respectively. Iraq has refused to submit itself to its quota and Iran may not be able to fulfill its own production output target in view of Iraq's successful attacks.

It is likely that the existing depressed tanker market and oversupply situation will persist during at least 1987, unless the tonnage scrapping level increases significantly. The number of tankers employed as floating oil storage will probably again continue downwards, creating more surplus tonnage. In addition, it is feared that the laid-up tankers reactivated during 1986 in the Arabian Gulf trade may not find business in 1987.

It can be estimated that the demand for crude oil carriers on inter-area employment will increase by about 6.5 million dwt during 1987 or by 3.7 per cent compared to the previous year. The significant reduction in VLCC trading in oil experienced since 1982 may come to a halt and could even show a small growth of about 2 million dwt. ULCCs are expected to record an increase of 0.5 million dwt. The small and medium-sized range categories could witness a rise in demand of about 2 million dwt each and for the combined carrier fleet, it can be assumed that the level to be used in oil trading will remain about the same as 1985 and 1986, which, for both years, represented about 40 per cent of the shipments.

Freight futures market for tankers

Since the establishment of the Baltic International Freight Future Exchange (BIFFEX) on 1st May 1985, traders and shipowners in the oil market sector showed a certain interest in using this new trading index. As 1986 progressed, however, it became clear that the enthusiasm experienced during the previous year was falling and it has therefore been decided to discontinue BIFFEX in the oil tanker trade altogether.

Liner freight market

The German Liner Freight Index (recorded over the last three years in Table XXII of the Statistical Annex) indicates a 1986 annual decrease from the previous year of about 17 per cent from 141 in January to a gradual and constant decline to 124 in December. The softening of the Index is once again largely attributed to the currency exchange rate fluctuations between the Deutsche Mark and the US dollar.

The longstanding overcapacity situation in the liner trades once again made rate stability impossible during 1986. It was estimated that the gap between slot capacity and container transport demand stood at about 25 to 30 per cent. In addition, a number of newbuilding orders were placed for large containerships of above 2 500 teu. Rates were kept low throughout the year (estimated to be at the level of 15 years ago in real terms), in view of the strong competition existing among various shipping conferences and also between conferences and outsider lines. Certain members of conferences could no longer continue to operate at a loss and were forced to abandon their operations. This trend was mainly observed in the North Atlantic and Middle East trades. In January 1987, Evergreen Lines decided to return to being an independent operator across the Pacific, which could influence other shipping lines to follow suit, thus triggering an upset in the whole of the liner trade.

As rates fell dramatically during the first half of the year on the transpacific trades, confidence grew on the transatlantic routes. The latter seemed to maintain healthier rates, which could have been threatened if too many ships were transferred to them. The liner market started to pick up in July as trade volumes increased, prompting a few conferences to announce rate increases.

Bunker prices

Bunker prices are determined by the price for international crude oil. As the price for the latter fell precipitously since the second half of 1985, so did the one for bunker. Table 4.D indicates the estimated bunker prices for 1986 in the major areas. Bunker prices recorded a spectacular collapse during the first seven successive months of 1986. In January, one tonne of Bunker 'C' fuel on the Rotterdam spot market cost $135, while in July, it was worth only $45/tonne, representing approximately a 66 per cent drop. In August, prices for the same bunker recovered and, due mainly to OPEC's production controls, continued to increase between September and December, with the exception of a slight dip in October. Bunker prices in the other key areas also picked up during the same period.

T.4.D

MONTH-BY-MONTH ESTIMATED BUNKER PRICES

in dollars per long ton

	Rotterdam		Caribs	Japan	Ras Tanura
	180 CS		Bunker "C"		
1986					
January	140	135	149	169	157
February	125	121	132	151	131
March	113	107	103	128	91
April	79	73	96	115	91
May	65	61	81	81	71
June	69	64	76	72	56
July	50	46	76	71	51
August	66	64	69	70	61
September	75	73	82	90	76
October	73	70	82	88	76
November	85	83	82	86	76
December	82	79	84	88	81

SOURCE: "World Tanker Fleet Review", John I. Jacobs, London, July-December 1986.

Fluctuations in fuel prices have had consequences on freight charters. During the first half of 1986, low prices gave owners a reason for hope of a further decrease, which led them to offer voyage charters, expecially in the dry bulk trades. When prices regained momentum later in the year, carriers were prompted to switch their ships to time charters in order not to risk an even greater increase. It is estimated that bunker prices will rise slightly in 1987 and will continue to do so steadily until 1990.

Coinciding with the fluctuation of bunker prices, shippers exerted more and more pressure on the owners to pass on the savings effected from lower bunker costs. In addition, there was a growing feeling among shippers to urge carriers to discontinue the usage of the Bunker Adjustment Factor (BAF).

NOTES AND REFERENCES

Material was derived from:

"Review 1986", Fearnleys, Oslo 1987.

"Shipping Statistics", Institute of Shipping Economics and Logistics, Bremen, 1986-early 1987 issues.

"Shipping Statistics and Economics", Drewry Shipping Consultants Ltd., London, 1986-early 1987 issues.

"Forecast Tanker Profitability, 1986-1990", No. 86/9, Drewry Shipping Consultants Ltd., London, November 1986.

"World Tanker Fleet Review", John I. Jacobs PLC, London, 1986 issues.

"Lloyd's Shipping Economist", Lloyd's of London Press, 1986 issues.

Chapter V

COMMON PRINCIPLES OF SHIPPING POLICY FOR MEMBER COUNTRIES

INTRODUCTION: THE INVISIBLES CODE

Shipping has been one of the principal concerns of the OECD and its predecessor, the OEEC, right from its inception. Indeed, even in the weeks of 1947 which followed General Marshall's speech at Harvard University, the Committee which was established to draw up a programme covering the requirements and future plans for the restoration of Europe, decided that maritime transport was one of the key sectors. It established Technical Committee IVb which is the direct antecedent of the present Maritime Transport Committee of the OECD, and as a result the Committee celebrates this year the fortieth anniversary of the first meeting, on 22nd July 1947. The report of this Technical Committee contains the first common statement of principle on shipping which was adopted by Western countries, which stated:

> "The shipping practices of the participating countries is based on the free circulation of shipping in international trades, in free and fair competition. Any interference with this free circulation is liable to reduce efficiency of the total shipping available and hence to increase the cost of shipping services."

This principle has remained the key to the approach first of the OEEC and then of the OECD to maritime transport and it is as valid in today's conditions as it was in 1947, during the aftermath of the Second World War.

During the early fifties, the OEEC drew up its Code of Liberalisation and the Maritime Transport Committee was invited to put forward ideas for the liberalisation of invisible transactions in the shipping account. The outcome of this was the formulation contained in Note 1 to Annex A of the Code of Liberalisation of Current Invisible Operations, which was promulgated during 1957, was retained when the Code was taken over by the OECD and adopted in December 1961, and remains the statement of common obligations accepted by Member countries. It reads as follows:

> "The provisions of C/1 [Maritime freights including chartering, harbour expenses, disbursements for fishing vessels, etc. ...] and of the other items which have a direct or indirect impact on international maritime transport, are intended to give residents of one Member State the unrestricted opportunity to avail themselves of, and pay for, all

services in connection with international maritime transport which are offered by residents of any other Member State. As the shipping policy of the Governments of the Members is based on the principle of free circulation of shipping in international trade in free and fair competition, it follows that the freedom of transactions and transfers in connection with maritime transport should not be hampered by measures in the field of exchange control, by legislative provisions in favour of the national flag, by arrangements made by governmental or semi-governmental organisations giving preferential treatment to national flag ships, by preferential shipping clauses in trade agreements, by the operation of import and export licensing systems so as to influence the flag of the carrying ship, or by discriminatory port regulations or taxation measures -- the aim always being that liberal and competitive commercial and shipping practices and procedures should be followed in international trade and normal commercial considerations should alone determine the method and flag of shipment."

At the time of the establishment of the OECD, the United States, because of its national legislation, was unable to associate itself with the whole of Note 1 and accordingly the Note in its present form ends with the statement, "The second sentence of this Note does not apply to the United States". Nevertheless, Note 1 to Annex B of the Code of Liberalisation of Current Invisible Operations remains as the cornerstone of Member countries' approach to liberalisation in the area of maritime transport.

NEW INSTRUMENTS COMPLEMENTING THE INVISIBLES CODE

During the fifties and sixties, the main problems which had concerned Member countries had been between themselves. However, in the seventies and more recently, the ever-growing influence by governments, primarily of developing and state trading countries, upon ocean shipping has led to significant departures from free circulation of shipping and fair competition in this area, with the resulting need for OECD Member countries to defend the principles of liberalisation and, where possible, to extend its scope in the maritime sector. For this reason, the Maritime Transport Committee decided to initiate a programme of work which led it to cover a number of shipping policy issues directed towards harmonising the policies of individual Member countries, the objective being to implement, in new areas, the co-operative approach set out in the Invisibles Code.

The programme was intended to cover both the relations between Member countries and the relations between Member and non-Member countries. For both types of problem, the approach was first to identify and evaluate the principle difficulties which existed in international shipping relations and then to try and establish common ground which Member countries would accept to ameliorate and remedy these problems. The Inventory of problems and difficulties which was the result of this work was summarised in the Maritime Transport Committee's Annual Report for 1983 in a special Chapter.

The assembly of an inventory was complicated and time-consuming, but the negotiations of common ground proved to be much more difficult. The OECD is based on the principle of consensus and particularly in the shipping sector, the interests of Member countries are widely different. This largely results from the fact that there are three fairly distinct categories of countries:

-- those with extensive trade but only a small fleet, who rely on ships operating under other flags to transport their cargoes;

-- those with extensive trade and substantial fleets which may handle their own imports and exports or operate as crosstraders in general world-wide trade; and

-- those with large fleets but little cargo of their own, whose role is to provide services to other countries.

It can well be imagined that it was not easy to reach agreement on such widely different matters as the application of competition policy to liner shipping, the operation of mobile offshore units, consultation procedures on how to react to external pressures or the negotiation of bilateral agreements. As a result, the agreement to a series of common principles and guidelines took several years and it was not finally until February 1987 that the Council of the OECD gave its approval to a Recommendation on Common Principles of Shipping Policy for Member Countries and an associated Resolution on the follow-up to the Recommendation and on work to be undertaken on the sections of the OECD Code of Liberalisation of Current Invisible Operations relating to Maritime Transport. These Instruments were generally accepted by all 24 Member countries. However, Australia, while voting in favour of the Instruments as a whole, and indicating its support for the general principle of fair competitive markets for international shipping, was unable to accept the approach to developing countries advocated in Principles 2-6. In Australia's view, the principles relating to the co-ordinated adoption of countermeasures tended to be contrary to broader OECD objectives which advocate assistance to developing countries. Australia was concerned that their use could be directed against the valid national shipping development aspirations of such countries. The full text of these Instruments is annexed to the present Chapter.

THE CONTENT AND IMPORTANCE OF OECD INSTRUMENTS

The main body of the Recommendation is based on five elements:

-- the maintenance of open trades and free competitive access to international shipping operations;

-- co-ordinated response to external pressures, based on full consultations between Member countries;

-- the role and recognition of governmental involvement by Member countries to preserve free competitive access and the provision of choice to the shippers;

-- a common approach to the application of competition policy to the liner shipping sector;

-- guidelines concerning the transport activities of mobile offshore vessels.

These elements, embodied in thirteen principles, together with Note 1 to Annex A of the Code of Liberalisation of Current Invisible Operations (see the second paragraph), form a new and coherent common approach to international shipping policy between Member countries and their relations with countries outside the Organisation.

However, this work was not conceived as an end but as a continuing process forming part of the overall work of the OECD towards the further liberalisation of all sectors of trade in the service industries. The development of the Principles was also closely interlinked with the organisation's work on updating the Invisibles Code. It was thus decided that it was essential that the provisions of the Recommendation should be accompanied by a commitment to work towards further liberalisation in the maritime transport policies of Member countries. This commitment is embodied in the Resolution which spells out the programme of work to be undertaken jointly by the Maritime Transport Committee and the Committee for Capital Movements and Invisible Transactions. The Resolution also provides for a general review of the Recommendation and for examinations of the observance of its individual elements. This work has been started but is expected to continue for some time.

Why are these two Instruments, taken together with the Invisibles Code, important? There are three main counts which made their formal adoption by the OECD Council on 13th February 1987 a milestone for international shipping.

a) At the meeting of GATT in Punta del Este, it was decided that the service industries would form part of the Uruguay round of negotiations. Although no decision has yet been taken on how far shipping questions will be directly or indirectly involved in these discussions, it is most important that the Member countries of the OECD should have a common approach in this sector, which is of basic significance to the growth of international trade.

b) For the first time, the developed market economy countries have together drawn up a detailed document covering a large number of facets of international maritime transport, which can be used as a yardstick for national policies.

c) The Recommendation and Resolution which have been adopted are essentially aimed at preserving and encouraging the freedom of worldwide seaborne trade. The Member countries of the OECD have thus asserted that the present economic difficulties which beset this sector can only be made worse by protectionism. Such a declaration at the present time is a noteworthy event.

The Instruments thus form a single entity which complements the obligations under the Invisibles Code and widens the work being undertaken in other international groupings. Chapter I of the Report described how the European Communities reached agreement during December 1986 on four Resolutions covering some of the sectors which are taken up in the Instruments. The approach of the United States and the Consultative Shipping Group also touches upon some of the same ground and in the same direction. However, the OECD Invisibles Code and Instruments are the most comprehensive and they bring together much larger numbers of countries in the implementation of three major themes.

a) **The preservation and encouragement of the policy of free competition on a fair and commercial basis**

The Recommendation is the basis for national policies in the trades inside the OECD as well as those with third countries, as much for the liner sector as for the transportation of commodities in bulk. This means that the trades must be open to competition, and that competition must respect a number of clearly defined rules. For this reason, an important section of the Recommendation is concerned with the application of competition policy to liner shipping. The document establishes the framework within which national legislation should be set. In particular, it stresses the need to avoid and resolve conflicts between Member countries by appropriate arrangements, especially by bilateral or multilateral consultations. But in addition to this, it sets out the basic concepts for competition policy in shipping:

-- the balance of interest between ship operators, shippers and consumers;

-- the prevention of any abuse of a dominant position;

-- the definition of specific practices of liner conferences which are desirable or undesirable in relation to shippers and lines outside the conferences as well as to their member lines;

-- action against unfair or non-commercial practices;

-- the need to ensure the freedom of choice for the shipper between conference and non-conference lines.

In more general terms, the Recommendation stresses that commercial competition between conferences and independent lines must be preserved and calls upon governments to take any measures which may be needed with regard to third countries which impede such competition.

b) **The strengthening of the Invisibles Code and the movement towards greater liberalisation**

As a result of the encouragement given by the OECD Council meeting at Ministerial level in 1986, Member countries decided to include in the Recommendation and Resolution a number of elements and to establish a procedure whereby the liberalisation commitments concerning maritime transport can be strengthened. Among these are the agreement not to introduce any new measures restricting competitive access to international trade and cargoes, and the alignment of a large number of countries towards the freedom of transport services rendered by mobile offshore vessels outside territorial waters and the harmonisation of social and technical regulations.

The Member countries also considered that it was not reasonable to put forward so strongly the principle of free circulation of shipping to the outside world without taking some care that their own house was in order. Accordingly, it has been agreed to thoroughly examine all existing measures such as bilateral agreements and national regulations concerning access to cargo, which are restrictive in the sense of the Invisibles Code. The programme also envisages an examination of the problems which have been raised by governmental support measures which distort competition and prolong the imbalance between supply and demand in shipping. Finally, Member countries will consider what further liberalisation is possible by extending the existing maritime obligations under the Code of Liberalisation of Current Invisible Operations to new areas.

c)   The rejection of the protectionist measures of non-Member countries

The countries of the OECD are anxious to encourage the freedom of maritime trade with third countries. To this end, they have taken part, both multilaterally and bilaterally, in programmes for co-operation in the maritime sector and recognise the right of each country to establish its own shipping policies. However, there has been considerable uneasiness caused by the unilateral introduction of protectionist measures by third countries and by certain non-commercial and non-reciprocal practices of state-trading countries.

Member countries have, therefore, come together to resist such practices and they are seeking, as far as possible on a common basis, the necessary means to put an end to them, even to the extent of using countermeasures as a last resort, on a concerted basis. It is emphasised that before any such action is taken, all attempts must be made to initiate consultations with the country concerned as well as with the governments of other Member countries concerned or affected. The aim of those Member countries which support this approach is to react in a firm but defensive way. Finally, if and when agreements are concluded with third countries, they should contain, to the maximum extent possible, clauses which guarantee the competitive access of carriers from OECD countries to the ports and national trades of the countries who have made the agreement.

The adoption of the Resolution and Recommendation marks the end of a longdrawn out process of investigation and negotiation. Member countries have now reasserted in unambiguous terms their opposition to protectionism and their commitment to the principle of free circulation of shipping in international trade. However, these Instruments together with the Invisibles Code will only be of value if their content is progressively incorporated into national legislation and policy and if concrete steps towards increased liberalisation of the existing situation are taken. If this is to occur, it will require the will of the governments of Member countries to make it happen; the OECD Instruments have opened the door. It is for Member countries to decide to go through this door and to press on in the direction which it has indicated.

ATTACHMENT

RECOMMENDATION OF THE COUNCIL*
concerning Common Principles of Shipping Policy
for Member countries

(Adopted by the Council at its 656th meeting
on 13th February 1987)

THE COUNCIL,

Having regard to Article 5 b) of the Convention on the Organisation for Economic Co-operation and Development of 14th December 1960;

Having regard to the Declaration on Trade Policy as adopted by Governments of OECD Member countries on 4th June 1980;

Having regard to the Code of Liberalisation of Current Invisible Operations of 12th December 1961 and in particular to Note 1 to Annex A of that Code; (1)

Having regard to the Revised Recommendation of the Council of 21st May 1986 concerning co-operation between Member countries on Restrictive Business Practices affecting International Trade [C(86)44(Final)] and the Second Revised Decision of the Council on the Guidelines for Multinational Enterprises, adopted on 17th May 1984 [C(84)90];

Recognising the special character of shipping as an international activity;

Noting that differences exist in the application of competition legislation to liner shipping by Member countries;

Recalling the fact that the major shipping policy problems in the liner trades with which Governments of Member countries or their commercial interests are confronted in their relations with other countries relate to the growth of direct or indirect governmental intervention in shipping affairs by other countries;

---

*This Recommendation is complemented by the Resolution of the Council concerning work to be undertaken on the sections of the Code of Liberalisation of Current Invisible Operations relating to maritime transport and in following up the Recommendation concerning Common Principles of Shipping Policy for Member countries, adopted at the same date.

Noting that the United Nations Conference of Plenipotentiaries on a Code of Conduct for Liner Conferences adopted on 6th April 1974 a Convention on a Code of Conduct for Liner Conferences and a Resolution concerning non-conference shipping lines, and that the Convention came into force on 6th October 1983;

Considering that it is desirable that the policies of Member countries on shipping matters in their relations with non-Member countries, as well as their relations among themselves, should be harmonised as far as possible;

Recalling that the Council of the OECD at Ministerial level on 17th and 18th April 1986 in their Press Communiqué addressed trade policy and trade-in-services [C(86)56];

Recalling also that Ministers underlined the importance of extending and making more effective the Code of Liberalisation of Current Invisible Operations and other existing instruments which are applicable to trade-in-services among OECD Members, in order to promote liberalisation in as many sectors as possible;

Recalling further that the Ministers considered that increased attention should be paid to trade-distorting effects of government subsidies to specific sectors;

Emphasising the particular importance in the field of maritime transport of the Code of Liberalisation of Current Invisible Operations, under which all Member countries have accepted obligations which they must continue to observe;

Considering that the principle of free circulation of shipping in international trade in free and fair competition, which is elaborated in Note 1 to Annex A of the OECD Code of Liberalisation of Current Invisible Operations (1), forms a guarantee of adequate and economic world shipping services and of maximum economic benefit for shipowners, shippers and consumers;

Recognising the need to maintain an equitable balance of interest between shippers and ship operators, bearing in mind the repercussions upon the consumer;

Noting that the Maritime Transport Committee of the OECD has carried out a review of the shipping policy problems of OECD Member countries and has reached a number of general conclusions and statements of policy concerning common principles of shipping policy for Member countries and that the Committee on Capital Movements and Invisible Transactions has examined these conclusions and statements in relation to the Code of Liberalisation of Current Invisible Operations.

On the proposal of the Maritime Transport Committee and the Committee on Capital Movements and Invisible Transactions:

I. CONFIRMS that nothing in this Recommendation shall be interpreted as diminishing in any way the obligations accepted by Member countries under the Code of Liberalisation of Current Invisible Operations (hereinafter referred to as "the Code").

II. AGREES that, in pursuance of, and/or in addition to, the obligations under the Code, no Government of a Member country should introduce new and/or additional measures restricting competitive access to international trade and cargoes.

III. RECOMMENDS that the Governments of Member countries should endeavour, in pursuance of, and/or in addition to, their obligations under the Code, when contemplating the introduction of new laws and regulations relating to shipping policy, or the amendment of existing ones, to ensure that they are in conformity with the following general principles*, and with the guidelines contained in Annexes I and II to this Recommendation.

Principle 1 -- The bases of Member countries' shipping policies

The shipping policies of Member countries should be directed to safeguarding and promoting open trades, and a situation of free competition on a fair and commercial basis in international shipping in their mutual relations, as well as in their relations with non-Member countries. These policies should also prevent the abuse of a dominant position by any commercial party. These general elements form the bases for the following Principles and for Annexes I and II to this Recommendation.

Principle 2 -- Principles to follow for Normal Resolution of Problems

In resolving problems arising in trades with non-Member countries, the aim of Member countries should be to prevent the introduction by non-Member countries of measures that would run contrary to the general aims of OECD, inter alia, the expansion of world trade on a multilateral non-discriminatory basis. Member countries should thus actively oppose the imposition of régimes which restrict the access to cargo moving internationally by shipping companies adhering to the principle of free competition on a commercial basis, in conformity with Note 1 of Annex A to the Code.

In the case of state-trading countries and their carriers, it is necessary to take account of non-commercial and non-reciprocal practices with the aim of arriving at a situation of reciprocity and equality of opportunity.

Principle 3 -- Consultations among Member Countries

When the trade between a Member and a non-Member country is subject to pressures for cargo sharing or cargo reservation in favour of the national flag by the policies of the non-Member country, including an expansion of the definition of "Government Cargoes" the government of the Member country should be prepared to enter into consultations with the governments of other Member countries concerned, with a view to defending the aims of this Recommendation, and exploring the possibility of a co-ordinated response. Such consultations may be initiated by the Member country whose national trade is concerned or the other interested Member countries. While fully endorsing the principle of consultations with other Member governments at the earliest practicable stage, as stated in this Principle and Principle 6, a Member government may, on occasion, be obliged to act in advance of consultations with other Member

---

*Australia is unable to accept the recommendations contained in Principles 2-6.

countries, pursuant to its maritime legislation or policy requirements, actions of its regulatory bodies, or the need for a speedy response to restrictive measures of non-Member countries. A Member country contemplating action in respect of a trade between another Member country and a non-Member country will whenever possible undertake prior consultations with that Member country. (2)

Principle 4 -- Response to Pressures from Non-Member Countries

All reasonable endeavours should first be made to solve any problems with non-Member countries via consultations and/or negotiations. If circumstances should arise when such government-to-government consultations or negotiations cannot resolve conflicting interests or when the non-Member country refuses to enter into these procedures, the governments of Member countries should be in a position to react and, to this end, should provide themselves with such countervailing powers as they consider necessary. In the final analysis, countermeasures may be necessary, and, in their application, the aim should be to secure arrangements in accordance with the principles expressed in this Recommendation.

Principle 5 -- Availability of Countervailing Powers

Where the free competitive sea transport market is undermined by actions of third countries or where such a country disregards its relevant international obligations, Member countries should have at their disposal powers to react to such a situation.

Principle 6 -- Use of Countervailing Powers

When the introduction of countermeasures is contemplated, there should be, subject to what is contained in Principle 3, consultations among the OECD Member governments concerned with a view to the co-ordinated use of these powers. If countermeasures are decided upon following these consultations, the Member country whose national trade is involved can reasonably look to the Member countries with companies in the trade as cross-traders for support in the form of the joint introduction of countermeasures by all the Member countries concerned. In those exceptional cases in which prior consultation has not been possible, each Member country undertakes to inform other Member countries as soon and as fully as possible, of countermeasures adopted. Member countries acknowledge that the imposition of countermeasures or the participation in harmonised response as stated in Principle 3 above, is subject to the foreign policy considerations of individual Member countries in each case. A Member country may decline a request to participate in concerted countermeasures if, in its view, the Member country requesting countermeasure actions itself operates practices similar in effect to those against which the countermeasures are proposed to be directed. (2)

Principle 7 -- Equitable Treatment in Shipping Agreements

OECD Member countries should ensure wherever appropriate the equitable treatment of their shipping through the inclusion, in trade, navigation and other agreements with non-Member countries, of clauses aimed at ensuring competitive access of the carriers of all Member countries to both ports and cargo in the trades concerned.

Principle 8 -- Freedom of Shipping in the Bulk Trades

OECD Member countries reaffirm their commitment to a free and fair competitive environment in the dry and liquid bulk trades. They are convinced that cargo sharing in the bulk trades leads to substantial increases in transportation costs and has a serious effect on the trading interests of all countries.

Principle 9 -- Governmental Supervision of the Trade

OECD Member governments acknowledge that in order to give full effect to international obligations which they assume in connection with other countries, their supervisory powers should, as far as possible, be harmonised on an OECD-wide basis.

Principle 10 -- The Role of Government and Competition Policy in Liner Shipping

The role of government is to safeguard and promote a situation of open and fair competition and to prevent the abuse of a dominant position by any commercial party. Its involvement should be on a basis of such minimum intervention as may be adequate in the particular situation and consistent with the maintenance of a free and fair competitive and commercial environment. (3)

In determining how national competition policy should be applied in international shipping, it is essential for governments to give adequate consideration to the way their measures will affect the activities of foreign companies or might interfere with the competition policies and the interests of other OECD Member countries' governments.

Principle 11 -- The Relationship of Governments to the Activities of Shipping Lines and Conferences

In determining what activities of shipping lines and conferences are desirable or undesirable, in accordance with the guidelines set out in Annex II to this Recommendation, governmental involvement should be directed towards the maintenance of a balance between the interests of shippers and shipowners, bearing in mind the repercussions on the end-users of the cargoes. If it appears that these interests and repercussions are not being sufficiently taken into account it is the responsibility of governments to redress the balance as appropriate. However, in doing so the normal commercial activities of shippers, shipowners and conferences should not be unduly impeded or distorted.

Principle 12 -- Avoidance and Resolution of Conflict in Matters of Competition Policy Concerning Shipping

If agreement could be reached concerning what activities should be controlled from the point of view of competition and on how this should be done, there would be no source of conflict between regulatory authorities. However, this may prove to be impossible and, because of its inherent character, international shipping will be particularly affected by conflicts of law and policy.

When such conflicts emerge, or appear imminent to any party, either because of the enactment of new competition legislation affecting shipping, by modifications to existing legislation, or as a result of the application by a government or one of its agencies of existing laws or policy in a particular case, governments of Member countries should endeavour as appropriate and practicable to minimise these and arrive at mutually acceptable solutions through bilateral or multilateral consultations. Such consultations should be in accordance with mutually acceptable arrangements adopted on a bilateral or multilateral basis between Member countries.

Governments of Member countries should make full use of existing OECD fora including the Maritime Transport Committee. These arrangements and the spirit in which they are implemented should be in accordance with the general considerations and practical approach established under the Revised Council Recommendation of 21st May 1986 and the second Revised Council Decision of 17th May 1984, to ensure full mutual comprehension by Member countries of the philosophies and practical effects of the application of competition policy to shipping in Member countries.

Principle 13 -- Non-Conference Shipping

The protection of free circulation of international shipping in a competitive commercial environment requires that opportunities for fair competition on a commercial basis by non-conference shipping lines continue to exist and that shippers are not denied an option in the choice between conference and non-conference shipping lines, subject to loyalty arrangements where they exist. Restrictions should not be imposed by governments on the right of individual shipping lines to decide whether they want to operate inside or outside the conference system. Governments of Member countries should take appropriate steps when another country adopts measures or practices that prevent fair competition on a commercial basis in their liner trades and should, under such circumstances, consult with each other, upon request, with the objective of remedying the situation.

Annex I

GUIDELINES CONCERNING THE TRANSPORT ACTIVITIES OF MOBILE OFFSHORE VESSELS (4)

Offshore vessels

Governments of Member countries of the OECD should secure free trade in transport services rendered by mobile offshore vessels and refrain from measures giving preferential treatment to national flag vessels with the aim of promoting free and fair competition on a commercial basis.

In order to facilitate the free circulation of transport services rendered by mobile offshore vessels, Governments of Member countries will encourage the harmonisation of social and technical regulations concerning the maritime activities of mobile offshore vessels by appropriate international organisations, including IMO and ILO.

This statement applies to the transport activities of mobile offshore vessels beyond the territorial waters of a Member country.

Mobile offshore vessels are defined as vessels which are engaged in activities associated with the exploration or exploitation of the non-living natural resources on or below the seabed.

Note:

The MTC, in formulating these guidelines, noted that the non-transport activities by mobile offshore vessels are closely associated with the transportation activities. The MTC therefore invites the CMIT and other appropriate OECD bodies to consider the scope for liberalisation of those services rendered by mobile offshore vessels which are not transport services.

Annex II

GUIDELINES CONCERNING COMPETITION POLICY AS APPLIED TO LINER SHIPPING

Section A - General

i)   **Agreement upon common rules on what activities should be controlled**

Agreement should be reached on those activities of shipping lines and conferences which are undesirable and should be discouraged or prevented, and those which are desirable and should be encouraged or required. Some of these activities are set out in Section B but this Section should not be regarded as necessarily exclusive.

Conferences as such are generally accepted as a satisfactory means of organising liner shiping trade. However, because they are usually exempted from the full impact of cartel legislation, to avoid abuses of a dominant or monopolistic position it is necessary that they should be exposed to counter-balancing forces notably by competition or the possibility of competition from lines outside the conference, and strong shippers or shippers' councils. The activities of conferences should also be exposed to administrative regulation where this appears necessary. By the existence of these checks, conferences or the shipping lines within them should not be in a position to abuse a dominant or monopolistic position which they may have achieved by reason of their exemption from cartel legislation.

Governments should take the necessary steps to prohibit any abuse of a dominant position by a conference. If a conference by abusing its dominant position causes the elimination or exclusion of competition from non-conference lines or if a member line, including a cross-trader line, is driven out of a specific conference trade in defiance of the conference agreement, governments should be able to take measures to ensure that such lines have the opportunity to compete in that trade. Governments should also take the necessary steps to prohibit any abuse of a dominant position by independent lines.

Governments should take the necessary steps to ensure that no line engages in unfair or non-commercial practices. In acting against unfair or non-commercial practices, without inhibiting the right of independent lines to compete freely and fairly with conferences, governments should endeavour to reach consensus on those practices which should be regarded as unfair or non-commercial.

ii)   Agreement upon common principles of enforcement

In cases where direct governmental intervention is deemed necessary, any regulatory body established for this purpose should be provided with clearly defined powers and authority, including the activities to be controlled as agreed under (i). Prohibited practices should be clearly defined. Where there is more than one such regulatory body within a national framework, their respective jurisdictions also need to be clearly defined.

Non-national lines and shippers should be treated in the same manner and according to the same criteria as national lines and shippers, provided that the other country operates in the same manner.

It is for individual governments to select how enforcement should be undertaken such as whether a first approach could be to assure themselves of the existence and effective operation of self-policing systems within the conferences. With respect to relations between conferences and shippers, procedures should be provided whereby complaints of activities which are prohibited by national competition legislation can be received and legally remedied. Similarly, procedures should be provided to promote or maintain fair competition on a commercial basis between conferences and non-conference lines.

Alternatively, or in addition, some governments may choose to establish systems of prior approval by regulatory bodies and enact legislation prohibiting or requiring certain actions under the sanctions of penalites as necessary.

In any case, mechanisms should exist whereby consultations can be initiated both with national and non-national private organisations in advance of substantial new developments in the field of competition policy as applied to shipping or of important new applications of existing regulations in specific cases. (5)

Section B - Specific practices of Conferences and Conference Members which can be generally considered desirable or undesirable.

i)   Specific practices with relation to shippers

Among the desirable practices of conferences, which may be required of them by governmental regulation or by common agreement, are the following:

a) The provision of tariffs and related rules and conditions of carriage and their ready availability to any interested party at reasonable cost.

b) The organisation of prior meaningful consultations and/or negotiations with shippers, shippers' organisations or other bodies directly involved concerning inter alia changes proposed in tariffs, conditions of carriage or provision of services and the introduction of new technology, except where national law provides other means of protecting shippers' interests.

On the other hand certain practices appear undesirable including:

- c) The offering of special terms or rebates to particular shippers which are not available to other shippers similarly situated or which are not in accordance with service contracts.

- d) Any refusal to carry goods of a shipper because he has used non-conference carriers or specific inland transport services or the imposition of excessive penalties for so doing.

- e) The introduction of loyalty contracts which tie the shipper to the conference by such means as making excessive differences between contract and non-contract rates, or by not providing arrangements for short-term termination.

- f) The introduction of surcharges which more than recoup the extra expenditure caused by the particular situation for which the surcharge was imposed. Prior or, if necessary, subsequent consultations should always accompany the introduction of, and, where relevant, amendments to, surcharges, unless national law provides other means of protecting shippers' interests.

ii) **Specific practices with relation to lines outside the conference**

Possible practices in which conferences might indulge with regard to non-conference lines, which could be regarded as abuse of their dominant position, include:

- a) The use of fighting ships or similar means to forestall a non-conference line in obtaining cargo.

- b) The deliberate conclusion of agreements with governmental or quasi-governmental authorities which have the effect of restricting competition by the exclusion of non-member lines from participation in the trade or of placing them at a substantial disadvantage vis-à-vis conferences lines. (6)

- c) The establishment of unreasonable, discretionary criteria for lines seeking to join the conference. Cross trading and national lines of OECD countries should continue to have the opportunity to serve the trades of any OECD country as members of conferences or as outsiders competing with the conferences.

iii) **Specific practices with relation to lines inside the conference**

The relations between lines within a conference and between the conference and its members are governed by the terms of the conference agreement in conformity with applicable national laws. The efficient operation of a conference implies the existence of conference machinery to police the terms of the conference agreement, to ensure, for example, that member shipping lines do not offer individual shippers terms which are not in accordance with the tariffs of the conference as published or otherwise made available to shippers. (7)

Conference agreements are agreed between the members at the time of establishment and subsequent participants may find it difficult to amend the agreement. It is therefore important that the initial agreement, which may or may not require governmental approval, should be equitable between present and future members over such matters as the duration of notice that a line wishing to leave the conference must give, the penalties that might be incurred as a result of doing so and the procedure for handling reports of malpractices by member lines.

OBSERVATIONS

Preamble

(1) <u>Preambular paragraphs 3 and 14</u>: The United States wishes to draw attention to the fact that the second sentence of Note 1 to Annex A of the Code of Liberalisation of Current Invisible Operations, "does not apply to the United States".

Principles 1-13

(2) <u>Principles 3 and 6</u>: It is agreed that the term "national trade" refers to cargoes moving to and from the Member country concerned.

(3) <u>Principle 10</u>: Australia accepts this text as being compatible with ensuring the equitable participation of its national-flag shipping on a fair commercial basis.

Annex I

(4) These guidelines are initially introduced for a number of Member countries in the hope that the others will be progressively able to adhere to them. The following countries cannot, at the present stage, associate themselves with these Guidelines: Australia, Canada, Italy, Japan, New Zealand, Portugal, Spain, Turkey, United States and United Kingdom.

Annex II

(5) <u>Paragraph 9</u>: The United States accepts this paragraph on the understanding that US law and legislative procedures provide adequate opportunity for interested parties to comment on new developments.

(6) <u>Paragraph 11 b)</u>: This clause does not concern commercial agreements between quasi-governmental authorities and conferences or individual lines which were awarded on a commercial basis but during their duration limit the transport of a particular commodity in the trade to the conference or line having received the contract.

(7) <u>Paragraph 12</u>: The United States accepts this paragraph on the understanding that it allows individual lines to exercise the right of independent action on any rate or service item required to be filed in a tariff under Section 8(a) of the Shipping Act of 1984 and as allowing conferences or carriers to offer service contracts to individual shippers or shippers' associations as provided for in Section 8(c) of the Shipping Act of 1984. Canada would broadly interpret the last clause of this paragraph to mean that independent action and service contracts are available.

RESOLUTION OF THE COUNCIL*

concerning work to be undertaken on the sections of
the Code of Liberalisation of Current Invisible Operations
relating to maritime transport
and in following up the Recommendation of the Council
concerning Common Principles of Shipping Policy for Member countries

(Adopted by the Council at its 656th meeting
on 13th February 1987)

THE COUNCIL,

Having regard to the Recommendation of the Council concerning Common Principles of Shipping Policy for Member countries and, in particular, to its preamble,

I. DECIDES that Member countries' existing obligations under the Code of Liberalisation of Current Invisible Operations (hereinafter referred to as "the Code") in the field of maritime transport shall be defined as precisely as possible in order to achieve full uniformity of interpretation and that relevant maritime measures and practices shall be examined to determine whether they are consistent with the existing obligations under the Code, in accordance with the procedure as set out in the Annex to this Resolution; and that, in the field of international maritime transport, Member countries, taking into account the conclusions and agreements reached at the meeting of the Council at Ministerial level on 17th and 18th April 1986 [C(86)56], and the mandate of the Committee on Capital Movements and Invisible Transactions (CMIT) to update the Code [C(79)113(Final)], shall proceed towards extending and making more effective the Code to promote further liberalisation, also in accordance with the procedure in the Annex.

II. INSTRUCTS the Maritime Transport Committee to undertake a general review of the actions taken by Member countries in the implementation of the Recommendation of the Council concerning Common Principles of Shipping Policy for Member countries not more than two years after its adoption, ensuring that, where elements fall within the scope of other existing OECD Instruments, the review is undertaken in co-operation with the appropriate body or bodies of the Organisation, and report thereon jointly to the Council.

III. INSTRUCTS the Maritime Transport Committee, in co-operation, where relevant, with other appropriate bodies of the Organisation, to establish procedures whereby the observation of individual elements or guidelines contained in the Recommendation or its Annexes can be discussed upon the request of any Member country.

---
*This Resolution is complementary to the Recommendation of the Council concerning Common Principles of Shipping Policy for Member countries, adopted at the same date.

Annex

PROCEDURE FOR IMPLEMENTING OPERATIVE PARAGRAPH I

Member countries agree to accomplish, within a determined timeframe which should not extend beyond the end of 1988, the following tasks:

a) to define precisely existing obligations under the Code, as set out in Operative Paragraph I;

b) to identify:

  i) any relevant maritime measures and practices which may be incompatible with Member countries' obligations under the Code; and

  ii) any relevant measures and practices associated with an exemption under the Code;

c) to determine how, and according to what time scale, the measures and practices identified under b)i) above will be modified to bring them into conformity with the Code, in accordance with its provisions;

d) to examine how Member countries' existing reservations and derogations to the maritime sections of the Code could be lifted;

e) to examine other measures having the effect of distorting free and fair competition in shipping and/or creating or prolonging a structural imbalance in the shipping industry;

f) to consider the scope for the extension of maritime obligations under the Code;

g) to decide how to incorporate in the Code the relevant results of the foregoing examinations.

The Maritime Transport Committee and the CMIT will cooperate closely in undertaking, through a Joint Working Group, the work set out in the foregoing paragraphs, the CMIT retaining all its responsibilities relating to the Code and its mandate for updating the services sections of that Code.

Chapter VI

DEVELOPING COUNTRY PROTECTIONISM
IN INTERNATIONAL MARITIME TRANSPORT SERVICES

INTRODUCTION

The problem of protectionism in international shipping is not a new one, nor is it confined to any one group of countries. Most if not all Member countries of the international shipping community (including OECD Member countries) have at one time or another engaged in such practices to varying degrees, for national fleet development reasons. An inventory of such practices exercised by OECD Member countries is to be found in Chapter V of the Committee's 1983 Annual Report. However, whereas OECD Member countries (with the exception of the US), as a result of their obligations to observe the concept of free circulation of shipping in free and fair competition, have had limited freedom to introduce __new__ direct measures of this kind, no such restrictions apply to CMEA or developing countries. The last several decades have witnessed increased government involvement, particularly by developing countries and state trading nations in international maritime transport services. A large number of these nations have to date adopted measures and practices restricting free access to cargoes with the ultimate aim of increasing the participation of their fleets in the carriage of their countries' trade.

Over the years, OECD Member countries opposed, and are still opposing, these discriminatory measures but they have stressed at the same time that the aim of an increasing and equitable participation developing countries in the world shipping tonnage can best be met by attempting to increase the competitiveness of the fleets of developing countries and by eliminating obstacles to free and fair competition, where they exist, so that these countries can participate on equal terms in the transport of all types of cargo on a world-wide basis. Nevertheless, in spite of all efforts made by OECD Member countries to encourage trading partners engaged in discriminatory practices to discontinue their application of "non-commercial" and "non-reciprocal" measures or to find possible compromise solutions acceptable to all parties concerned, protectionist measures have been increasingly adopted by a large number of developing countries.

Against this background, the OECD Council recently adopted a Recommendation on Common Principles of Shipping Policy which, _inter alia_, provides for co-ordinated countermeasures against countries restricting the access of OECD

Member country shipping lines to their trades. At the same time, the Council adopted a parallel Resolution implicitly recognising the persistence within the OECD itself of a number of restrictive or distortive measures and practices. The Council Resolution provides for completion of an examination by the end of 1988 of all such measures and practices and determination how and according to what time scale the identified measures and practices will be modified to bring them into conformity with the OECD Code of Liberalisation. The Recommendation and Resolution have been discussed in detail in the previous Chapter.

Flag discrimination covers a wide range of practices and is, at first sight, not always evident; buying f.o.b. and selling c.i.f. can be, for example, normal commercial practice, but if this practice is applied to cargoes over which a government or a semi-governmental body has some kind of control, its strict application can easily favour ships of a particular flag and lead to some sort of discrimination. On the whole, two categories of unilateral impediments in the maritime transport services could be identified:

i) direct government controls on cargoes (i.e. cargo sharing legislation); and

ii) indirect, and often commercial, restrictions (i.e. CIF sales/FOB purchases).

These direct and indirect controls appear in various forms (elaborated on later). Firstly, they affect foreign carriers' access to trade and, secondly, they neutralise the competitive market forces in the relevant trade.

Although such practices are common in the socialist countries of Eastern Europe, these countries have not been considered in the present chapter because of the different economic structures inherent in centrally-planned developed economy countries. The analysis was restricted to developing market-economy and state trading countries. The following paragraphs review the various types of developing country protectionist measures which have been encountered and list the countries which have adopted them. A detailed inventory of these measures is contained in Annex I, by country. Annexes II and III set out, in a summarised form, which countries operate the various direct and indirect measures of protectionism considered in the chapter.

TYPES OF CONTROLS IN MARITIME SERVICES

a) <u>Direct control of cargoes</u>

Most of the countries examined exercise direct controls on cargoes through unilateral protectionist measures, often referred to as "cargo reservation" or "cargo sharing" policies, legislation and practices (see Annex II). Cargo reservation is one of the most widespread forms of protectionism in the shipping sector. With this type of non-commercial control provided in legislation, a government allows itself the right to claim the seaborne carriage of a certain share or 100 per cent of its import and export trade in national flag ships, which is often called the "cargo generators' right".

Although many of these countries might wish to reserve 100 per cent of cargoes for national registered ships, in practice, market conditions and availability of national shipping services have made the attainment of this goal difficult. A good number of governments have decided to allocate only a share to their fleet, which often amounts to about 50 per cent of their international waterborne trade.

In spite of the fact that "cargo sharing" schemes are often initiated unilaterally, they are generally implemented bilaterally by two trading partners who mutually agree on a division of their seaborne trade in the form of a shipping agreement. (The details of a number of such agreements are contained in Annex I, "Implementation and Practices").

i) <u>Government cargoes</u>

Bearing in mind that the term "government cargoes" encompasses a broad range of cargoes and is defined at present differently in many countries, the following seven types of governmental or commercial activity, involving or involved in the seaborne carriage of cargo, have been identified as falling under the "government cargo" category though no common definition has been agreed internationally:

i) Government departments in pursuit of their own mandate, inter alia, defence supplies and mail;

ii) Government departments engaged in commercial operations for their own accounts;

iii) Quasi-governmental bodies (including local government authorities);

iv) Nationalised corporations;

v) Commercial organisations in which governments hold a majority shareholding;

vi) Commercial organisations engaged in operations involving government grants, loans, guarantees or subsidies, or tax exemptions;

vii) Commercial organisations dealing with commodities regarded as of strategic importance.

This list is not exhaustive, but may provide a basis for the following classification of measures and practices concerning governmental cargoes. Such practices exist, for example, in the following countries:

Argentina	India	Pakistan
Bolivia	Indonesia	Philippines
Brazil	Jamaica	Saudi Arabia
Cameroon	Malaysia	Sri Lanka
Côte d'Ivoire	Mexico	Sudan
Dominican Republic	Morocco	Thailand
Ecuador	Nicaragua	Venezuela
Egypt		

ii) **Specific commodities included or excluded**

The legislation of a certain number of countries provides for the inclusion or exclusion of a share of specific commodities to be carried by national flag ships.

In most cases, this form of cargo reservation concerns outbound cargoes. Coffee, cocoa beans, cotton and petroleum products are among the most common.

Of those countries examined, the following reserve specific commodities to their merchant fleets:

Brazil	Ghana	Philippines
Colombia	Guinea	Singapore
Côte d'Ivoire	Indonesia	Venezuela
Ecuador		

There are a small number of countries that possess cargo reservation legislation from which certain commodities such as sugar, garments, handicrafts and oil are excluded. Such provisions exist in the following countries:

Bangladesh
Colombia
Thailand

iii) **Cargo reservation through legislation**

This type of cargo reservation is primarily based on a quantitative restriction of cargo. By law, several countries claim up to 100 per cent of the cargo for carriage by their merchant marines. Others demand a 50 per cent share or less which, in practice, seems to generate sufficient trade for the development and safeguard of national merchant fleets. Almost all the countries examined have in place this type of measure in one form or another. In many cases, it provides for the carriage of cargo by trading partners via, inter alia, reciprocal treatment and bilateral agreements and also, sometimes, by crosstraders. In some cases, waivers can be obtained.

Of those countries examined, the following have adopted legislation containing general cargo reservation provisions:

Algeria	Cuba	Morocco
Angola	Dominican Republic	Nicaragua
Argentina	Ecuador	Nigeria
Bangladesh	Egypt	Pakistan
Benin	Ethiopia	Paraguay
Bolivia	Gabon	Peru
Brazil	Ghana	Philippines
Burma	Guatemala	Saudi Arabia
Cameroon	Honduras	Senegal
Chile	India	Taiwan
People's Republic of China	Indonesia	Togo
Colombia	Korea (South)	United Arab Emirates
Congo	Libya	Uruguay
Costa Rica	Malta	Venezuela
Côte d'Ivoire	Mexico	Zaïre

iv) Specific flags excluded

Another measure is specifically aimed at blocking ships flying certain foreign flags and employing certain crews from carrying the cargo and from entering the ports of implementing countries. Madagascar has adopted such measures and Nigeria has done so on an earlier occasion.

b)   Indirect protectionist measures

Although many countries have adopted direct and strict cargo reservation measures, some have also chosen, as part of their broad national shipping policy, to impose indirect governmental or commercial restrictions which translate into prohibiting foreign flag carriers from trading and discouraging national shippers from buying their shipping services. About eighteen of these measures have to date been identified, based on the information available on the countries studied.

i)   Financial incentives to shippers

Certain countries offer financial incentives to their shippers who use the services of national flag carriers. These incentives can take the form, for example, of rebates or tax credits, lower rates of interest on funds borrowed from government finance institutions, waivers of import duties on goods and grants of export subsidies. Such incentives are granted by:

        Argentina   Philippines
        Malaysia   Thailand
        Mexico   Zaïre
        Pakistan

ii)   Currency regulations

A small number of countries examined exercise some control over currency in one form or another with the aim to save foreign exchange in ocean shipping and to earn extra foreign exchange revenue. For example, one such government, Honduras, requires that all Honduran freight charges be paid in local currency. Another country, Chile, gives national line ships a 20 per cent advantage in conversion of foreign exchange. Furthermore, Algeria enforces strong exchange control regulations.

iii)   CIF sales/FOB purchases

Although CIF sales and FOB purchases are generally normal commercial practices, some governments encourage their strict application to imports and exports in order to favour the carriage of their seaborne trade in national flag ships. In both cases, the shipper pays the freight and selects the carrier. This type of dominance is mainly practised by certain developing countries, but in particular by the state trading countries of Eastern Europe. In these countries, trading is carried out by state corporations and agencies, in which case the foreign importers and exporters are to a very large extent unable to participate in the process of determining the terms of shipment of their import and/or export cargoes. Of the countries examined, the following maintain a CIF sales/FOB purchase policy.

           Angola   Congo
           Bangladesh   Ghana
           People's Republic of China

However, the list is not exhaustive.

   iv) <u>Central Freight Bureaux</u>

      Some of the countries studied have established a "central booking arrangement" on the territories of their trading partners. This arrangement is known as the Central Freight Bureau (CFB), which has some control of its country's ocean transport market. It has been reported that CFBs have been opened in about ten OECD Member countries. This is a development that gives cause for alarm, since in essence all shippers must channel their shipments to and from the country concerned through the latter's CFB or its designated agent, which in turn uses its powers to allocate cargoes to national flag ships. Most OECD Member countries in which these agencies operate have reported having taken measures to discourage the establishment of such operations or to put an end to their activities. Some deterrents have been successful, but at least one OECD country is still trying to find a solution.

      CFBs mainly originate in the following countries:

           Argentina   Gabon   Sri Lanka
           Benin   Indonesia   Tanzania
           Brazil   Iraq   Togo
           Cameroon   Malta   Uruguay
           Congo (People's Republic)   Peru   Zaïre
           Côte d'Ivoire   Senegal

   v) <u>Associate line status</u>

      An associate line status can be obtained when a foreign shipping line negotiates and concludes a pooling arrangement or commercial agreement with an individual state line or the major private line of the trading partner in order to gain access to the trade on a shared basis with the latter. Such status can also be acquired through intergovernmental bilateral shipping agreements. This form of cargo sharing is more often practised in South America. It should be noted that associate status is not automatic upon signature of a commercial agreement; it is usually subject to approval by the regulatory agency. Countries that require associate line status for foreign shipping companies are:

           Argentina   Ecuador
           Bolivia   Peru
           Brazil   Venezuela
           Colombia

   vi) <u>Discriminatory freight tax</u>

      A few of the countries examined have adopted measures with respect to charges imposed on foreign flag carriers that load or unload goods in their ports in the form of a freight tax. These charges are discriminatory, creating competitive distortions between countries and often translate into higher freight rates for the foreign carrier, who in turn passes these costs on to the shipper. Some exemptions have been granted, but this practice remains one of the prevalent forms of government intervention. The following developing countries have been identified as those collecting this type of tax:

    Ecuador   Sri Lanka
    India   Tanzania
    Pakistan   Zaïre
    Panama

vii) **Charges for marine services**

In several of the countries studied, national carriers pay less for various marine services than foreign flag ships, or in some cases, even benefit from an exemption. These marine services include various port charges such as mooring, dockage, demurrage and pilotage. This preference sometimes extends to bunker charges or to taxes on bunkers. Of the countries examined, the following allow their national lines to benefit from reduced charges for different marine services:

    Angola   Peru
    Argentina Venezuela
    Brazil

viii) **Other restrictions**

The following are other types of indirect restrictions practised by governments which can prohibit foreign carriers from participating in the national trade. These measures have not necessarily been adopted by the countries studied:

a) berthing priorities to national ships;

b) restrictions in the investment in facilities by a foreign carrier; for example a foreign shipowner cannot own capital assets in South Korea. In Taiwan, the law prohibits non-Taiwanese from establishing container terminals;

c) restrictions in the purchase of land, etc.;

d) prohibition of foreign carriers to act as multimodal transport operators (MTO). For example, the Mexican International Multimodal Container Transport Decree establishes government controlled MTO to direct the inland movement of all container traffic;

e) prohibition of transhipment or imposition of higher duties on transhipped cargoes;

f) non-standard dimension of container equipment;

g) cargo insurance and credit; for example, Algeria requires that all import and export cargoes be insured with the state-owned insurance company. In Bangladesh, it has been reported that Bengali banks have issued letters of credit in which shipment by national lines is required.

h) translation of documents. Libyan Port Authority Decree of January 1984 requires that ships' documents, cargo manifests and crew lists be translated into Arabic;

i) failure to provide facilities required by high-technology systems;

j) all cargo restrictions; for example, in Cuban trade almost all the cargo is allocated to domestic or Soviet flag ships; and

k) preferential foreign exchange rates.

CONCLUSION

Of the countries examined, forty-six have adopted direct cargo reservation legislation, which accounts for about 78 per cent of those listed. When compared with the other measures and practices identified, cargo reservation is by far the most widespread barrier to trade in maritime transport. If strictly applied, it is also the most important since it affects, inter alia, industry structure, technology, investment, freight rates and services. Despite this high percentage, the conditions in shipping have made the achievement of the goals set regarding cargo reservation to national ships difficult for many countries. Although in most cases the principles set out in the laws are clear, it has been a major task to establish the monitoring and enforcement procedures that would fully implement them. Another factor, which has played a major role in the delay in fulfilling the ideal of carrying all trade in national ships, is the "infant" state of many fleets; in other words there is not enough national tonnage available to carry the trade.

The second most popular measure to exercise a direct control of cargoes is the reservation of a share of government cargoes to national flag ships. Twenty-two countries in the list have adopted the necessary policies and legislation. Eleven reserve specific commodities to their fleet and four exclude certain merchandise in their legislation. One country has included in its law specific flags that do not have access to its trade.

Among the indirect measures of protectionism identified, the establishment of Central Freight Bureaux within the territories of the trading partner takes the lead, with twelve countries that have such bureaux in OECD Member countries and one that exercises control of cargo through a bureau within its own borders. Financial incentives and the associate line status come in second place, with seven countries for each. The next indirect measure is the discriminatory freight tax charged to foreign ships, which has been adopted by six countries. Close behind are the CIF sales, FOB purchases and the charges for certain marine services, which are each practised by five different countries.

The effects of protectionism are well known, as a large number of OECD shipowners have experienced difficulties and frustrations which have been very costly. They made strong representations to their governments urging them to find solutions or practical alternatives but they obtained very little success. Since it is unlikely that in the next few years governments can come together in an international agreement to prohibit discriminatory measures which support national fleets through cargo reservation policies, OECD Member countries will have to turn to other alternatives, based on mutual understanding and co-operation with developing countries, as envisaged in the Recommendation described in the previous Chapter.

Annex I

INVENTORY OF EXISTING DISCRIMINATORY CARGO LEGISLATION AND PRACTICES
BY DEVELOPING COUNTRIES

Note: UN/C indicates whether country is contracting party to the UN Liner Code Convention

ALGERIA

UN/C: No
No. of vessels: 145
000 GRT: 881.7

1) Legislation and Government Orders:	None.
2) Implementation and Practices:	- 50/50 agreements (most of which cover all cargoes) with a number of countries (France, Brazil, Guinea, PRC, Cape Verde). - Exchange control regulations which block remittances; obligatory insurance of cargoes with state-owned insurance co. - Imposition of an additional 10% freight on its imports and exports through CNAN. This measure does not apply to ships flying the flags of France, Tunisia and Belgium, since these countries have concluded bilateral tax agreements with Algeria.
3) Central Freight Bureaux:	-
4) Additional Information: a) are outsiders free to compete?	-
b) restrictions on cross-trader entry and participation in the Conference?	50/50 agreements in certain trades exclude cross-traders.
c) shipper consultations?	-
d) other?	Strong and sometimes exclusionary preference for CNAN (national co.).

ANGOLA

UN/C: No
No. of vessels: 100
000 GRT: 92.3

1) Legislation and Government Orders:	March 1976 decree gives priority to national line for imports and exports. Use of foreign flag vessel only with waiver from government.
2) Implementation and Practices:	- Preferential customs treatment and port fees for national vessels. - All FOB cargoes are controlled by ARGONAVE, the national line. CIF shipments may be shared 50/50.
3) Central Freight Bureaux:	-
4) Additional Information: a) are outsiders free to compete?	Most Angolan liner trade is with state-trading countries and the trade is said to be served primarily by non-conference Eastern Bloc lines. European lines find difficulty in obtaining cargo.
b) restrictions on cross-trader entry and participation in the Conference?	Not known.
c) shipper consultations?	-
d) other?	-

ARGENTINA

UN/C: No
No. of vessels: 454
000 GRT: 2 117

1) Legislation and Government Orders:	- Law 18.250 of 10/6/67 reserves 100% of government cargo (broadly defined) to Argentinian vessels. - Amended by Law 19.877 of 10/6/72 to allow participation by foreign vessels if government or commercial agreement exists granting at least 50% share to Argentinian vessels. Waivers available. - Law 20.447 of 22/5/73 asserts claim to 50% of all cargo. - Legislation (1976) reserves 50% of Southbound cargo to Argentinian flag; waivers on a case-by-case basis. - Resolution 509 of 19/1/77 reserves 50% of imports from the US to Argentinian flag vessels. - Resolution 619, rescinded on 14/4/86, requires all export cargo be carried by members of approved pool or conference.
2) Implementation and Practices:	- 50% reservation all cargoes, not effectively applied. In practice a liner conference which gives Argentina at least 50% of the pool may carry cargo up to a maximum of 50%. 50/50 intergovernmental agreements with Brazil, Chile (not yet ratified), Cuba (not yet ratified), Ecuador, Mexico, Peru, Uruguay and USSR. - 50/50 agreements reserve trade to conference vessels of two parties; then preference given to national non-conference lines and then to other - preferably Latin American - 3rd flags. - US-Argentina agreement gives "Equal Access" to government cargoes. Commercial pool agreement divides liner cargo 50/50 southbound, 40/40/20 northbound.
3) Central Freight Bureaux:	- Letters of credit and licences sometimes stipulate shipment by Argentine national lines, ELMA and CIAMAR. - For the full Hamburg/Bordeaux range, a waiver for shipment by any other conference line can be requested from ELMA office in Hamburg and must be obtained before shipment.
4) Additional Information: a) are outsiders free to compete? b) restrictions on cross-trader entry and participation in the Conference? c) shipper consultations? d) other?	Very small percentage (10%-15%) of trade carried by non-conference lines. No. Are permitted in some trades but with severely limited shares. No. Argentinian vessels pay reduced port fees and receive rebates of wharfage fees. Freight costs rebated to exporters who use national flag.

BANGLADESH

UN/C: Yes
No. of vessels: 274
000 GRT: 378.6

1) Legislation and Government Orders:	Bangladesh Flag (Protection) Ordinance No.14 of 28/6/82 implemented by decree of 26/9/82 reserves 40% to national flag vessels.

2) Implementation and Practices:	General waiver automatically granted for: 1) trades where Bangladesh flag vessels are not operated; or 2) certain export cargoes (e.g. garments, handicraft); or 3) export cargoes less than 350 WT per vessel per loading port and import cargoes less than 1 000 WT (500 WT in Bay of Bengal/Japan/Bay of Bengal Conference) per vessel per loading port. Specific waiver is required for cargoes not covered by general waiver. Total Bangladesh lines' share in Japan/Bangladesh trade far exceeds 40%. Bangladesh lines operate as both conference lines and outsiders in the trade.
3) Central Freight Bureaux:	-
4) Additional Information: a) are outsiders free to compete? b) restrictions on cross-trader entry and participation in the Conference? c) shipper consultations? d) other?	 Yes. Uncertain, but most likely yes. Yes. There have been reports that Bengali banks have issued letters of credit requiring shipment on national lines. Bangladesh shipping authorities have backed away from their April 6 decision to tighten restrictions on foreign-flag carriage of FOB-nominated export cargo. On April 14, the Department of Shipping published a notice stating that the procedure "for granting waiver to FOB cargo being nominated by the buyers is hereby revived with immediate effect". The Government of Bangladesh reserves the right to refuse to grant a waiver for FOB nominated cargo if the overseas buyer does not confirm the nomination by telex to the Dept. of Shipping. The notice encourages local agents of FOB buyers to nominate Bangladesh-flag vessels "for at least a certain percentage of FOB cargo" but stipulates no penalty for failure to do so.

BENIN (PR)

UN/C: Yes
No. of vessels: 15
000 GRT: 4.9

1) Legislation and Government Orders:	Ordinance No.49 and Decree No.240 of 13/9/79 require cargo sharing on 40/40/20 basis (whole trade). But Interministerial Order of 14/5/84 requires ships operated or chartered by COBENAM (national line) to have priority to all cargo and requires submission of freight manifests. Waivers granted where national flag unavailable.
2) Implementation and Practices:	Effective use made of Central Freight Booking Offices. (Benin Shippers' Council - CNCB).
3) Central Freight Bureaux:	- An attestation from the CNCB (Conseil National des Chargeurs du Bénin) is required for shipments with COBENAM, the national line. For shipments with any other line, a waiver must be obtained from the local CNCB representative. It is reported that waivers are difficult to obtain.

4) Additional Information:
   a) are outsiders free to compete? No.
   b) restrictions on cross-trader entry and participation in the Conference? Yes.
   c) shipper consultations? Yes.
   d) other? –

BOLIVIA

UN/C: No
No. of vessels: 2
000 GRT: 14.9

1) Legislation and Government Orders:
   - 50% reservation to national flag including general reefer and bulk cargo. Remaining 50% open to "associate" foreign lines which have a "pool agreement" with the Bolivian national line.
   - 100% of government import cargoes are served to Bolivian line.

2) Implementation and Practices:
   Associate status granted to a number of lines which have a "pool agreement" with Bolivian national line.

3) Central Freight Bureaux: –

4) Additional Information:
   a) are outsiders free to compete? Yes, but in practice members of pool agreements are required to be members of the relevant conference and thus outsiders are unable to become "associated lines".
   b) restrictions on cross-trader entry and participation in the Conference? Yes.
   c) shipper consultations? No.
   d) other? –

BRAZIL

UN/C: No
No. of vessels: 697
000 GRT: 6 212

1) Legislation and Government Orders:
   - According to Decree 666 of 2/7/69, Brazil reserves for its ships 100% of "prescribed cargo". 70% is for prescribed dry bulk only. General cargo is shared. Exports are free.
   - Petroleum and related cargoes reserved to national line. Cargo preference waivers up to 50% on basis of reciprocity, subject to agreement by SUNAMAM. Waivers occasionally also to outsiders.

2) Implementation and Practices:
   - Legislation applies in the absence of intergovernmental and commercial agreements. Associated status is, however, granted to a number of lines which have "pool agreements" with Brazilian lines.
   - Government agreements with Argentina, Chile, Ecuador, Mexico and Peru establish 50/50 division of all liner cargo. Agreements with Portugal, Nigeria, France and US divide government cargo. Commercial pools agreements give 50/50 or 40/40/20 split.
   - National carriers exempt from light duties, pay reduced pilotage fees.

3) Central Freight Bureaux: — Letters of credit and licences sometimes stipulate shipping by Brazilian national lines, Lloyd Brasileiro and Alianca.
— For the full Hamburg/Bordeaux range, a waiver for shipment by any other conference line can only be obtained from the SUNAMAM office in Hamburg. SUNAMAM, which is subordinate to the Ministry of Transport, is the regulatory body charged, among other responsibilities, with overseeing Brazil's cargo reservation rules.

4) Additional Information:
   a) are outsiders free to compete? Yes. However foreign shipping companies cannot operate to Brazil unless co-members with a Brazilian line of a conference. Most conference agreements cover whole trade. Thus opportunities for outsiders are very restricted.

   b) restrictions on cross-trader entry and participation in the Conference? SUNAMAM Resolution 5246 prohibits cross-trading. Exemptions are granted to certain Latin American countries which have bilateral agreements with Brazil granting access to each other's crosstrades.

   c) shipper consultations? No.
   d) other? On the whole government agreements do not recognise 3rd flag rights.

BURMA

UN/C: No
No. of vessels: 106
000 GRT: 125.5

1) Legislation and Government Orders: Existing legislation reserves all cargo to the national flag except for certain regional trades where Burma operates in a conference.

2) Implementation and Practices: —

3) Central Freight Bureaux: —

4) Additional Information:
   a) are outsiders free to compete? No competition from outsiders is possible.
   b) restrictions on cross-trader entry and participation in the Conference? Not known.
   c) shipper consultations? —
   d) other? —

CAMEROON

UN/C: Yes
No. of vessels: 49
000 GRT: 76.7

1) Legislation and Government Orders: Decree No.709 of 13/10/75 and Order No.39 of 16/1/76 reserve govt cargo to CAMSHIP (state line) unless 40/40/20 agreement divides the whole trade. Order No.317 of 1977 requires all conferences to negotiate rates with Cameroon National Shipowners' Council.

2) Implementation and Practices: — Cameroon Nat. Shipowners' Council implements the regulations on 40/40/20 cargo division.
— CAMSHIP takes best cargoes – probably 50-60% – in the European trades through operation of a waiver system. Since 1983, waiver system has also been implemented in Far East trade. CAMSHIP takes around 40% of cargoes.

3) Central Freight Bureaux:	- For shipments with CAMSHIP, the national line, attestations are not required. For shipments with any other line, a waiver must be obtained from the local representatives of CNCC (Conseil National des Chargeurs Camerounais). As CAMSHIP gives a regular service, it is difficult to obtain a waiver.
4) Additional Information: a) are outsiders free to compete?	Excluded entirely in the absence of bilateral agreement.
b) restrictions on cross-trader entry and participation in the Conference?	Yes.
c) shipper consultations?	Yes.
d) other?	-

CHILE

UN/C: Yes
No. of vessels: 255
000 GRT: 566.9

1) Legislation and Government Orders:	Law No. 18.454 of 11/11/85 applies basic 50% liner cargo reservation. Based on reciprocity, in which access by foreign carrier determined by degree of access permitted to Chilean vessels by foreign flag country.
2) Implementation and Practices:	- Law has little effective impact. Chile has entered bilateral agreement establishing 50/50 division of all liner cargo. Has agreements with Argentina (not yet ratified) and Brazil, and a protocol with Peru. - National lines given 20% advantage in conversion of foreign exchange.
3) Central Freight Bureaux:	-
4) Additional Information: a) are outsiders free to compete?	Yes.
b) restrictions on cross-trader entry and participation in the Conference?	Crosstrading also determined on reciprocal basis.
c) shipper consultations?	No.
d) other?	-

CHINA (PR)

UN/C: Yes
No. of vessels: 1 562
000 GRT: 11 567

1) Legislation and Government Orders:	New maritime code being drafted which is likely to contain protectionist clauses.
2) Implementation and Practices:	Chinese lay down all conditions on which cargo moves in their trades, e.g. they discriminate by buying fob and exporting cif and fix freight rates. Currently much cargo carried in foreign ships although the PRC fleet is rapidly growing.
3) Central Freight Bureaux:	-

4) Additional Information:
   a) are outsiders free to compete?   No.
   b) restrictions on cross-trader entry and
      participation in the Conference?   No conference.
   c) shipper consultations?   -
   d) other?   -

COLOMBIA

UN/C: No
No. of vessels: 90
000 GRT: 380

1) Legislation and Government Orders: According to Decree 1208 of 21/7/69, Colombia reserves minimum of 50% of all general cargo to Colombian companies. Maximum of 50% for bulk commodities.

2) Implementation and Practices:
   - Provision supported by requirement that foreign carrier be granted associate status by national carrier to gain permission to load and discharge goods.
   - Import and Export licences; once approved the goods are transported either by a ship of a Colombian company or an associate line.

3) Central Freight Bureaux: -

4) Additional Information:
   a) are outsiders free to compete?   Licensing procedure precludes, with minor exceptions, the operation of non-conference lines except for very small amount of unstamped cargoes.

   b) restrictions on cross-trader entry and
      participation in the Conference?   Conference cross-traders are not necessarily excluded, provided they do not, with minor exceptions, take away from Colombian 50% share.
   c) shipper consultations?   No.
   d) other?   -

CONGO (PR)

UN/C: Yes
No. of vessels: 21
000 GRT: 8.5

1) Legislation and Government Orders: Decree No. 85/045 of 22/1/85 divides conference trade 40/40/20.

2) Implementation and Practices: Cargo division regulated by system of loading permits awarded to lines guaranteeing regular sailings and adherence to officially approved tariffs. Exports must be CIF, imports FOB, unless expressly regulated otherwise.

3) Central Freight Bureaux:
   - The national line, COTRAM, has no sailings. Its rights are passed on to other lines. The "Marine Marchande de la République Populaire du Congo" have indicated agents who deliver a loading authorisation which must be obtained before shipment. If not, the importer is fined at arrival in the port of destination. The system is effectively applied since 1/5/85.

4) Additional Information:
   a) are outsiders free to compete?   No.
   b) restrictions on cross-trader entry and
      participation in the Conference?   Not known.
   c) shipper consultations?   Yes.
   d) other?   Semi-Congo National Line status has been given to foreign shipping lines in trades between Congo and following countries/regions: France, Scandinavia, FRG, Netherlands, Belgium, Italy, Spain, Far East.

COSTA RICA

UN/C: Yes
No. of vessels: 25
000 GRT: 13.3
(the regional carrier NAMUCAR was liquidated in March 86)

1) Legislation and Government Orders: Law No. 5873 of 12/75 reserves 80% of all cargo for regional carrier, NAMUCAR, placed in liquidation 3/86.

2) Implementation and Practices: Never implemented.

3) Central Freight Bureaux: -

4) Additional Information:
   a) are outsiders free to compete?   Yes.
   b) restrictions on cross-trader entry and
      participation in the Conference?   No.
   c) shipper consultations?   No.
   d) other?   -

COTE D'IVOIRE

UN/C: Yes
No. of vessels: 58
000 GRT: 120.7

1) Legislation and Government Orders: Law No. 75-940 of 26/12/75; Decree No. 617 of 3/9/75, and Decree No. 576 of 25/8/77 apply 40/40/20 principle to both conf. & non-conf. cargoes, including bulk & other cargoes.

2) Implementation and Practices: Cargo booking offices direct cargo with following priorities:
a) IC flag ships; b) conf. ships of bilateral trading partner; c) regular line vessels of trading partner; d) crosstraders in conf.; e) IC non-conf. lines, if any; f) outsiders.

3) Central Freight Bureaux: - An attestation from OIC (Office Ivoirien des Chargeurs) is required for all shipments including those with SITRAM, the national line, and must be obtained from the local OIC representative in the ports of the Hamburg/Antwerp range.

4) Additional Information:
   a) are outsiders free to compete?   See cargo allocation rules.
   b) restrictions on cross-trader entry and
      participation in the Conference?   See cargo allocation rules.
   c) shipper consultations?   Yes.
   d) other?   Agreements (40/40/20) with France, FRG, Belgium, Spain, Senegal, Cameroon, Italy.
State mktg boards control coffee & cocoa exports as govt cargo.

CUBA

UN/C: Yes
No. of vessels: 422
000 GRT: 958.6

1) Legislation and Government Orders:	Not known.
2) Implementation and Practices:	Most cargo is allocated to Cuban or Soviet flag ships. Although fixtures with 3rd party flags are reported, regulations prohibit non-Cuban flag vessels from loading/discharging Cuban cargo.
3) Central Freight Bureaux:	-
4) Additional Information:	
a) are outsiders free to compete?	No.
b) restrictions on cross-trader entry and participation in the Conference?	Yes.
c) shipper consultations?	-
d) other?	-

DOMINICAN REPUBLIC

UN/C: No
No. of vessels: 35
000 GRT: 42.2

1) Legislation and Government Orders:	Law No. 180 of 31/5/75 reserves 60% of govt. and 40-50% of general cargo reserved to national flag.
2) Implementation and Practices:	Not applied in practice.
3) Central Freight Bureaux:	-
4) Additional Information:	
a) are outsiders free to compete?	Yes.
b) restrictions on cross-trader entry and participation in the Conference?	Not known.
c) shipper consultations?	No.
d) other?	-

ECUADOR

UN/C: No
No. of vessels: 155
000 GRT: 437.7

1) Legislation and Government Orders:	- According to Decree No. 3367 of 6/8/69, for both imports and exports of general cargoes minimum of 50% reserved for national flag. All government cargoes are reserved. All petroleum and petroleum products (100%) are reserved for Ecuadorian state-owned lines. As for other cargoes the percentages are fixed from time to time, but the aim is 50% for Ecuadorian line ships. - Foreign carriers subject to 0.952 per cent freight charge (other Latin American carriers not charged).

2) Implementation and Practices: — Implementation taking place route by route as Ecuadorian vessels become available in the trade. Associate status granted to a number of lines which have a "pool agreement" with Ecuadorian Lines.
— Waivers available but granted on preferential basis to carriers of nations with which Ecuador has bilateral agreement.
— Bilaterals with Argentina, Brazil, Honduras and Panama.
— Regulation on the import side. Shipping lines are required to send copies of their manifests to DIGMAR.

3) Central Freight Bureaux: —

4) Additional Information:
 a) are outsiders free to compete? In practice outsiders are not allowed to join "pool agreements" and thus are unable to be "associate lines". One of the two Ecuadorian lines operates as conference member, the second as an active outsider.
 b) restrictions on cross-trader entry and participation in the Conference? Cross-trading takes place in practice only between non-Latin American pool members.
 c) shipper consultations? No.
 d) other? —

EGYPT

UN/C: Yes
No. of vessels: 422
000 GRT: 1 063

1) Legislation and Government Orders: 1976 decree of Council of State directs govt. cargo & 30% of all imports & exports to Egypt-flag vessels. Art.1 of Decree 221 of 1974 requires all organisations with 25% or more govt. ownership to give priority to national flag vessels.

2) Implementation and Practices: Egyptian Co for Maritime Transport and agents give priority to state line and 2nd preference to Egyptian private lines; bilateral agreements with cargo clauses with Sri Lanka, Indonesia, Libya, Pakistan.

3) Central Freight Bureaux: —

4) Additional Information:
 a) are outsiders free to compete? Not known.
 b) restrictions on cross-trader entry and participation in the Conference? Not known.
 c) shipper consultations? —
 d) other? —

ETHIOPIA

UN/C: Yes
No. of vessels: 23
000 GRT: 66.9

1) Legislation and Government Orders: Not known.

2) Implementation and Practices: Import licences bear the words "to be shipped in Ethiopian flag vessels", however fleet is very small and waivers given automatically.

3) Central Freight Bureaux: -

4) Additional Information:
   a) are outsiders free to compete? Unclear.
   b) restrictions on cross-trader entry and participation in the Conference? Only in certain cases.
   c) shipper consultations? -
   d) other? -

GABON

UN/C: Yes (reservation that govt & quasi-govt cargo reserved for nat. flag)
No. of vessels: 23
000 GRT: 98

1) Legislation and Government Orders: Decree No.54 of 7/9/78 introduced 40/40/20 division of the trade.

2) Implementation and Practices: Since July 1980, cargo has been controlled by Gabon Shippers' Council. When SONATRAM (national line) does not have adequate capacity to carry its 40%, the remainder may go on foreign lines. Agreement (40/40/20) with Belgium.

3) Central Freight Bureaux: - An attestation from CGC (Conseil Gabonais des Chargeurs) is in principle required for all shipments including those with SONATRAM, the national line, and must be obtained from the local CGC representative in the ports of the Hamburg/Antwerp range.

4) Additional Information:
   a) are outsiders free to compete? Not known.
   b) restrictions on cross-trader entry and participation in the Conference? No.
   c) shipper consultations? Yes.
   d) other? -

GHANA

UN/C: Yes
No. of vessels: 137
000 GRT: 165.6

1) Legislation and Government Orders: Not known.

2) Implementation and Practices:
   - Ghana Supply Commission (govt purchasing agent) imports via state-owned Black Star Line. Import licences require use of Black Star Line. 25% of national timber exports via national line.
   - Ghana favours FOB purchasing as a means of discrimination, but due to political situation, virtually no trade.

3) Central Freight Bureaux: -

4) Additional Information:
   a) are outsiders free to compete?   Yes.
   b) restrictions on cross-trader entry and
      participation in the Conference?   No.
   c) shipper consultations?   -
   d) other?   -

GUATEMALA

UN/C: Yes
No. of vessels: 8
000 GRT: 9.4

1) Legislation and Government Orders: Several decrees regulate access to cargoes.

2) Implementation and Practices: Substantially ineffective.

3) Central Freight Bureaux: -

4) Additional Information:
   a) are outsiders free to compete?   Yes.
   b) restrictions on cross-trader entry and
      participation in the Conference?   No.
   c) shipper consultations?   -
   d) other?   -

GUINEA (PR)

UN/C: Yes
No. of vessels: 19
000 GRT: 7.2

1) Legislation and Government Orders: 50% bauxite & alumina exports reserved to national flag. Legislation in preparation.

2) Implementation and Practices: Partners in CBG Consortium are bound by a clause in the bauxite agreement reserving, under certain conditions, 50% of bauxite exports from Port Kamsar for Guinean or assimilated flags. Alumina exports ex Conakry are not affected.
Guinean operator for CBC tonnage is Guinomar (50% WABS, 50% Government).

3) Central Freight Bureaux: -

4) Additional Information:
   a) are outsiders free to compete?   Not known.
   b) restrictions on cross-trader entry and
      participation in the Conference?   Not known.
   c) shipper consultations?   Yes.
   d) other?   -

HONDURAS

UN/C: Yes
No. of vessels: 424
000 GRT: 555.2

1) Legislation and Government Orders: 1970 legislation reserves imports of certain "privileged" companies to Honduran vessels.

2) Implementation and Practices:	Not effective so far as we know - fleet too small to cope. Market therefore free in practice.
3) Central Freight Bureaux:	-
4) Additional Information:	
a) are outsiders free to compete?	Yes.
b) restrictions on cross-trader entry and participation in the Conference?	No.
c) shipper consultations?	-
d) other?	All Honduran freight charges must be paid in local currency.

INDIA

UN/C: Yes
No. of vessels: 736
000 GRT: 6 540.1

1) Legislation and Government Orders:	Government cargoes reserved to national flag. Further legislation under consideration to reserve 40% of all cargoes to Indian vessels.
2) Implementation and Practices:	- Foreign shipping companies taxed about 5% of gross freight revenues (some exempted by bilateral agreement). (Domestic firms are taxed on income in lieu of freight tax). - Number of 50/50 agreements with USSR, Peru, Romania, Iran, Czechoslovakia, Hungary. 40/40/20 agreements with Poland and GDR. - In Dec.1985 Dir.Gen. of Shipping issued instructions that exp. to Bangladesh ports of Chittagong and Chalna were regarded as domestic trade and reserved to Indian vessels.
3) Central Freight Bureaux:	-
4) Additional Information:	
a) are outsiders free to compete?	50/50 agreements extend to whole trade. Neither Indian nor foreign outsiders may participate where trade is subject to bilateral agreements.
b) restrictions on cross-trader entry and participation in the Conference?	Yes.
c) shipper consultations?	Yes.
d) other?	-

INDONESIA

UN/C: Yes
No. of vessels: 1 707
000 GRT: 2 085.6

1) Legislation and Government Orders:	- Presidential Decree 18-82 (4/12/82) reserves broadly-defined government cargoes to national-flag carriers. - 20% of timber exports to Japan are reserved for national-flag vessels, as are 50% of CIF fertilizer imports and 100% of FOB fertilizer imports. - Ministry of Communications Decree KM/16/PR.302/PHB-82 (18/1/82) provides for a 50% reduction in port and bunkering charges for national carriers, except those carrying oil or natural gas.

2) Implementation and Practices: - The Indonesia/Japan/Indonesia Freight Conference (IJJIFC) agreed in Feb.1986 to restrict bookings based on trade shares of 43% for Indonesian and Japanese conference members and 14% for other members.
- After withdrawal of Presidential Decree 4185 open trading is operative

3) Central Freight Bureaux: - Certain flag prescriptions still exist; however, outsiders can participate to a certain extent.

4) Additional Information:
   a) are outsiders free to compete?   Yes.
   b) restrictions on cross-trader entry and participation in the Conference?   Unclear.
   c) shipper consultations?   Yes.
   d) other?   -

IRAQ

UN/C: Yes
No. of vessels: 149
000 GRT: 1 016.3

1) Legislation and Government Orders:

2) Implementation and Practices: -

3) Central Freight Bureaux: - Letters of credit or import licences often indicate shipment by national line, Iraqi Line and ISEMT. Waivers must be obtained from the local agents of the national line for cargoes destined for Antwerp.

4) Additional Information:
   a) are outsiders free to compete?   -
   b) restrictions on cross-trader entry and participation in the Conference?   -
   c) shipper consultations?   -
   d) other?   -

JAMAICA

UN/C: Yes
No. of vessels: 13
000 GRT: 9.4

1) Legislation and Government Orders: Cargo preference act of 1979 reserves natural resources (bauxite, alumina and agric. products) to Jamaican owned or chartered vessels.

2) Implementation and Practices: - Not applied in practice. Waivers are not even currently required.
- Liner cargoes are not affected by cargo preference acts but strong directive to government departments to use the Jamaican national line which, however, is not very effective. Market is therefore fairly open.

3) Central Freight Bureaux: -

4) Additional Information:
   a) are outsiders free to compete?   Yes.
   b) restrictions on cross-trader entry and
      participation in the Conference?   No.
   c) shipper consultations?   Yes.
   d) other?   -

KOREA (South)

UN/C: Yes
No. of vessels: 1 837
000 GRT: 7 183.6

1) Legislation and Government Orders:
   - Marine Trade Promotion (Law 1895, 28/2/67) amended by Law 3146 (12/5/78) reserves 100% of all Korean export and import liner cargoes for national-flag vessels. Act supplemented by Presidential Enforcement Decree 4283 (20/1/79).
   - Since 1979 waivers must be obtained before carrying cargoes on non-Korean ships.

2) Implementation and Practices:
   - Foreign-flag vessels may be exempted from Act by FCN Treaty or inter-governmental agreement.
   - The FEFC has gained exemption from Korean cargo reservation in the Europe trade route.

3) Central Freight Bureaux: -

4) Additional Information:
   a) are outsiders free to compete?
      Ceiling of 20% imposed on non-conference lines to Northern Europe. In practice Koreans constantly demanding more of trade.
   b) restrictions on cross-trader entry and
      participation in the Conference?
      - Cross traders in trans-Pacific trade whose government have no bilateral agreements have been affected.
      - Foreign carriers cannot own capital assets in Korea.
   c) shipper consultations?
      Joint co-operation between Korean shippers & shipowners may promote protectionist measures.
   d) other?   -

LIBYA

UN/C: No
No. of vessels: 104
000 GRT: 825.2

1) Legislation and Government Orders:
   - 1982 decree reserves all imports to nat. owned or chartered vessels.
   - Port authority decree of Jan.84 requires translation of ship's documents, cargo manifests and crew lists into Arabic.

2) Implementation and Practices:
   - Implementation reportedly delayed.
   - Ships calling at western Libyan ports detained for failure to comply.
   - Imposition of inward freight commission which for Mediterranean cargoes is 4% and for non Mediterranean cargoes is 3%. The calculation made by Libyan authorities is based on freight rates which are estimated without taking into account the actual freights and which in any case are much higher than the actually contracted ones to the detriment of the vessel's earnings.
   - Imposition of high compensation penalties, declaring that there are missing parcels from all cargoes discharged.

3) Central Freight Bureaux: —

4) Additional Information:
   a) are outsiders free to compete?   Yes.
   b) restrictions on cross-trader entry and
      participation in the Conference?   No.
   c) shipper consultations?   —
   d) other?   —

MADAGASCAR

UN/C: Yes
No. of vessels: 71
000 GRT: 73.7

1) Legislation and Government Orders: 1980 decree blocks ships flying FOC, Israel, South African, South Korean and Formosan flags and crews.

2) Implementation and Practices: —

3) Central Freight Bureaux: —

4) Additional Information:
   a) are outsiders free to compete?   See legislation.
   b) restrictions on cross-trader entry and
      participation in the Conference?   See legislation.
   c) shipper consultations?   —
   d) other?   —

MALAYSIA

UN/C: Yes
No. of vessels: 498
000 GRT: 1 743.6

1) Legislation and Government Orders: Government and quasi-Government cargoes reserved to national flag. Also fiscal incentives.

2) Implementation and Practices: Ineffective.

3) Central Freight Bureaux: —

4) Additional Information:
   a) are outsiders free to compete?   Yes.
   b) restrictions on cross-trader entry and
      participation in the Conference?   Yes.
   c) shipper consultations?   Yes.
   d) other?   —

MALTA

UN/C: No
No. of vessels: 246
000 GRT: 2 014.9

1) Legislation and Government Orders: Maltese Minister for Ports may exclude from trade with Malta those lines not party to an agreement of which he approves.

2) Implementation and Practices: Legislation led to a number of 50/50 commercial deals (in UK trades, UK share is open to European cross-traders).

3) Central Freight Bureaux: - Shipment destined for Antwerp is compulsory by the national line, Sea Malta & Co., Ltd., or by accepted lines, DNOL and NECOL.

4) Additional Information:
   a) are outsiders free to compete? Previous non-conference lines accommodated in agreement - presumably there would be difficulties for new non-conference lines.

   b) restrictions on cross-trader entry and participation in the Conference? Cross traders have been accommodated in agreement but on a limited basis.

   c) shipper consultations? -
   d) other? -

MEXICO

UN/C: Yes
No. of vessels: 642
000 GRT: 1 520.2

1) Legislation and Government Orders:
   - 1981 legislation reserves 50% of general cargo and up to 50% of bulk and homogeneous cargo plus all Government cargoes to national flag.
   - Decree of January 1985 authorises 10% rebate of import duties to importers using national flag.
   - International Multimodal Container Transport Decree establishes government controlled MTO to direct inland movement of all container traffic.

2) Implementation and Practices:
   - Cargo reservation law is rigidly enforced, 50/50 agreements divide liner cargo with Brazil and Argentina.
   - Tax rebate only partially effective.

3) Central Freight Bureaux: -

4) Additional Information:
   a) are outsiders free to compete? Yes. High proportion of liner trade is non-conference even though legislation attempts to prevent outsiders from acquiring cargo; fiscal benefits to Mexican outsiders.

   b) restrictions on cross-trader entry and participation in the Conference? No, provided their share does not come out of the Mexican line's 50%.

   c) shipper consultations? Yes.
   d) other? -

MOROCCO

UN/C: Yes
No. of vessels: 294
000 GRT: 416.5

1) Legislation and Government Orders: 40% imports and 30% exports required to be shipped on national flag ships; but 50/50 oriented.

2) Implementation and Practices: Agreements (40/40/20) with Spain and Italy interpreted by Morocco to include bulk. National lines pref. for govt cargo.

3) Central Freight Bureaux: —

4) Additional Information:
   a) are outsiders free to compete? Not in practice.
   b) restrictions on cross-trader entry and participation in the Conference? Agreements currently restrict conference cross-trade share.
   c) shipper consultations? —
   d) other? —

MOZAMBIQUE

UN/C: No
No. of vessels: 104
000 GRT: 42.8

1) Legislation and Government Orders: —

2) Implementation and Practices: Mozambique-Portugal trade reserved to Portuguese flag vessels, which get 20% reduction in taxes.

3) Central Freight Bureaux: —

4) Additional Information:
   a) are outsiders free to compete? Not known.
   b) restrictions on cross-trader entry and participation in the Conference? Not known.
   c) shipper consultations? —
   d) other? —

NICARAGUA

UN/C: No
No. of vessels: 24
000 GRT: 22.9

1) Legislation and Government Orders: Decree No.299 of 24/3/72 reserves 100% of government cargo, 50% of other liner cargo to nat'l carrier; balance on flag carriers of trading partners; reserves 80% where other party does not have shipping service. 40% of imports/exports must move on govt owned carrier. 20% of cargo available to other Central American cross-traders.

2) Implementation and Practices: Enforcement not effective due to lack of fleet.

3) Central Freight Bureaux: —

4) Additional Information:
   a) are outsiders free to compete? Yes, in principle, but competition from outsiders is restricted due to legislation.
   b) restrictions on cross-trader entry and participation in the Conference? No.
   c) shipper consultations? —
   d) other? —

NIGERIA

UN/C: Yes
No. of vessels: 206
000 GRT: 563.9

1) Legislation and Government Orders:	None at present, but number of attempts made at drafting legislation to implement code - latest policy indicates that it may extend 40/40/20 to all cargoes including bulk (or even 50/50).
2) Implementation and Practices:	50/50 agreement with Brazil. Attempts being made to enter into bilateral cargo-sharing agreements (covering whole trade), with other countries.
3) Central Freight Bureaux:	-
4) Additional Information:	
a) are outsiders free to compete?	High proportion of trade currently carried by non-conference lines.
b) restrictions on cross-trader entry and participation in the Conference?	No.
c) shipper consultations?	Yes.
d) other?	-

PAKISTAN

UN/C: Yes
No. of vessels: 78
000 GRT: 434.1

1) Legislation and Government Orders:	Freight tax of 8.1% on gross freight earnings of foreign shipping firms (bilateral exceptions for some countries; tax collection provisionally suspended for US vessels in March 1986).
2) Implementation and Practices:	Most government cargo is shipped via Pakistan National Shipping Corporation. Bilateral cargo-sharing agreements with Egypt, India, Malaysia, Korea. (Nat. firms pay tax on income instead of freight tax).
3) Central Freight Bureaux:	-
4) Additional Information:	
a) are outsiders free to compete?	Yes, but dependent on bilateral agreements.
b) restrictions on cross-trader entry and participation in the Conference?	In practice, cross-traders are eliminated.
c) shipper consultations?	Yes.
d) other?	

PANAMA

UN/C: No
No. of vessels: 5 252
000 GRT: 41 305

1) Legislation and Government Orders:	Freight tax on foreign flag vessels loading or discharging.
2) Implementation and Practices:	Exemption on the basis of reciprocity - but several European countries have had their claims for exemption rejected.

3) Central Freight Bureaux: -

4) Additional Information:
   a) are outsiders free to compete?   Yes.
   b) restrictions on cross-trader entry and
      participation in the Conference?   No.
   c) shipper consultations?   -
   d) other?   -

PARAGUAY

   UN/C: No
   No. of vessels: 41
   000 GRT: 43.3

1) Legislation and Government Orders: Law No.295 of 17/11/71 reserves 100% of import cargo to Paraguayan owned or chartered vessels; up to 50% reserved in trade with other Latin American countries.

2) Implementation and Practices: Paraguay seeks to control cargo allocation at both ends of trade. Cargoes loaded in order of priority to: (a) Paraguayan state shipping line; (b) Other Paraguayan flag vessels; (c) Vessels of countries with which an agreement exists.

3) Central Freight Bureaux: -

4) Additional Information:
   a) are outsiders free to compete?   In practice, no.
   b) restrictions on cross-trader entry and
      participation in the Conference?   No conferences serve Paraguayan ports. Bilateral agreements in some trades exclude cross-traders.
   c) shipper consultations?   No.
   d) other?   -

PERU

   UN/C: Yes (reservation on cargo sharing)
   No. of vessels: 632
   000 GRT: 754.2

1) Legislation and Government Orders: Decree 009-86-TC of 21/2/86 reserves 100% of import & export cargo to nat'l lines except where government or commercial agreement establishes 50/50 division. Changed 1982 Decree 36-82-TC which reserved 50% of liner cargo to national flag.

2) Implementation and Practices: - Implementing regulations still under preparation. Intent appears to be to deny third flag access.
                                         - If pool agreement exists agreed share is respected with dominant operational right given to CPV among Peruvian lines.
                                         - National vessels pay lower port fees.

3) Central Freight Bureaux: - A Government decree imposes shipment by Peruvian national line or by lines associated to Peruvian lines, Consorcio Naviero Peruano, Empresa Maritima del Estado and Campania Peruana de Vapores. For inbound cargo to Europe, there is no pool which means that an associated line is not available. For non-bulk shipments, waivers are to be obtained in Peru from the Direccion General de Transporte Acuatico (DGTA), when no national line is available.

4) Additional Information:
   a) are outsiders free to compete? No.
   b) restrictions on cross-trader entry and participation in the Conference? Cross-traders not permitted unless they have pool agreements with Peruvian flag Line.
   c) shipper consultations? No.
   d) other? –

PHILIPPINES

UN/C: Yes
No. of vessels: 1 131
000 GRT: 6 922.5

1) Legislation and Government Orders:
   - Presidential Directive 1466 (11/6/78) directs govt-impelled cargoes to national-flag vessels (waiver available).
   - Memorandum Order No.6 (23/8/84) reserves 50% of the log trade with Japan, Korea and Taiwan for national-flag carriers.
   - The Merchant Shipping Act of 1985 allows exporters to deduct 150% of overseas freight and port charges from their taxable income if they use national-flag carriers. Enterprises registered with the Board of Investments may deduct 200%.
   - Executive Order No.769 of 19/1/82 provides authority for implementation of 40/40/20 cargo reservation in all trades (government cargoes excepted).

2) Implementation and Practices:
   Implementing regulations for E.O.769 issued for US route but rescinded on 30/5/84. Combination of two decrees could mean 60% trade reserved for Philippine ships but current strength of national fleet means this is not possible.

3) Central Freight Bureaux: –

4) Additional Information:
   a) are outsiders free to compete? Yes, very active, both east and westbound.
   b) restrictions on cross-trader entry and participation in the Conference? No.
   c) shipper consultations? Yes.
   d) other? –

SAUDI ARABIA

UN/C: Yes
No. of vessels: 380
000 GRT: 2 978

1) Legislation and Government Orders:
   Feb.1985 royal decree directs govt agencies to prefer Saudi vessels. Decree of Nov.24 1985 calls for 40% of liner imports to go via national vessels.

2) Implementation and Practices:
   National lines (National Shipping Corp. of Saudi Arabia and United Arab Shipping Co.) now have about 22% of liner trade; they have insufficient capacity to carry 40%. Both have pressured importers to use national lines, in some cases suggesting to foreign contractors that govt would cancel contracts if nat. lines were not used. In September 1985 the Saudi Monetary Authority (central bank) telexed banks urging them to specify use of national lines in letters of credit.

3) Central Freight Bureaux: —

4) Additional Information:
   a) are outsiders free to compete? Yes.
   b) restrictions on cross-trader entry and
      participation in the Conference? No.
   c) shipper consultations? Yes.
   d) other? —

SENEGAL

UN/C: Yes
No. of vessels: 148
000 GRT: 50.4

1) Legislation and Government Orders: Decree 179 of 2/3/78 and Order 454 of 25/7/80 apply 40/40/20 to all cargoes.

2) Implementation and Practices: Cargo-sharing agreement, administered by "shipowners' committee", concluded with France. Other cargo-sharing agreements administered by Senegal authority.

3) Central Freight Bureaux: - The national line, COSENAM, offers no sailings at present. Its rights are passed on to other lines. The Senegalese Shippers' Council (COSEC) has indicated agents in the ports of the Hamburg/Antwerp range. These agents deliver the attestation required for all shipments.

4) Additional Information:
   a) are outsiders free to compete? Not in trades where cargo sharing agreements are concluded.
   b) restrictions on cross-trader entry and
      participation in the Conference? See legislation.
   c) shipper consultations? Yes.
   d) other? —

SINGAPORE

UN/C: No
No. of vessels: 716
000 GRT: 6 267.6

1) Legislation and Government Orders: Defence contracts require preference to be given to state shipping line, but impact negligible.

2) Implementation and Practices: Cargo-sharing agreement with Indonesia (45% cargo from Indonesia to Singapore flag ships remaining 55% to Indonesian ships) has become obsolete since Indonesian SKU system was abolished in 1985 and trade has been opened for cross-traders.

3) Central Freight Bureaux: —

4) Additional Information:
   a) are outsiders free to compete? Yes.
   b) restrictions on cross-trader entry and
      participation in the Conference? No.
   c) shipper consultations? —
   d) other? —

SRI LANKA

UN/C: Yes
No. of vessels: 91
000 GRT: 622.2

1) Legislation and Government Orders:	- All government cargoes must be carried by the state line.
2) Implementation and Practices:	- Discriminatory tax on foreign lines of 3.3% of gross freight revenues. Freight tax exemptions for China, Poland, UK. - 50/50 agreement with Malaysia.
3) Central Freight Bureaux:	- Law No.26 of 1973 established Central Freight Bureau, which: 1) centralises booking for all goods; 2) allocates export freights by line & by vessel; 3) negotiates freight rates, surcharges, service conditions, frequency of service for all lines calling in Sri Lanka. - CFB closely controls all bookings and strictly regulates conditions of service, frequency of calls, and tariffs so as to protect CSC. CSC is given first priority on shipments, and diversion is not possible unless no CSC vessels is available within 14 days.
4) Additional Information: a) are outsiders free to compete?	CFB practices severely restrict non-conference lines.
b) restrictions on cross-trader entry and participation in the Conference?	Yes.
c) shipper consultations?	-
d) other?	-

SUDAN

UN/C: Yes
No. of vessels: 23
000 GRT: 95.7

1) Legislation and Government Orders:	-
2) Implementation and Practices:	Virtually all governmental or quasi-government cargo (about 75% of total) uses Sudan national line.
3) Central Freight Bureaux:	-
4) Additional Information: a) are outsiders free to compete?	Not known.
b) restrictions on cross-trader entry and participation in the Conference?	Not known.
c) shipper consultations?	-
d) other?	-

SYRIA

UN/C: No
No. of vessels: 57
000 GRT: 63.1

1) Legislation and Government Orders:

2) Implementation and Practices: —

3) Central Freight Bureaux: - All shipments are controlled by SYRIAMAR which
                                                is not a national line but a state institution in
                                                control of certain traffics and which prescribes
                                                line, vessel and freight conditions. SYRIAMAR has
                                                certain agreements with the lines available.

4) Additional Information:
   a) are outsiders free to compete?   —
   b) restrictions on cross-trader entry and
      participation in the Conference?   —
   c) shipper consultations?   —
   d) other?   —

TAIWAN

UN/C: No
No. of vessels: 587
000 GRT: 4 272.8

1) Legislation and Government Orders: Shipping Enterprise Act (6/3/81) authorises
                                                government to designate bulk and liner cargoes for
                                                which national-flag vessels will have priority of
                                                carriage. The Act prohibits non-Taiwanese
                                                nationals from establishing container terminals.

2) Implementation and Practices: Some Act provisions do not apply where a contract,
                                                agreement, or international convention require
                                                otherwise or depending on quantity or nature of
                                                cargo. Foreigners may be exempt if their country
                                                grants reciprocal rights to Taiwanese nationals.

3) Central Freight Bureaux: —

4) Additional Information:
   a) are outsiders free to compete?   Yes.
   b) restrictions on cross-trader entry and
      participation in the Conference?   No.
   c) shipper consultations?   Yes.
   d) other?   —

TANZANIA

UN/C: Yes
No. of vessels: 41
000 GRT: 50.7

1) Legislation and Government Orders: 1981 legislation established Tanzania Central
                                                Freight Bureau with control over exports and
                                                imports. Income tax on foreign lines of 3.575% of
                                                gross outbound freight (some countries exempted).

2) Implementation and Practices: —

3) Central Freight Bureaux: - Tanzania has not yet a national line.
                                                - Shipment is to be realised by the line indicated
                                                by the Tanzania Central Freight Bureau (TCFB) or
                                                its agent who chooses a conference line or an
                                                outsider.
                                                - The LCs must indicate the freight applied. The
                                                importer in Tanzania must contact the local
                                                Tanzanian Freight Bureau in order to obtain
                                                freight level as well as space on board a ship.
                                                The local Tanzanian Bureau passes this information
                                                to its agent in the port of shipment.
                                                - The TCFB Agents in the port of shipment require
                                                a 2.5% commission on the freight for their
                                                intervention.

4) Additional Information:
   a) are outsiders free to compete? Yes.
   b) restrictions on cross-trader entry and participation in the Conference? No.
   c) shipper consultations? Yes.
   d) other? –

THAILAND

UN/C: No
No. of vessels: 243
000 GRT: 533.1

1) Legislation and Government Orders:
   – Mercantile Marine Promotion Act (B.E. 2521, 1978) requires government-impelled cargoes to be carried by national-flag vessel, when available (waivers available). Act establishes fiscal incentives for shippers to use national-flag vessels, including allowing them to deduct 50% of transport costs by national-flag vessel from net before tax profits.
   – Ministerial Regulation No.2527, adopted July 1984 requires all private firms engaged in business transactions with government agencies/state enterprises to hire Thai flag ships for imports to Thailand in trades where Thai ships are in operation.

2) Implementation and Practices:
   – Ministerial Regulation No.2 (B.E.2524, 10/8/81) implements the Act by designating government exports and imports to be carried by national-flag vessels as well as major trade routes on which all government imports must be carried by national-flag vessel.
   – Oil and cargoes financed by foreign governments or international banks are exempted.
   – Waiver available if requirement conflicts with Thai treaty or agreement with a foreign government.

3) Central Freight Bureaux: –

4) Additional Information:
   a) are outsiders free to compete? Yes.
   b) restrictions on cross-trader entry and participation in the Conference? No.
   c) shipper consultations? Yes.
   d) other? –

TOGO

UN/C: Yes
No. of vessels: 11
000 GRT: 54.9

1) Legislation and Government Orders: Decree No.8 of 9/1/80 and Order No.4 of 19/2/80 apply 40/40/20 principle to whole trade. Freight agency allocates cargo and determines rates.

2) Implementation and Practices: Cargo-sharing agreement with France administered by "Shipowners' Committee". Other agreements administered by Togo Shippers' Council – CNCT.

3) Central Freight Bureaux: — An attestation from the CNCT (Conseil National des Chargeurs Togolais) is required for all shipments from the Hamburg/Antwerp range, and must be obtained from the local CNCT representative. It is reported that attestations for shipments with lines other than SOTONAM, the national line, are difficult to obtain.

4) Additional Information:
   a) are outsiders free to compete? Not in trades where cargo-sharing agreements are concluded.
   b) restrictions on cross-trader entry and participation in the Conference? Yes.
   c) shipper consultations? Yes.
   d) other? —

TUNISIA

UN/C: Yes
No. of vessels: 71
000 GRT: 285.5

1) Legislation and Government Orders: —

2) Implementation and Practices:

3) Central Freight Bureaux: —

4) Additional Information:
   a) are outsiders free to compete? According to the terms of a bilateral agreement with Spain, third country flag ships may participate in the bilateral trade to a maximum of 20% only.
   b) restrictions on cross-trader entry and participation in the Conference? Yes.
   c) shipper consultations? —
   d) other? —

UNITED ARAB EMIRATES

UN/C: No
No. of vessels: 220
000 GRT: 653.5

1) Legislation and Government Orders: 1982 law gives priority to vessels with national flag and other Arab flags.

2) Implementation and Practices:
   - Legislation not implemented.
   - Abu Dhabi Ch. of Commerce requests banks (since 1983) to include preferential clauses in letters of credit.

3) Central Freight Bureaux: —

4) Additional Information:
   a) are outsiders free to compete? Yes.
   b) restrictions on cross-trader entry and participation in the Conference? Not known.
   c) shipper consultations? —
   d) other? —

URUGUAY

UN/C: Yes
No. of vessels: 89
000 GRT: 149.8

1) Legislation and Government Orders:	- Merchant Marine Policy Law of May 1977 reserves 100% of all import cargo to Uruguayan ships and minimum of 50% of export cargo. If no flag ships available, priority is given to: (1) foreign flag conference vessels; (2) non-conference lines. - Waivers not granted 10 days before and 10 days after port call of a national line.
2) Implementation and Practices:	- 100% southbound Europe cargo is reserved to National flag. Waivers very difficult to obtain. - Cargo restrictions not applied to northbound Europe trade as Uruguayan Lines are not River Plate Conference members. - Exports are free but regulations are placed on imports. Import documents are used in the reservation control system.
3) Central Freight Bureaux:	- The Uruguay national line, MONTEMAR, must be used for all shipments. To enable shipment by another line, the agents of MONTEMAR have to provide an attestation by telex that there is no Uruguayan ship available ten days prior to or after the loading date on a non-Uruguayan ship. This telex is accepted as an official document by the customs in Uruguay.
4) Additional Information: a) are outsiders free to compete? b) restrictions on cross-trader entry and participation in the Conference? c) shipper consultations? d) other?	 Yes. Heavy presence of outsiders. Yes. - -

---

VENEZUELA

UN/C: Yes
No. of vessels: 279
000 GRT: 998.3

1) Legislation and Government Orders:	Decree 1570 Jan.74 stipulates 50% of all general cargo plus all government cargoes and government assisted cargoes reserved to state line. In addition not less than 10% of exports and imports of petroleum and its by-products - this amount gradually to increase to 50% - was reserved for national line ships, according to the merchant marine law of 18/7/73.
2) Implementation and Practices:	- In practice the national line gets approximately 50% of the conference trade. More concentration of enforcement made on the import side than export. - Associated line status granted to a number of lines which have a "pooling agreement" with Venezuelan national lines. - Although bulk exports appear to be fairly free, a waiver has to be obtained. Usually, to obtain the waiver, this must be approved by the national carrier.
3) Central Freight Bureaux:	-

162

4) Additional Information:
   a) are outsiders free to compete?   Non-conference lines have free access to
                                              non-reserved cargoes, but rarely to reserved
                                              cargoes.
   b) restrictions on cross-trader entry and
      participation in the Conference?   Yes, in theory, but permitted only if they do not
                                              detract from Venezuela's 50% share.
   c) shipper consultations?   -
   d) other?   National flag vessels pay 50% less in pilotage
                                              fees.

ZAIRE

UN/C: Yes
No: of vessels: 31
000 GRT: 65.8

1) Legislation and Government Orders: Ordinance No.256 of Nov.1980 & No.192 of Dec.1982
                                        as implemented by Decree No.1 of 17/1/83, apply
                                        40/40/20 principle to all cargo and grant the
                                        Zaïre Office of Maritime Freight Management
                                        (OGEFREM) extensive powers, including the fixing
                                        of freight rates.

2) Implementation and Practices: Mid-1983 Zaïre demanded deposits of US$ 10 000
                                        from each line for the right to continue trading,
                                        plus 3% freight tax backed up by requirement to
                                        submit freight manifests. (Freight tax is reduced
                                        to 1.2% in trades where Zaïre line participates).
                                        1.2% freight tax on all import cargoes are
                                        collected by OGEFREM in trades between Zaïre and
                                        following countries/regions: FRG, Scandinavia,
                                        Belgium, Netherlands, Italy, Spain, Far East.

3) Central Freight Bureaux: - The OGEFREM must put their stamp of approval on
                                        the shipping documents before shipment.

4) Additional Information:
   a) are outsiders free to compete?   No.
   b) restrictions on cross-trader entry and
      participation in the Conference?   Not known.
   c) shipper consultations?   Yes.
   d) other?   -

Annex II

DIRECT CONTROL OF CARGOES

	Country	Government cargoes	Specific commodities included or excluded	Cargo Reservation through legislation	Specific Flags excluded
1.	Algeria			X	
2.	Angola			X	
3.	Argentina	X		X	
4.	Bangladesh		X	X	
5.	Benin (PR)			X	
6.	Bolivia	X		X	
7.	Brazil	X	X	X	
8.	Burma			X	
9.	Cameroon	X		X	
10.	Chile			X	
11.	China (PR)			X	
12.	Colombia		X	X	
13.	Congo (PR)			X	
14.	Costa Rica			X	
15.	Côte d'Ivoire	X	X	X	
16.	Cuba			X	
17.	Dominican Republic	X		X	
18.	Ecuador	X	X	X	
19.	Egypt	X		X	
20.	Ethiopia			X	
21.	Gabon			X	
22.	Ghana		X	X	
23.	Guatemala			X	
24.	Guinea (PR)		X		
25.	Honduras			X	
26.	India	X		X	
27.	Indonesia	X	X	X	
28.	Iraq				
29.	Jamaica	X	X		
30.	Korea (South)			X	
31.	Libya			X	
32.	Madagascar				X
33.	Malaysia	X			
34.	Malta			X	
35.	Mexico	X		X	
36.	Morocco	X		X	
37.	Mozambique			X	
38.	Nicaragua	X		X	
39.	Nigeria			X	
40.	Pakistan	X		X	
41.	Panama				
42.	Paraguay			X	
43.	Peru			X	
44.	Philippines	X	X	X	
45.	Saudi Arabia	X		X	
46.	Senegal			X	
47.	Singapore		X		
48.	Sri Lanka	X			
49.	Sudan	X			
50.	Syria				
51.	Taiwan			X	
52.	Tanzania				
53.	Thailand	X	X		
54.	Togo			X	
55.	Tunisia				
56.	United Arab Emirates			X	
57.	Uruguay			X	
58.	Venezuela	X	X	X	
59.	Zaïre			X	

Annex III

INDIRECT MEASURES OF PROTECTIONISM

	Country	Financial Incentives	Currency Regulations	CIF/FOB	CFBs	Associate Line	Marine Services	Freight Tax
1.	Algeria		X					
2.	Angola			X			X	
3.	Argentina	X				X	X	
4.	Bangladesh			X				
5.	Benin (PR)				X			
6.	Bolivia					X		
7.	Brazil					X	X	
8.	Burma							
9.	Cameroon				X			
10.	Chile		X					
11.	China (PR)			X				
12.	Colombia					X		
13.	Congo (PR)			X	X			
14.	Costa Rica							
15.	Côte d'Ivoire				X			
16.	Cuba							
17.	Dominican Republic							
18.	Ecuador					X	X	
19.	Egypt							
20.	Ethiopia							
21.	Gabon							
22.	Ghana			X	X			
23.	Guatemala							
24.	Guinea (PR)							
25.	Honduras		X					
26.	India							X
27.	Indonesia							
28.	Iraq				X			
29.	Jamaica							
30.	Korea (South)							
31.	Libya							
32.	Madagascar							
33.	Malta							
34.	Malaysia	X						
35.	Mexico	X						
36.	Morocco							
37.	Mozambique							
38.	Nicaragua							
39.	Nigeria							
40.	Pakistan	X						X
41.	Panama							X
42.	Paraguay							
43.	Peru					X	X	
44.	Philippines	X						
45.	Saudi Arabia							
46.	Senegal				X			
47.	Singapore							
48.	Sri Lanka				X			X
49.	Sudan							
50.	Syria				X			
51.	Taiwan							
52.	Tanzania				X			X
53.	Thailand	X						
54.	Togo				X			
55.	Tunisia							
56.	United Arab Emirates							
57.	Uruguay							
58.	Venezuela					X		
59.	Zaïre	X			X			X

STATISTICAL ANNEX

STATISTICAL ANNEX

Page

Tables relating to Chapter II

Table I	Development of World International Seaborne Trade	170
Table II	Suez Canal Traffic	171
Table III(a)	Development of World Seaborne Trade of Main Bulk Commodities	172
Table III(b)	World Seaborne Trade carried by dry Bulk Carriers in 1985	173
Table IV	Iron Ore: World Seaborne Trade in 1985	174
Table V	Coal: World Seaborne Trade in 1985	175
Table VI	Grain: World Seaborne Trade in 1985	176
Table VII	Bauxite and Alumina: World Seaborne Trade in 1985	177
Table VIII	Phosphate Rock: World Seaborne Trade in 1985	178
Table IX	Sugar: Movements in 1985	179
Table X(a)	Softwood: Movements in 1984	180
Table X(b)	Softwood: Movements in 1985	181
Table XI	Other Bulk Commodities: Major Trades in 1985	182
Table XII(a)	Oil: Inter-Regional Movements in 1985	183
Table XII(b)	Oil: Inter-Regional Sea Transport Performance in 1985	184

Tables relating to Chapter III

Table XIII(a)	OECD Seaborne Trade: Total Tonnage Imported in 1985	185/186
Table XIII(b)	OECD Seaborne Trade: Total Tonnage Exported in 1985	187/188
Table XIII(c)	OECD Seaborne Trade: Total Tonnage Traded by certain countries in 1985	189
Table XIII(d)	OECD Seaborne Trade: Flag Shares in Total Trade 1985	190/191/192
	Notes to Tables XIII(a)-(d)	193/194
Table XIV	Development of World Fleet	195

Table XV(a)	World Fleet as at mid-1985 in grt and dwt	196
Table XV(b)	World Fleet: Analysis by Principal Types as at mid-1986	197
Table XVI(a)	Size Distribution of World Fleet as at mid-1986 (in grt)	198
Table XVI(b)	Size Distribution of World Fleet as at mid-1986 (in dwt)	199
Table XVII	Age Distribution of World Fleet as at mid-1986	200
Table XVIII(a)	Age Distribution of Principal Fleets as at mid-1986	201
Table XVIII(b)	Age Distribution of Principal Tanker Fleets as at mid-1986	202
Table XVIII(c)	Age Distribution of Principal Dry Bulk Carriers Fleets as at mid-1985	203
Table XIX	Tonnage Lost and Scrapped	204
Table XX(a)	Personnel Employed in the Merchant Marines of OECD Member countries: by Occupation	205
Table XX(b)	Personnel Employed in the Merchant Marines of OECD Member countries: by Nationality	206

Tables relating to Chapter IV

Table XXI	Development of Dry Cargo and Tanker Voyage Charter Freight Indices	207
Table XXII	Dry Cargo Voyage and Trip Charter and Liner Freight Indices	208
Table XXIII	Dry Cargo Time Charter Freight Indices	209
Table XXIV	Tanker Voyage Freight Indices	210

Table I

DEVELOPMENT OF WORLD INTERNATIONAL SEABORNE TRADE

YEAR	DRY CARGO		OIL		CARGO	
	MILLION METRIC TONS	PER CENT INCREASE/ DECREASE OVER PREVIOUS YEAR	MILLION METRIC TONS	PER CENT INCREASE/ DECREASE OVER PREVIOUS YEAR	MILLION METRIC TONS	PER CENT INCREASE/ DECREASE OVER PREVIOUS YEAR
1965	780	8	860	9	1 640	9
1966	830	6	940	9	1 760	7
1967	860	4	1 010	7	1 870	6
1968	930	8	1 130	12	2 060	10
1969	990	6	1 260	11	2 250	9
1970	1 125	14	1 422	13	2 545	13
1971	1 140	1	1 516	7	2 656	4
1972	1 216	7	1 648	9	2 864	8
1973	1 346	11	1 868	13	3 014	8
1974	1 440	7	1 810	-3	3 250	12
1975	1 373	-5	1 652	-9	3 025	11
1976	1 471	7	1 838	11	3 309	-7
1977	1 515	3	1 898	3	3 413	9
1978	1 602	6	1 949	3	3 551	3
1979	1 731	8	2 038	5	3 769	4
1980	1 833	6	1 871	-8	3 704	6
1981	1 866	2	1 693	-10	3 559	-2
1982	1 793	-4	1 480	-13	3 273	-4
1983	1 770	-1	1 461	-1	3 231	-8
1984	1 886	7	1 478	1	3 364	-1
1985(est)	1 871	-1	1 459	-1	3 330	-1

NOTE: Excluding international cargoes of main bulk commodities loaded at ports of the Great Lakes and St. Lawrence system for unloading at ports of the same system. Including imports into Netherlands Antilles and Trinidad for refining and re-export. Figures are the average of loaded and unloaded quantities. Comparable figures for the period 1950-65 can be found in 'Maritime Transport, 1978', Table I.

SOURCE: United Nations Monthly Bulletin of Statistics. 1980-1985, UNCTAD Review of Maritime Transport, 1985.

Table II

SUEZ CANAL TRAFFIC

in million metric tons

YEAR	NORTHBOUND			SOUTHBOUND			TOTAL		
	OIL	DRY CARGO	TOTAL	OIL	DRY CARGO	TOTAL	OIL	DRY CARGO	TOTAL
1955	66.9	20.5	87.4	1.9	18.2	20.1	68.8	38.7	107.5
1956(1)	65.8	17.1	82.9	1.8	16.3	18.1	67.6	33.4	101.0
1957(2)	54.1	13.1	67.2	0.8	13.3	14.1	54.9	26.4	81.3
1958	94.4	20.0	114.4	2.4	22.5	24.9	96.8	42.5	139.3
1959	98.7	23.0	121.7	2.5	23.5	26.5	101.7	46.5	148.2
1960	114.4	25.2	139.6	3.0	26.3	29.3	117.4	51.5	168.9
1961	114.3	25.3	139.6	6.3	26.5	32.8	120.6	51.8	172.4
1962	124.6	26.6	151.2	5.5	25.7	31.2	130.1	52.3	182.4
1963	133.0	26.5	159.5	5.0	29.1	34.1	138.0	55.6	193.6
1964	144.7	27.8	172.5	6.1	32.4	38.5	150.8	60.2	211.0
1965	155.1	28.3	183.4	7.9	34.1	42.0	163.0	62.4	225.4
1966	166.7	27.5	194.2	9.0	38.7	47.7	175.7	66.2	241.9
1967(3)	75.8	11.4	87.2	3.2	20.0	23.2	79.0	31.4	110.4
1975(4)	5.3	13.2	18.5	2.0	17.1	19.1	7.4	31.4	38.8
1976	29.9	42.1	72.0	4.0	41.6	45.6	33.8	83.8	117.6
1977	30.9	41.7	72.6	4.1	52.0	56.1	35.0	93.7	128.7
1978	28.4	41.2	69.6	4.8	75.4	80.2	33.2	116.6	149.8
1979	27.3	51.4	78.7	9.0	72.9	81.9	36.3	124.3	160.6
1980	28.5	58.0	86.5	14.0	75.7	89.7	42.5	133.7	176.2
1981	36.6	57.3	93.9	18.2	84.2	102.5	54.8	141.6	196.4
1982	63.1	61.7	124.8	20.3	86.3	106.6	83.4	158.0	231.4
1983	81.2	59.8	141.0	17.0	98.7	115.7	98.2	158.5	256.7
1984	86.6	67.6	154.2	11.1	98.4	109.5	97.7	166.0	263.7
1985	81.8	70.1	151.9	12.2	93.5	105.7	94.0	163.6	257.6
1986	92.2	72.8	165.0	12.8	84.9	97.7	105.0	157.7	262.7

1. 1/1/56 to 31/10/56
2. 10/4/57 to 31/12/57
3. 1/1/67 to 31/5/67
4. 5/6/75 to 31/12/75

SOURCE: Suez Canal Authority

Table III(a)
DEVELOPMENT OF WORLD SEABORNE TRADE OF MAIN BULK COMMODITIES

YEAR	IRON ORE MILLION METRIC TONS	IRON ORE '000 MILLION TONNE-MILES	GRAIN MILLION METRIC TONS	GRAIN '000 MILLION TONNE-MILES	COAL MILLION METRIC TONS	COAL '000 MILLION TONNE-MILES	BAUXITE AND ALUMINA MILLION METRIC TONS	BAUXITE AND ALUMINA '000 MILLION TONNE-MILES	PHOSPHATE ROCK MILLION METRIC TONS	PHOSPHATE ROCK '000 MILLION TONNE-MILES	TOTAL MILLION METRIC TONS	TOTAL '000 MILLION TONNE-MILES
					TOTAL SHIPMENTS							
1970	247	1 093	89	475	101	481	34	99	33	116	504	2 264
1971	250	1 185	91	487	94	434	35	108	35	121	505	2 335
1972	247	1 156	108	548	96	444	35	109	38	143	524	2 400
1973	298	1 398	139	760	104	467	38	133	43	159	622	2 917
1974	329	1 578	130	695	119	558	42	158	48	168	668	3 157
1975	292	1 471	137	734	127	621	41	168	38	127	635	3 121
1976	294	1 469	146	779	127	591	42	158	37	125	646	3 122
1977	276	1 386	147	801	132	643	46	167	44	160	645	3 157
1978	278	1 384	169	945	127	604	46	162	47	168	667	3 263
1979	327	1 599	182	1 026	159	786	46	169	48	177	762	3 757
1980	314	1 613	198	1 087	188	952	48	188	48	171	796	4 011
1981	303	1 508	206	1 131	210	1 120	45	172	42	139	806	4 070
1982	273	1 443	200	1 120	208	1 094	38	153	40	142	759	3 952
1983	257	1 320	199	1 135	197	1 057	36	145	43	159	732	3 816
1984	306	1 631	207	1 157	232	1 270	44	172	44	162	833	4 392
1985	321	1 675	181	1 004	272	1 479	40	166	43	156	857	4 480
					BULK CARRIER SHIPMENTS*							
1970	148	718	10	61	39	246	5	18	2	7	204	1 050
1971	160	827	12	75	38	223	5	20	2	12	217	1 157
1972	173	880	16	96	47	258	5	21	5	21	246	1 276
1973	217	1 084	18	112	55	300	6	25	5	21	301	1 542
1974	257	1 297	21	130	65	369	8	38	6	25	357	1 859
1975	233	1 220	43	260	75	436	10	55	4	16	365	1 987
1976	244	1 252	57	312	80	428	13	61	5	22	399	2 075
1977	235	1 206	60	337	88	449	16	65	8	34	407	2 091
1978	240	1 209	74	436	89	422	15	60	8	32	426	2 159
1979	294	1 475	81	486	105	565	17	72	8	35	505	2 633
1980	286	1 469	88	502	133	746	19	88	8	35	534	2 840
1981	281	1 448	103	604	143	817	18	80	7	30	552	2 979
1982	246	1 347	112	665	147	842	16	71	7	34	528	2 959
1983	235	1 205	115	698	144	860	18	80	9	52	491	2 895
1984	285	1 532	119	721	175	1 044	21	94	11	61	611	3 452
1985	295	1 551	117	690	210	1 238	21	90	11	58	654	3 627

*By ships of more than 40 000 dwt.

NOTE: Comparable figures for the period 1960-1970 are contained in Table III(a) of 'Maritime Transport, 1975'. A geographical analysis of bulk carrier movements for 1985 is contained in Table III(b).

SOURCE: Fearnleys

Table III(b)
WORLD SEABORNE TRADE CARRIED BY DRY BULK CARRIERS IN 1985
(ships of 40 000 dwt and over)

In thousand metric tons

TO / FROM	UNITED KINGDOM/ CONTINENT	MEDITER- RANEAN	OTHER EUROPE	NORTH AMERICA	SOUTH AMERICA	JAPAN	OTHER ASIA	OTHERS	WORLD 1985	WORLD 1984	WORLD 1983
United Kingdom/Continent	210	1 890	4 620	1 610	100	–	2 890	1 190	12 510	9 010	10 690
Mediterranean	1 650	550	310	1 020	50	–	1 490	620	5 690	6 500	5 660
Other Europe	18 100	2 750	4 760	930	2 680	510	2 520	1 310	33 560	32 810	25 950
Africa	30 050	15 490	7 850	4 700	470	13 150	7 310	80	79 100	76 280	63 450
North America	50 060	21 240	29 420	11 460	12 060	61 650	31 920	4 270	231 080	231 750	213 620
South America	46 630	13 730	19 140	10 840	5 760	35 920	15 490	280	147 790	130 860	108 350
Asia	6 740	1 980	4 030	2 390	100	20 310	10 410	450	46 410	40 970	35 890
Australia	25 160	7 370	7 440	3 890	1 420	104 480	37 630	2 340	189 730	178 580	142 600
World 1985	187 600	65 000	77 570	36 840	22 640	236 020	109 660	10 540	745 870		
World 1984	175 530	62 310	73 720	35 350	20 650	231 440	97 230	10 530		706 760	
World 1983	151 760	56 220	64 920	25 470	15 800	203 560	79 280	9 200			606 210

NOTE: These include dry cargo transported by combination carriers but exclude grain shipments by tankers and the transport of cars by cars/bulk carriers. Information for years prior to 1980 given in earlier reports related to vessels over 18 000 dwt.

SOURCE: Fearnleys

Table IV

IRON ORE: WORLD SEABORNE TRADE IN 1985

in thousand metric tons

FROM \ TO	UNITED KINGDOM/ CONTINENT	MEDITER- RANEAN	OTHER EUROPE	UNITED STATES	JAPAN	OTHER FAR EAST	OTHERS	WORLD 1985	WORLD 1984	WORLD 1983
Scandinavia	15 890	223	2 467	42	–	1 099	555	20 276	18 978	15 734
Other Europe	2 107	91	1 383	130	–	–	3	3 714	3 968	3 696
West Africa	14 723	6 151	764	2 163	374	–	902	25 077	25 359	22 238
Other Africa	2 383	744	235	4	6 586	–	–	9 952	13 161	9 947
North America	16 120	2 144	894	5 000	2 791	209	307	27 465	24 196	20 531
South America (Atlantic)	35 175	9 991	7 802	4 899	29 064	5 070	10 658	102 659	95 500	74 457
South America (Pacific)	658	608	–	290	6 219	1 605	415	9 795	8 905	9 635
Asia	347	1 047	3 724	–	22 809	3 202	2 747	33 876	27 675	24 120
Australia	13 049	2 181	627	–	56 669	15 055	241	87 822	87 969	77 086
World 1985	100 452	23 180	17 896	12 528	124 512	26 240	15 828	320 636		
World 1984	95 723	20 810	22 278	11 591	125 371	23 445	6 493		305 711	
World 1983	79 135	15 147	17 255	8 336	109 144	21 526	6 901			257 444

NOTE: Import statistics are used wherever possible. The Group 'Others' is partly estimated. Exports from Canada to the United States via Great Lakes are excluded.

SOURCE: Fearnleys

Table V

COAL: WORLD SEABORNE TRADE IN 1985

in thousand metric tons

FROM \ TO	UK/ CONTINENT	MEDITER- RANEAN	OTHER EUROPE	SOUTH AMERICA	JAPAN	OTHER FAR EAST	OTHERS	WORLD 1985	WORLD 1984	WORLD 1983
Eastern Europe	8 132	2 418	10 278	2 086	3 890	-	161	26 965	28 515	20 967
Other Europe	2 138	1 678	3 475	32	-	468	245	8 036	6 850	10 004
North America	18 658	13 461	11 055	7 797	32 249	10 975	2 552	96 747	79 688	71 980
Australia	9 811	2 974	5 082	1 330	44 508	18 848	3 011	85 564	74 211	58 347
South Africa	12 785	6 215	5 245	-	8 623	8 241	2 991	44 100	35 049	28 203
Others	538	156	1 719	38	4 736	2 371	618	10 176	7 988	7 558
World 1985	52 062	26 902	36 854	11 283	94 006	40 903	9 578	271 588		
World 1984	50 007	23 356	28 858	9 458	86 601	25 502	8 519		232 301	
World 1983	39 471	20 347	25 958	7 243	74 784	20 134	9 122			197 059

NOTE: The term 'coal' comprises anthracite and bituminous coal. Export statistics are used whenever possible. Exports from the United States to Canada are excluded. Exports from Siberia to Japan are included under Eastern Europe-Japan. Coal transportation between most continental countries as well as between East European countries is considered as overland transportation.

SOURCE: Fearnleys

Table VI

GRAIN: WORLD SEABORNE TRADE IN 1985

In thousand metric tons

TO / FROM	UNITED KINGDOM/ CONTINENT	MEDITER- RANEAN	EASTERN EUROPE	OTHER EUROPE	AFRICA	AMERICAS	NEAR EAST	INDIAN OCEAN	JAPAN	OTHER FAR EAST	NOT SPECI- FIED	WORLD 1985	WORLD 1984	WORLD 1983
United States	7 492	5 986	15 313	2 919	9 191	14 327	2 723	2 375	21 023	12 056	220	93 625	118 649	115 458
Canada	1 169	538	7 094	159	1 522	2 413	702	628	2 308	2 934	57	19 524	25 429	28 451
Argentina	1 801	2 299	8 847	353	885	3 589	483	1 479	1 873	1 373	18	23 000	20 140	23 433
Australia	102	55	2 503	–	2 778	347	4 613	3 622	2 772	3 551	212	20 555	20 996	7 833
Others	2 100	1 576	8 363	440	5 410	834	2 274	775	539	2 395	78	24 784	21 453	24 308
World 1985	12 664	10 454	42 120	3 871	19 786	21 510	10 795	8 879	28 515	22 309	585	181 488		
World 1984	13 395	11 509	46 040	4 895	23 023	23 260	11 278	13 370	30 743	28 036	1 118		206 667	
World 1983	15 988	12 860	38 264	5 592	17 689	25 841	7 500	12 543	29 532	33 079	585			199 483

NOTE: Export Statistics are used whenever possible. The figures comprise wheat, maize, barley, oats, rye, sorghum and soya beans. Tapioca, (which in 1985 amounted to about 6 million metric tons), rice, millet and all kinds of flour are excluded.

SOURCE: Fearnleys

Table VII

BAUXITE AND ALUMINA: WORLD SEABORNE TRADE IN 1985

in thousand metric tons

FROM \ TO	UNITED KINGDOM/ CONTINENT	OTHER EUROPE	NORTH AMERICA	JAPAN	OTHERS	WORLD 1985	WORLD 1984	WORLD 1983
Mediterranean	592	862	14	2	-	1 470	1 883	1 864
Africa	2 262	6 400	3 913	-	300	12 875	12 072	10 575
Jamaica	366	875	2 663	-	50	3 954	6 607	5 204
Other Americas	777	1 558	3 495	68	1 102	7 000	7 997	6 997
Asia	121	203	561	1 252	146	2 283	2 680	2 120
Australia	1 635	1 263	4 155	2 239	2 300	11 592	11 771	8 600
Others	365	257	221	2	17	862	1 048	450
World 1985	6 118	11 418	15 022	3 563	3 915	40 036		
World 1984	6 430	10 517	18 756	4 003	4 352		44 058	
World 1983	4 904	9 492	15 395	3 613	2 406			35 810

NOTE: Import statistics are used whenever possible. 'Others' and 'Other Europe' are partly estimated.

SOURCE: Fearnleys

Table VIII

PHOSPHATE ROCK: WORLD SEABORNE TRADE IN 1985

in thousand metric tons

FROM \ TO	UNITED KINGDOM/ CONTINENT	MEDITER-RANEAN	OTHER EUROPE	AMERICAS	JAPAN	AUSTRALIA(1)	OTHERS	WORLD 1985	WORLD 1984	WORLD 1983
Morocco	5 074	3 896	3 254	899	599	96	972	14 790	14 979	14 653
Other Africa	2 182	1 460	1 464	158	45	11	879	6 199	6 655	5 716
United States	2 498	109	1 133	2 932	1 349	334	1 928	10 283	11 301	12 196
Pacific Islands	–	–	–	–	39	2 091	566	2 696	2 595	2 750
Others	1 849	1 478	2 756	6	347	67	2 395	8 898	8 755	8 030
World 1985	11 603	6 943	8 607	3 995	2 379	2 599	6 740	42 866		
World 1984	12 292	7 200	8 615	4 380	2 334	2 648	6 816		44 285	
World 1983	12 697	6 804	8 669	4 022	2 465	2 986	5 702			43 345

1. Australia includes New Zealand.

NOTE: Import statistics are used whenever possible. Apatite shipments are included. Exports from United States to Canada via the Great Lakes and from USSR to Eastern Europe are excluded.

SOURCE: Fearnleys

Table IX

SUGAR: MOVEMENTS IN 1985

in thousand metric tons

TO / FROM	CANADA	UNITED STATES	EEC	OTHER WESTERN EUROPE	USSR	OTHER EASTERN EUROPE	NORTH AFRICA (1)	WEST AFRICA (2)	MIDDLE EAST (3)	S.E. ASIA (4)	CHINA	SOUTH KOREA	JAPAN	OTHERS/ UNALLO- CATED (5)	WORLD 1985	WORLD 1984	WORLD 1983
Cuba	140.5	-	13.5	64.5	3 684.8	897.1	439.1	51.0	188.2	53.4	680.0	-	467.1	529.8	7 209.0	7 016.5	6 792.0
Dominican Republic	-	429.8	-	-	231.3	-	-	-	-	-	-	-	-	60.5	721.6	885.1	956.2
Jamaica	-	-	131.6	-	-	-	-	-	-	-	-	-	-	20.5	152.1	160.4	157.1
Other Carib/ Central America	39.2	480.7	130.2	-	65.4	-	-	-	-	25.7	-	-	-	48.7	789.9	1 026.8	1 195.3
Argentina	-	147.9	-	11.0	-	-	-	-	-	-	-	-	-	-81.7	157.2	528.5	738.7
Guyana	9.4	46.8(6)	167.5	64.7	-	67.0	13.0	-	-	53.0	-	-	-	-111.0	230.4	214.9	226.6
Brazil	43.2	308.8	-	-	278.4	-	613.0	386.0	370.0	-	-	-	-	609.3	2 608.7	3 039.5	2 800.6
Peru	-	90.5	-	-	-	-	-	-	-	-	-	-	-	-	90.5	98.7	91.3
Other South America	-	46.7	0.1	41.0	-	-	41.3	-	-	-	-	12.0	24.6	176.1	341.7	307.7	378.2
Australia	475.8	121.4	107.9	-	-	-	-	-	-	533.9	452.0	376.3	561.3	130.7	2 651.4	2 590.6	425.3
Fiji	19.0	-	-	-	-	-	-	-	-	77.2	58.0	-	30.1	126.9	419.1	385.5	345.1
Taiwan	-	23.9	0.2	-	-	-	-	-	11.0	26.5	-	58.3	74.2	11.7	205.6	129.8	186.2
India	-	18.4	-	-	-	-	-	-	-	-	-	-	-	22.2	40.8	308.8	782.6
Thailand	-	33.8	-	-	36.4	-	-	-	-	118.1	911.0	133.6	316.4	231.7	1 781.0	1 443.6	1 410.7
Philippines	-	314.9	0.1	-	-	-	-	-	-	28.5	95.0	75.9	119.5	-39.1	594.8	1 200.2	998.8
Mauritius	-	10.1	416.9	-	-	-	-	-	-	-	-	-	-	144.2	571.2	561.9	643.6
South Africa	186.9	52.4	-	227.0	-	-	-	-	74.0	20.1	-	202.0	393.1	96.7	1 025.2	687.1	569.1
Other Africa	150.0	106.6	237.2	-	-	-	13.0	20.4	-	-	-	-	-	196.6	950.8	932.6	939.9
EEC	2.6	0.4	-	663.9	-	14.0	560.0	520.1	274.0	36.1	13.0	-	-	1 207.4	1 291.5	4 392.7	4 909.9
Czecho- slovakia	-	-	15.0	-	-	-	-	2.0	150.0	-	-	-	-	81.3	248.3	233.7	115.3
Poland	-	-	0.4	-	-	-	47.0	-	14.0	-	-	-	-	124.9	186.3	300.9	192.4
USSR	-	-	-	-	-	4.0	13.0	-	39.0	23.8	-	-	-	95.3	175.1	203.6	148.0
Other Countries	91.3	41.5	118.4	45.5	180.7	-	157.3	4.9	410.3	313.6	5.0	-	0.1	725.1	2 094.0	1 786.7	1 774.3
World 1985	1 157.9	2 274.6	1 338.9	1 117.7	4 477.0	982.1	1 896.7	984.4	2 530.9	1 310.0	2 214.0	858.2	1 986.4	4 407.8	27 536.6		
World 1984	1 054.2	2 771.3	1 571.8	1 071.7	5 704.2	1 160.7	2 118.7	849.1	2 881.8	1 158.7	1 348.0	838.2	1 902.5	4 004.9		28 435.8	
World 1983	1 000.6	2 666.9	1 403.4	1 055.3	5 998.0	1 123.9	1 824.8	134.5	2 386.8	1 226.5	1 776.1	775.2	1 868.0	4 424.7			28 777.9

1. Algeria, Egypt, Libya, Morocco, Sudan, Tunisia.
2. Coastal and land-locked West African States from Mauritania to Angola.
3. Iran, Iraq, Israel, Jordan, Kuwait, Lebanon, Saudi Arabia, Syria, Yemen Arab Republic, Yemen Democratic Republic.
4. Hong Kong, Indonesia, Malaysia, Singapore, Sri Lanka, Vietnam.
5. Includes quantities in transit and other differences due to the use of both import and export statistics.
6. British West Indies and Guyana.

NOTE: Import statistics have been used whenever possible for the breakdown, but total exports by exporting countries and world totals are shown according to export statistics. In all cases, movements of refined sugar are expressed in terms of their raw sugar equivalent. The table includes certain overland movements.

SOURCE: Calculated from International Sugar Council, Sugar Year Book, 1985.

Table X(a)

SOFTWOOD: MOVEMENTS IN 1984 (1)

In thousand cubic metres

FROM \ TO	UNITED KINGDOM	IRELAND	GERMANY (F.R.)	ITALY	NETHER- LANDS	FRANCE	BELGIUM	DENMARK	SPAIN	UNITED STATES	AUSTRA- LIA	JAPAN	EGYPT	OTHERS	WORLD 1984	WORLD 1983	WORLD 1982
Norway	162	8	125	–	54	13	3	27	258	–	–	–	–	64	456	446	361
Sweden	1 950	103	1 110	316	740	445	64	860	42	–	–	–	675	1 487	8 008	8 446	7 466
Finland	905	110	531	169	383	442	131	330	–	–	5	–	454	1 296	4 805	4 911	4 576
USSR	1 103	17	515	375	239	172	200	86	90	7	–	143	327	3 827	7 094	7 205	7 094
Canada	1 313	24	88	46	33	250	120	–	10	30 866	341	2 092	99	2 111	37 393	33 946	27 589
United States	87	3	67	228	5	11	16	3	67	–	424	1 285	8	1 596	3 800	4 323	3 812
Czechoslo- vakia	241	–	209	135	62	21	11	–	–	–	–	–	–	458	1 137	1 126	1 051
Austria	29	–	499	2 330	24	5	3	1	–	–	–	–	23	1 046	3 960	4 195	3 533
Yugoslavia	–	–	1	44	–	–	–	–	–	–	–	–	58	163	266	241	174
Poland	258	–	80	1	25	88	27	16	–	–	–	–	–	29	524	507	570
Brazil	54	7	3	–	3	–	–	–	–	6	–	–	–	na	73	125	80
France	2	–	38	13	2	–	25	–	3	–	–	–	–	50	133	130	133
Others	582	70	307	303	440	70	175	37	19	–	214	108	na	–	2 325	2 275	1 857
World 1984	6 686	342	3 573	3 960	2 010	1 517	775	1 360	489	30 879	984	3 628	1 644	12 127	69 974		
World 1983	7 130	354	4 005	3 676	2 018	1 885	863	1 246	480	27 754	711	4 150	1 007	12 597		67 876	
World 1982	6 105	325	3 599	3 734	1 983	2 041	893	989	506	21 232	724	4 188	1 184	10 793			58 296

na: Data not available.

1. Due to unavailability of softwood data for the 1985 edition of this report, tables for both 1984 and 1985 have been included in this edition.

NOTE: The figures relate to sawn and planed softwoods and include sleepers, boxboards, staves and shingles. The table includes certain overland movements, especially between Canada and the United States and between continental European countries.

SOURCE: Wm. Brandts (Timber) Ltd., London.

Table X(b)

SOFTWOOD: MOVEMENTS IN 1985 (1)

in thousand cubic metres

TO / FROM	UNITED KINGDOM	IRELAND	GERMANY (F.R.)	ITALY	NETHER-LANDS	FRANCE	BELGIUM	DENMARK	SPAIN	UNITED STATES	AUSTRA-LIA	JAPAN	EGYPT	OTHERS	WORLD 1985	WORLD 1984	WORLD 1983
Norway	116	12	71	-	45	3	2	26	-	-	-	-	-	105	380	456	446
Sweden	1 900	82	1 005	245	762	463	79	847	286	1	-	-	780	1 411	7 861	8 008	8 446
Finland	863	83	530	130	432	440	228	327	42	-	6	-	584	1 217	4 884	4 805	4 911
USSR	1 033	43	435	446	186	223	99	66	67	2	-	150	378	4 502	7 629	7 094	7 205
Canada	895	7	76	42	15	134	108	-	6	34 000	390	2 348	10	928	38 959	37 393	33 946
United States	61	-	48	184	10	6	10	2	61	-	373	1 355	2	1 437	3 549	3 800	4 323
Czechoslo-vakia	240	-	209	111	78	23	10	-	-	-	-	-	24	353	1 024	1 137	1 126
Austria	33	-	392	2 247	18	13	2	1	-	-	-	-	27	859	3 589	3 960	4 195
Yugoslavia	-	-	-	21	-	-	-	1	-	-	-	-	-	107	155	266	241
Poland	222	-	84	1	16	90	14	19	-	-	-	-	-	28	474	524	507
Brazil	41	2	2	-	2	-	-	-	-	8	-	-	-	na	55	73	125
France	2	-	27	16	2	-	30	-	8	-	-	-	-	68	153	133	130
Others	705	50	307	128	469	129	208	41	72	71	304	187	na	-	2 671	2 275	1 857
World 1985	6 111	279	3 186	3 571	2 035	1 524	790	1 329	542	34 083	1 073	4 040	1 805	11 015	71 383		
World 1984	6 686	342	3 573	3 960	2 010	1 517	775	1 360	489	30 879	984	3 628	1 644	12 127		69 974	
World 1983	7 130	354	4 005	3 676	2 018	1 885	863	1 246	480	27 754	711	4 150	1 007	12 597			67 876

na: Data not available.

1. Due to unavailability of softwood data for the 1985 edition of this report, tables for both 1984 and 1985 have been included in this edition.

NOTE: The figures relate to sawn and planed softwoods and include sleepers, boxboards, staves and shingles. The table includes certain overland movements, especially between Canada and the United States and between continental European countries.

SOURCE: Wm. Brandts (Timber) Ltd., London.

Table XI

OTHER BULK COMMODITIES: MAJOR TRADES IN 1985

in thousand metric tons

		1985	1984	1983			1985	1984	1983
MANGANESE ORE					**CEMENT**				
Brazil	- U.K./Continent	297	93	190	Spain	- Middle East	1 110	4 580	6 540
Brazil	- USA/Canada	167	40	99	Spain	- Mediterranean	2 080	2 800	3 500
South Africa	- U.K./Continent	569	630	733	Spain	- Africa	1 100	1 220	1 560
South Africa	- Japan	772	1 209	872	Spain	- Americas	3 390	1 760	850
Other Africa	- U.K./Continent	785	858	590	France	- Africa	1 410	1 748	1 870
Other Africa	- USA/Canada	234	110	96	Japan	- Southeast Asia	3 791	4 383	5 595
India	- Japan	-	275	206	Japan	- Middle East	4 107	6 478	8 534
Australia	- Japan	495	532	404	Japan	- Others	1 232	629	184
					South Korea	- Southeast Asia	1 859	1 287	3 124
GYPSUM					South Korea	- Middle East	695	437	1 651
Canada	- United States	5 844	6 195	5 187	Greece	- Africa	391	372	102
Australia	- Southeast Asia	485	714	(1)	Greece	- Middle East	4 423	4 550	4 381
					Venezuela	- United States	2 130	2 513	3 240
SALT							1 569	1 022	(1)
Mexico	- Japan	2 846	2 764	2 717					
Australia	- Japan	3 305	3 028	3 057	**NON-FERROUS ORES**				
Australia	- South Korea	732	621	(1)	Copper: Canada	- Japan	804	797	788
Australia	- Taiwan	657	676	(1)	Copper: Philippines	- Japan	299	386	646
China	- Japan	681	666	608	Copper: Papua/New Guinea	- Japan	271	291	348
SULPHUR					Copper: Others	- Japan	1 636	1 456	1 353
USA/Canada	- U.K./Continent	977	990	810	Nickel: New Caledonia	- Japan	1 364	1 271	1 136
USA/Canada	- Far East	832	1 389	1 176	Nickel: Indonesia	- Japan	854	830	709
USA/Canada	- Mediterranean	414	388	316	Nickel: Philippines	- Japan	757	734	452
USA/Canada	- North Africa	1 000	968	(1)	Zinc : Canada	- U.K./Continent	299	420	362
USA/Canada	- South America	214	1 010	979	Zinc : Peru	- Japan	205	262	214
Canada	- Australia/N.Z.	610	639	523	Zinc : Australia	- Japan	498	459	407
Canada	- South Africa	418	533	367	Chrome: South Africa	- Japan	543	418	302
					Chrome: Others	- Japan	444	405	343
LIMESTONE									
Japan	- Australia	1 006	935	838	**PETROLEUM COKE**				
Japan	- Hong Kong	3	764	800	United States	- U.K./Continent	3 768	4 282	4 175
					United States	- Mediterranean	2 246	2 883	3 088
SCRAP IRON					United States	- Japan	3 303	2 772	3 265
United States	- Mediterranean	2 136	1 676	1 116	United States	- Others	3 040	2 900	2 369
United States	- Japan	1 914	2 430	2 357					
United States	- South Korea	1 795	661	1 340	**TAPIOCA**				
United States	- Other Asia	876	946	1 030	Thailand	- Continent	5 547	4 769	5 063
United States	- South America	1 238	1 093	468	Indonesia	- Continent	228	364	55
United Kingdom	- Spain	2 985	2 331	(1)					
USSR	- Spain	405	531	(1)					

1. No figure available

SOURCE: Fearnleys

Table XII(a)

OIL: INTER-REGIONAL MOVEMENTS IN 1985
(Excluding intra-regional movements)

in million metric tons

TO / FROM	UNITED STATES	CANADA	OTHER WESTERN HEMISPHERE	WESTERN EUROPE	AFRICA	SOUTH EAST ASIA	JAPAN	AUSTRALASIA	OTHER EASTERN HEMISPHERE	DESTINATION NOT KNOWN (1)	WORLD 1985	(TOTAL CRUDE)	(TOTAL PRODUCT)	WORLD 1984	WORLD 1983
United States	X	3.9	15.1	9.2	0.5	3.6	5.9	0.2	0.4	3.0	41.8	10.1	31.7	39.3	39.7
Canada	37.7	X	–	0.4	–	–	0.1	–	–	–	38.2	23.3	14.9	32.2	26.8
Latin America	102.6	6.1	16.5	41.4	2.8	3.6	7.5	–	2.3	–	182.8	126.1	56.7	202.4	200.3
Western Europe	24.1	3.5	0.7	X	3.2	0.2	0.2	0.1	4.5	4.2	40.7	19.4	21.3	42.2	41.6
North Africa	10.2	1.6	4.7	82.6	1.0	–	2.6	–	13.1	–	115.8	97.9	17.9	113.7	108.2
West Africa	25.2	0.6	8.4	48.3	4.0	0.5	–	0.1	1.2	–	88.3	86.4	1.9	83.3	70.6
Middle East of which:	[21.0]	[2.3]	[30.4]	[144.2]	[16.7]	[66.4]	[129.6]	[3.1]	[32.9]	[–]	[446.6]	[391.8]	[54.8]	[489.4]	[512.9]
– Cape	14.7	1.3	30.4	7.6	–	–	–	–	–	–	54.0	54.0	–	52.8	66.6
– E. Mediterranean	2.3	–	–	30.9	–	–	–	–	–	–	33.2	33.2	–	34.8	36.5
– Suez/Sumed	4.0	1.0	–	105.7	–	–	–	–	10.9	–	121.6	93.4	28.2	138.4	146.0
– Eastwards	–	–	–	–	16.7	66.4	129.6	3.1	22.0	–	237.8	211.2	26.6	263.4	263.9
South East Asia	20.3	–	–	2.1	1.3	–	38.4	4.3	3.7	3.7	73.8	49.6	24.2	79.2	70.3
USSR, Eastern Europe & China	5.2	–	15.2	83.3	0.2	23.5	14.2	0.2	80.8	2.6	225.2	76.9(3)	23.7(3)	141.1	130.5
Other Eastern Hemisphere	2.0	–	–	1.0	0.8	2.8	3.7	–	0.5	0.5	10.8	5.2	5.6	7.1	5.2
World 1985	248.3	18.0	91.0	412.5	30.5	100.6	202.2	8.0	138.9	14.0	1 264.0(2)				
(Total Crude)	159.9	13.4	71.8	311.6	21.3	79.9	169.4	2.4	27.2	7.7		886.7(3)			
(Total Product)	88.4	4.6	19.2	100.9	9.2	20.7	32.8	5.6	1.7(3)	6.3		–	302.3(3)		
World 1984	264.4	17.2	90.1	427.9	30.0	101.9	214.6	11.5	54.6	17.7				1 229.9(2)	
World 1983	245.7	16.1	97.4	430.0	34.0	99.1	205.7	11.5	55.0	11.6					1 206.1(2)

1. Includes changes of oil in transit, transit losses, minor movements not otherwise shown, unidentified military use, etc.
2. These totals include certain overland and intrazonal movements, especially between Canada and the United States and within Eastern Europe.
   The total seaborne interregional movements amounted to 1 147, 1 176 and 1 242 million tons respectively.
3. Excludes intraregional trade within Eastern Europe.

SOURCE: B.P. Statistical Review of World Energy 1985

Table XII(b)

OIL: INTER-REGIONAL SEA TRANSPORT PERFORMANCE IN 1985
(Excluding intra-regional movements)

in 10⁹ laden tonne-miles

TO / FROM	UNITED STATES	CANADA	OTHER WESTERN HEMISPHERE	WESTERN EUROPE	AFRICA	SOUTH EAST ASIA	JAPAN	AUSTRALASIA	OTHER EASTERN HEMISPHERE	DESTINATION NOT KNOWN (1)	WORLD 1985	WORLD 1984	WORLD 1983
United States	Overland		17	51	3	25	27	1	2	15	141	135	147
Canada	Overland		-	1	-	-	-	-	-	-	1	1	1
Latin America	103	20	54	195	13	23	60	-	14	-	482	538	534
Western Europe	135	12	3	-	10	1	2	1	7	21	192	208	192
North Africa	43	7	23	149	1	-	25	-	65	-	313	293	273
West Africa	131	3	34	184	18	4	-	-	9	-	384	364	312
Middle East, of which:	[212]	[21]	[313]	[417]	[48]	[252]	[868]	[19]	[161]	[-]	[2 312]	[2 551]	[2 695]
- Cape	176	16	313	84	-	-	-	-	-	-	589	595	744
- E. Mediterranean	13	-	-	68	-	-	-	-	-	-	81	111	108
- Suez/Sumed	23	5	-	264	-	-	-	-	18	-	310	383	386
- Eastwards	-	-	-	-	48	252	868	19	143	-	1 330	1 462	1 457
South East Asia	142	-	-	14	6	-	99	11	10	10	292	296	265
USSR, Eastern Europe and China	29	-	77	117	7	148	160	2	46	7	587	483	414
Other Eastern Hemisphere	8	-	-	5	2	14	16	-	-	2	47	31	24
World 1985	803	63	521	1 132	102	467	1 257	35	314	55	4 749		
World 1984	938	49	507	1 155	100	449	1 315	53	273	61		4 900	
World 1983	902	70	567	1 146	122	425	1 270	56	265	34			4 857

1. Includes increased quantities in transit, transit losses, minor movements not otherwise shown, military use, etc. calculated at average voyage length of movements with known destinations.

NOTE: This table corresponds to Table XII(a), but care should be taken in estimating transport distances from these tables which may be misleading for certain smaller movements because both tonnage and tonne-mile figures have been rounded. The tonne-mile figures relate to the laden voyage only and not to the round trip.

SOURCE: Derived by the Secretariat from Table XII(a).

Table XIII(a)

OECD SEABORNE TRADE: TOTAL TONNAGE IMPORTED IN 1985
(Basis: Loading/Unloading)

In thousand metric tons

EXPORTING COUNTRY	REPORTING COUNTRY							
	SPAIN	GERMANY	ITALY	NETHERLANDS	FINLAND	CANADA	AUSTRALIA	NEW ZEALAND
Belgium/Luxembourg	317	521	-	200	467	1 999	95	-
Denmark	4	3 952	-	1 528	357	30	1	-
France	959	821	-	2 224	89	424	161	-
Germany	308	-	-	1 637	2 373	975	549	-
Italy	502	272	-	1 120	30	809	394	-
Ireland	98	185	-	909	55	43	1	-
Netherlands	1 032	4 402	-	-	1 653	612	527	-
United Kingdom	4 948	15 120	-	33 329	1 997	4 920	501	-
Greece	83	71	-	947	17	120	58	-
Total EEC	8 251	25 343	-	41 894	7 040	9 933	2 287	-
Finland	214	3 280	-	2 769	-	59	77	-
Norway	156	7 629	-	11 624	703	445	22	-
Portugal	165	335	-	175	20	32	14	-
Spain	-	836	-	3 930	380	415	59	-
Sweden	309	5 197	-	2 485	3 431	198	202	-
Other OECD Europe	6 719	392	-	2 673	80	75	19	-
Non EEC OECD Europe	7 563	17 667	-	24 656	4 616	1 223	375	-
Japan	287	673	-	1 176	42	1 300	2 929	-
United States	8 937	6 678	-	26 147	1 446	34 289	2 745	-
Canada	644	3 148	-	8 773	425	-	1 465	-
Australia	2 236	4 465	-	11 174	342	831	-	-
New Zealand	2	71	-	264	-	44	1 132	-
Non Europe OECD	12 106	15 035	-	47 535	2 257	36 464	8 271	-
Total OECD	27 920	58 046	-	114 085	13 914	47 620	10 950	-
Eastern Europe	2 189	8 980	-	18 283	15 411	129	25	-
Mediterranean	15 886	2 663	-	17 505	556	1 581	255	-
Middle East	4 828	705	-	19 792	1 275	503	0	-
East Africa	20	235	-	502	2	-	14	-
South Africa	4 115	3 059	-	8 433	0	439	171	-
West Africa	9 414	3 833	-	18 566	7	1 266	0	-
South Asia	649	511	-	961	-	106	89	-
South East Asia	163	1 570	-	7 825	-	137	2 261	-
China Sea (CP)	17	273	-	772	4	68	1 145	-
China Sea (ME)	57	980	-	1 345	-	420	-	-
Oceania	15	264	-	310	-	21	1 175	-
Caribbean	10 640	4 992	-	10 425	417	5 687	9	-
South America (West)	201	832	-	1 050	31	196	31	-
South America (East)	5 306	4 738	-	29 723	26	2 495	147	-
Unspecified	-	188	-	84	-	-	4 248	-
Total Non OECD	53 500	33 824	-	135 576	17 733	13 049	9 571	-
Total	81 420	91 870	-	249 662	31 647	60 669	20 521	-

NOTES: See pages following Table XIII(d)

SOURCE: National Delegations' replies to the Annual Seaborne Trade Questionnaire

Table XIII(a) continued

OCED SEABORNE TRADE: TOTAL TONNAGE IMPORTED IN 1985
(Basis: Origin/Destination)

In thousand metric tons

EXPORTING COUNTRY	REPORTING COUNTRY						
	NORWAY	U.K.	PORTUGAL	JAPAN	DENMARK	BELGIUM/LUX.	USA	FRANCE
Belgium/Luxembourg	707	7 962	-	100	-	-	2 159	-
Denmark	792	2 112	-	137	-	202	549	-
France	620	7 736	-	345	-	1 397	4 557	-
Germany	1 803	8 086	-	706	-	584	5 986	-
Italy	123	3 635	-	315	-	741	6 739	-
Ireland	160	2 316	-	14	-	502	196	-
Netherlands	1 044	15 459	-	302	-	1 269	5 372	-
United Kingdom	3 455	-	-	461	-	8 307	18 350	-
Greece	31	1 016	-	139	-	473	1 436	-
Total EEC	8 735	48 322	-	2 520	-	13 476	45 344	-
Finland	197	2 938	-	250	-	777	939	-
Norway	-	10 019	-	233	-	1 089	2 851	-
Portugal	47	1 298	-	66	-	563	404	-
Spain	655	4 077	-	304	-	1 585	7 581	-
Sweden	1 800	4 868	-	295	-	3 807	-	-
Other OECD Europe	134	3 972	-	336	-	479	2 604	-
Non EEC OECD Europe	2 833	27 172	-	1 483	-	8 299	13 753	-
Japan	174	677	-	-	-	503	17 409	-
United States	863	6 290	-	62 118	-	11 688	-	-
Canada	227	8 733	-	31 992	-	3 503	31 371	-
Australia	466	6 896	-	117 185	-	3 623	8 564	-
New Zealand	2	391	-	4 274	-	173	545	-
Non Europe OECD	1 732	22 987	-	215 569	-	19 490	60 493	-
Total OECD	13 300	98 481	-	219 572	-	41 266	119 590	-
Eastern Europe	1 971	7 682	-	10 339	-	6 718	4 633	-
Mediterranean	288	6 622	-	3 907	-	3 165	12 327	-
Middle East	173	4 063	-	138 262	-	603	12 155	-
East Africa	1	301	-	209	-	117	180	-
South Africa	407	4 118	-	19 549	-	3 153	8 642	-
West Africa	308	5 149	-	736	-	4 770	27 906	-
South Asia	34	824	-	20 654	-	231	69	-
South East Asia	18	1 277	-	79 476	-	725	21 824	-
China Sea (CP)	11	354	-	24 957	-	396	11 139	-
China Sea (ME)	14	621	-	19 256	-	101	6 883	-
Oceania	3	219	-	2 846	-	44	146	-
Caribbean	1 162	7 532	-	12 414	-	3 615	106 962	-
South America (West)	3	314	-	7 760	-	639	11 699	-
South America (East)	396	3 225	-	33 054	-	7 747	15 082	-
Unspecified	25	-	-	6	-	-	3 325	-
Total Non OECD	4 814	42 301	-	373 426	-	32 861	242 972	-
Total	18 109	140 782	-	592 999	33 661	74 127	362 562	-

NOTES: See pages following Table XIII(d)

SOURCE: National Delegations' replies to the Annual Seaborne Trade Questionnaire

Table XIII(b)

OECD SEABORNE TRADE: TOTAL TONNAGE EXPORTED IN 1985
(Basis: Loading/Unloading)

in thousand metric tons

EXPORTING COUNTRY	REPORTING COUNTRY							
	SPAIN	GERMANY	ITALY	NETHERLANDS	FINLAND	CANADA	AUSTRALIA	NEW ZEALAND
Belgium/Luxembourg	1 346	540	-	720	829	3 954	2 639	-
Denmark	356	4 295	-	3 969	1 079	502	2 013	-
France	1 751	369	-	4 179	964	3 515	5 887	-
Germany	699	-	-	5 102	3 408	3 291	3 220	-
Italy	1 448	141	-	2 823	516	2 821	5 151	-
Ireland	137	369	-	1 749	92	38	77	-
Netherlands	3 700	1 473	-	-	2 754	8 493	9 903	-
United Kingdom	2 954	2 766	-	23 147	2 917	8 993	6 259	-
Greece	193	167	-	758	172	97	871	-
Total EEC	12 584	10 121	-	42 446	12 734	31 704	1 918	-
Finland	340	2 162	-	1 680	-	341	610	-
Norway	522	1 543	-	1 792	200	366	196	-
Portugal	529	265	-	764	59	388	60	-
Spain	-	271	-	1 865	239	959	2 746	-
Sweden	408	3 381	-	2 928	3 008	482	743	-
Other OECD Europe	1 209	649	-	935	246	1 169	1 061	-
Non EEC OECD Europe	3 008	8 272	-	9 964	3 755	3 705	444	-
Japan	231	722	-	726	109	33 795	113 196	-
United States	6 395	4 773	-	7 853	831	36 158	7 873	-
Canada	379	1 049	-	677	58	-	1 037	-
Australia	40	441	-	626	99	1 334	-	-
New Zealand	24	69	-	160	7	282	1 796	-
Non Europe OECD	7 069	7 055	-	10 042	1 106	71 570	7 591	-
Total OECD	22 661	25 447	-	62 453	17 596	106 979	16 533	-
Eastern Europe	1 597	6 533	-	2 798	690	7 880	4 659	-
Mediterranean	5 771	2 228	-	3 172	1 070	4 223	4 262	-
Middle East	2 753	1 605	-	2 064	274	620	1 272	-
East Africa	66	377	-	327	19	165	336	-
South Africa	190	613	-	670	-	550	486	-
West Africa	2 062	831	-	1 865	49	677	103	-
South Asia	335	543	-	1 397	85	2 467	4 428	-
South East Asia	209	1 086	-	970	34	1 503	5 598	-
China Sea (CP)	1 367	1 586	-	700	252	3 992	43 385	-
China Sea (ME)	249	1 046	-	837	13	7 815	-	-
Oceania	0	29	-	54	-	27	-	-
Caribbean	791	815	-	865	159	3 216	2 371	-
South America (West)	171	177	-	88	-	331	274	-
South America (East)	231	488	-	308	60	328	1 352	-
Unspecified	-	70	-	102	-	2 980	10 421	-
Total Non OECD	15 792	19 028	-	16 213	2 710	36 442	79 277	-
Total	38 453	44 475	-	78 671	20 307	143 421	244 614	-

NOTES: See pages following Table XIII(d)

SOURCE: National Delegations' replies to the Annual Seaborne Trade Questionnaire

Table XIII(b) continued

OECD SEABORNE TRADE: TOTAL TONNAGE EXPORTED IN 1985
(Basis: Origin/Destination)

in thousand metric tons

EXPORTING COUNTRY	REPORTING COUNTRY							
	NORWAY	U.K.	PORTUGAL	JAPAN	DENMARK	BELGIUM/LUX.	USA	FRANCE
Belgium/Luxembourg	701	5 137	-	357	-	-	10 108	-
Denmark	1 994	4 653	-	139	-	654	2 250	-
France	4 473	21 699	-	322	-	1 643	6 401	-
Germany	5 975	18 664	-	1 058	-	480	5 406	-
Italy	330	6 250	-	207	-	743	14 984	-
Ireland	104	5 847	-	52	-	524	710	-
Netherlands	4 826	25 292	-	569	-	182	20 767	-
United Kingdom	9 612	-	-	785	-	9 647	5 900	-
Greece	61	405	-	176	-	684	1 711	-
Total EEC	28 076	87 947	-	3 665	-	14 556	68 237	-
Finland	601	1 870	-	119	-	386	1 465	-
Norway	-	2 541	-	217	-	801	695	-
Portugal	59	907	-	77	-	360	3 728	-
Spain	171	5 212	-	84	-	491	9 710	-
Sweden	3 614	10 100	-	208	-	1 189	-	-
Other OECD Europe	859	1 132	-	532	-	556	7 027	-
Non EEC OECD Europe	5 304	21 762	-	1 238	-	3 783	17 433	-
Japan	165	360	-	-	-	144	66 521	-
United States	1 742	17 482	-	15 582	-	5 795	-	-
Canada	30	3 223	-	1 420	-	1 409	28 725	-
Australia	60	488	-	3 088	-	90	2 546	-
New Zealand	16	184	-	657	-	36	627	-
Non Europe OECD	2 013	21 737	-	20 748	-	7 475	105 446	-
Total OECD	35 393	131 446	-	25 650	-	25 814	191 116	-
Eastern Europe	657	2 636	-	3 715	-	3 717	16 530	-
Mediterranean	780	2 037	-	707	-	4 425	11 875	-
Middle East	74	2 161	-	9 591	-	4 213	3 565	-
East Africa	41	341	-	284	-	796	2 240	-
South Africa	29	530	-	603	-	501	1 549	-
West Africa	104	799	-	342	-	1 955	3 498	-
South Asia	179	841	-	2 673	-	1 265	258	-
South East Asia	239	724	-	8 697	-	941	4 155	-
China Sea (CP)	167	379	-	14 026	-	1 323	31 630	-
China Sea (ME)	75	592	-	12 960	-	479	8 170	-
Oceania	3	18	-	331	-	46	392	-
Caribbean	129	1 285	-	1 624	-	1 264	22 841	-
South America (West)	4	73	-	401	-	266	3 103	-
South America (East)	23	94	-	200	-	356	10 347	-
Unspecified	3	-	-	0	-	2 228	8 008	-
Total Non OECD	2 507	12 510	-	56 153	-	23 990	128 161	-
Total	37 906	143 956	-	81 803	10 361	49 804	319 277	-

NOTES: See pages following Table XIII(d)

SOURCE: National Delegations' replies to the Annual Seaborne Trade Questionnaire

Table XIII(c)

OECD SEABORNE TRADE: TOTAL TONNAGE TRADED BY CERTAIN COUNTRIES IN 1985
(Basis: Loading/Unloading, where Member countries provided data on both bases)

In thousand metric tons

REPORTING COUNTRIES	UNITED STATES		BELGIUM/LUXEMBURG		FRANCE	
	IMPORTS	EXPORTS	IMPORTS	EXPORTS	IMPORTS	EXPORTS
Belgium/Luxembourg	5 625	10 954	64	22	-	-
Denmark	184	2 387	150	393	-	-
France	3 237	6 208	1 314	1 696	-	-
Germany	4 738	5 159	601	522	-	-
Italy	6 027	14 828	914	693	-	-
Ireland	117	624	393	849	-	-
Netherlands	7 238	23 649	895	362	-	-
United Kingdom	18 921	5 400	12 736	13 236	-	-
Greece	1 574	1 727	652	572	-	-
Total EEC	47 661	70 936	17 719	18 395	-	-
Finland	881	1 394	836	450	-	-
Norway	1 441	636	4 534	867	-	-
Portugal	328	3 713	603	521	-	-
Spain	7 549	9 702	1 589	504	-	-
Sweden	-	-	1 566	1 200	-	-
Other OECD Europe	1 396	6 264	538	1 136	-	-
Non EEC OECD Europe	12 147	17 393	9 665	4 677	-	-
Japan	17 536	66 702	625	188	-	-
United States	-	-	12 402	5 111	-	-
Canada	32 430	30 235	4 095	2 285	-	-
Australia	8 583	2 528	1 589	82	-	-
New Zealand	551	627	163	12	-	-
Non Europe OECD	60 496	106 356	18 875	7 679	-	-
Total OECD	120 304	194 685	46 259	30 752	-	-
Eastern Europe	4 481	14 535	6 754	2 887	-	-
Mediterranean	12 352	12 850	3 549	4 966	-	-
Middle East	10 686	2 429	524	2 822	-	-
East Africa	100	2 193	141	812	-	-
South Africa	8 330	1 555	2 086	552	-	-
West Africa	23 804	3 426	4 291	916	-	-
South Asia	64	246	233	1 242	-	-
South East Asia	21 106	3 865	601	1 132	-	-
China Sea (CP)	12 033	3 222	466	1 157	-	-
China Sea (ME)	5 790	7 902	199	355	-	-
Oceania	157	392	119	48	-	-
Caribbean	112 729	23 498	3 615	1 170	-	-
South America (West)	11 952	3 033	599	282	-	-
South America (East)	15 307	10 412	7 462	485	-	-
Unspecified	3 357	6 055	2 356	1 276	-	-
Total Non OECD	242 248	124 613	32 993	22 102	-	-
Total	362 552	319 298	79 251	52 854	-	-

NOTES: See pages following Table XIII(d)

SOURCE: National Delegations' replies to the Annual Seaborne Trade Questionnaire

Table XIII(d)

OECD SEABORNE TRADE: FLAG SHARES IN TOTAL TRADE IN 1985

as percentage of total trade

REPORTING COUNTRIES	BELGIUM/LUXEMBOURG				FRANCE		GERMANY		ITALY		NETHERLANDS			
	I TOTAL	E	I LINER	E	I	E	I	E	I	E	I TOTAL	E	I NON-BULK	E
FLAG OF CARRIER														
Belgium/Luxembourg	8.6	6.9	11.2	7.3	-	-	0.9	0.7	-	-	0.8	0.9	0.9	0.4
Denmark	1.1	1.6	0.5	1.1	-	-	2.5	7.4	-	-	1.2	2.4	1.9	1.9
France	2.0	2.0	3.2	2.6	-	-	1.1	1.0	-	-	1.9	1.7	1.9	1.7
Germany	4.6	8.1	6.1	8.1	-	-	12.9	20.4	-	-	5.6	15.6	19.1	21.4
Italy	1.3	0.5	1.2	0.1	-	-	1.1	0.0	-	-	1.1	1.4	0.3	0.4
Netherlands	4.0	3.7	2.7	2.5	-	-	4.2	3.1	-	-	2.4	8.7	8.2	9.0
United Kingdom	13.6	16.2	17.0	14.8	-	-	8.9	4.7	-	-	7.4	15.9	12.5	15.9
Greece	5.7	7.0	3.6	7.1	-	-	6.0	1.8	-	-	6.6	3.5	0.9	1.4
Finland	1.3	0.8	1.0	0.9	-	-	3.1	3.1	-	-	1.9	2.1	2.0	1.0
Norway	4.6	1.9	2.8	1.5	-	-	6.7	1.8	-	-	10.1	4.8	2.7	2.5
Spain	1.4	1.7	1.0	1.2	-	-	0.7	0.6	-	-	1.2	1.5	1.7	1.5
Sweden	2.3	2.6	3.4	2.1	-	-	4.9	7.3	-	-	2.2	4.7	4.5	3.0
Japan	1.7	1.0	1.6	0.5	-	-	2.4	1.4	-	-	3.1	0.7	0.9	1.0
United States	0.1	0.2	0.0	-	-	-	0.9	1.9	-	-	1.4	3.3	10.4	8.7
Canada	0.1	0.1	-	0.1	-	-	0.1	0.5	-	-	0.0	0.1	-	-
Other OECD	1.3	2.3	1.0	2.2	-	-	0.6	1.2	-	-	0.9	1.7	3.1	3.4
Total OECD	53.7	56.7	56.3	52.1	-	-	57.1	60.0	-	-	47.9	68.9	70.7	73.2
USSR	6.0	5.6	2.0	6.7	-	-	6.2	10.0	-	-	5.0	2.9	1.3	2.0
Poland	0.7	0.9	0.6	1.2	-	-	2.4	2.4	-	-	1.4	1.5	1.3	1.2
Germany (DR)	0.3	0.9	0.5	1.3	-	-	0.6	0.6	-	-	0.3	0.6	0.4	0.5
Liberia	14.0	6.9	14.4	5.8	-	-	14.4	3.7	-	-	21.4	7.0	3.8	2.1
Panama	7.0	7.6	7.5	7.9	-	-	6.8	5.6	-	-	7.5	6.6	7.0	6.0
Cyprus	2.0	3.7	1.4	3.4	-	-	1.3	1.8	-	-	1.5	1.8	1.1	1.0
Singapore	2.9	2.9	3.0	3.8	-	-	2.3	2.0	-	-	2.4	1.9	3.0	3.5
Other	13.0	14.0	14.0	17.2	-	-	8.8	13.7	-	-	12.4	7.4	11.5	10.5
Total Non OECD	46.0	42.6	43.4	47.3	-	-	42.7	39.9	-	-	51.7	29.7	29.3	26.8
Total	79 251	52 854	37 723	33 025	-	-	91 870	44 475	-	-	249 662	78 671	22 187	26 256

NOTES: See pages following Table XIII(d)
I: Imports; E: Exports.
Values in percentage of total trade except for Total (which is in '000 metric tons).

SOURCE: National Delegations' replies to the Annual Seaborne Trade Questionnaire

Table XIII(d) continued

OECD SEABORNE TRADE: FLAG SHARES IN TOTAL TRADE IN 1985

as percentage of total trade

REPORTING COUNTRIES	UNITED KINGDOM			FINLAND			SPAIN		SWEDEN		
FLAG OF CARRIER	I TOTAL	E	I NON-BULK	I TOTAL	E	I NON-BULK	I	E	I TOTAL	E	I NON-BULK
Belgium/Luxembourg	2.2	1.1	3.5	0.5	–	–	0.3	0.5	0.3	0.2	0.0	0.1
Denmark	2.2	1.1	3.5	0.7	0.5	1.7	0.4	1.9	1.7	3.2	2.5	4.2
France	3.1	2.6	6.4	0.2	0.5	0.2	0.6	1.9	1.0	1.1	1.6	3.7
Germany	10.1	7.8	16.4	7.7	17.4	23.9	3.0	5.2	12.2	15.5	29.9	22.5
Italy	1.2	0.7	0.2	0.3	0.4	0.2	2.0	6.0	0.3	0.1	–	–
Netherlands	4.3	5.2	7.5	2.5	4.0	2.8	1.3	2.7	3.2	4.2	4.4	5.3
United Kingdom	23.1	22.9	31.3	2.4	3.6	3.0	3.5	3.7	5.7	3.1	5.8	5.5
Greece	5.4	6.2	1.3	1.0	2.6	–	7.5	10.4	5.8	4.3	0.0	1.7
Finland	1.7	6.5	2.7	46.0	41.8	34.5	0.7	0.6	10.2	8.2	11.1	5.9
Norway	10.7	7.0	2.9	1.7	2.7	1.7	1.9	4.6	10.5	8.4	5.3	7.1
Spain	1.2	2.0	1.6	0.1	0.2	0.1	43.7	9.0	0.7	0.6	0.2	0.1
Sweden	2.8	1.8	3.4	6.1	13.5	11.0	0.3	1.0	19.6	27.7	23.5	25.9
Japan	2.0	2.2	1.1	0.4	0.1	0.1	1.5	0.9	1.3	0.3	–	0.0
United States	0.5	2.6	0.4	–	–	–	0.1	0.6	1.1	0.0	–	0.2
Canada	0.1	0.1	0.1	–	–	–	0.0	–	–	0.0	–	–
Other OECD	2.3	2.8	3.1	0.4	0.6	0.8	1.4	5.5	0.6	0.7	0.2	0.5
Total OECD	72.9	72.4	85.4	70.0	87.9	80.0	68.3	54.3	74.2	77.9	84.4	82.6
USSR	2.4	1.2	1.2	20.4	2.9	14.1	2.2	4.7	7.3	3.1	3.4	2.9
Poland	0.7	0.7	0.5	2.2	1.6	2.6	0.2	0.5	1.2	5.6	0.1	0.6
Germany (DR)	0.3	0.1	0.5	1.2	1.0	1.6	0.0	0.2	1.2	1.0	0.1	0.5
Liberia	10.4	11.8	1.7	1.5	1.9	0.2	12.0	9.2	5.0	2.5	0.6	0.8
Panama	4.0	3.3	3.7	1.2	1.0	0.1	6.4	12.0	2.2	2.9	3.5	2.6
Cyprus	1.2	0.6	0.9	0.1	0.4	0.1	1.6	4.7	0.5	0.5	0.2	0.4
Singapore	1.6	3.2	1.2	0.7	0.2	0.0	1.9	1.6	1.5	0.4	–	0.1
Other	6.5	6.6	4.8	2.7	3.2	1.1	7.4	12.8	6.8	6.1	7.1	9.4
Total Non OECD	27.1	27.6	14.6	29.9	12.0	19.8	31.6	45.6	25.7	22.1	15.4	17.2
Total	140 782	143 956	39 504	31 647	20 307	6 044	81 420	38 453	43 933	33 326	4 420	7 661
			26 603			13 950						

NOTES: See pages following Table XIII(d)
I: Imports; E: Exports.
Values in percentage of total trade except for Total (which is in '000 metric tons).

SOURCE: National Delegations' replies to the Annual Seaborne Trade Questionnaire

Table XIII(d) continued

OECD SEABORNE TRADE: FLAG SHARES IN TOTAL TRADE IN 1985

as percentage of total trade

REPORTING COUNTRIES	PORTUGAL		JAPAN		UNITED STATES				CANADA				AUSTRALIA	
FLAG OF CARRIER	I	E	I	E	I TOTAL	E	I LINER	E	I TOTAL	E	I NON-BULK	E	I	E
Belgium/Luxembourg	-	-	-	-	0.8	1.3	1.4	0.8	1.1	0.7	3.8	1.3	0.9	1.4
Denmark	-	-	0.5	2.1	1.5	1.0	5.5	5.4	0.3	0.3	0.7	1.0	1.7	0.3
France	-	-	0.8	1.1	0.8	0.6	0.8	0.4	0.6	0.8	1.4	1.7	0.2	0.5
Germany	-	-	-	-	1.6	1.0	7.6	5.0	1.5	1.2	6.0	4.9	3.7	0.4
Italy	-	-	-	-	1.1	2.3	1.2	0.6	0.9	0.9	1.4	0.7	0.5	0.0
Netherlands	-	-	-	-	0.9	0.9	2.6	2.9	0.3	0.4	0.9	0.9	1.1	0.2
United Kingdom	-	-	3.8	2.0	5.8	5.9	7.3	5.6	3.8	5.1	8.2	6.8	1.2	0.1
Greece	-	-	3.0	3.5	7.6	9.1	0.8	3.9	4.0	5.1	2.9	5.8	5.0	4.1
Finland	-	-	-	-	0.3	0.2	0.2	0.2	0.5	0.2	0.0	0.6	0.0	0.0
Norway	-	-	2.1	1.7	6.3	3.3	3.2	4.0	3.3	3.5	6.3	8.3	2.5	1.4
Spain	-	-	-	-	0.9	1.8	0.5	0.3	0.1	0.6	0.4	1.2	0.0	0.0
Sweden	-	-	-	-	0.8	0.5	2.2	1.4	0.7	0.6	3.3	3.0	0.9	0.2
Japan	-	-	43.1	20.8	3.6	6.1	6.9	9.6	2.4	13.7	6.0	5.1	9.6	36.9
United States	-	-	2.1	4.4	4.7	4.3	21.5	20.4	3.7	2.3	3.8	2.9	0.0	0.1
Canada	-	-	-	-	4.1	8.1	0.0	0.2	44.3	11.0	8.9	8.5	-	-
Other OECD	-	-	1.0	0.3	0.4	1.4	0.9	0.5	1.0	0.8	2.6	2.1	1.4	0.6
Total OECD	-	-	56.3	35.8	41.3	47.8	62.7	61.4	68.6	47.9	56.5	55.0	28.8	46.4
USSR	-	-	1.0	4.0	0.2	0.6	-	-	0.4	3.4	2.5	1.8	1.3	0.9
Poland	-	-	-	-	0.3	0.5	1.4	0.8	0.4	0.5	0.8	0.3	0.9	0.9
Germany (DR)	-	-	-	-	-	0.0	-	-	-	-	-	-	-	-
Liberia	-	-	17.6	8.4	29.0	19.2	4.3	5.2	11.1	17.1	11.1	11.9	10.0	6.6
Panama	-	-	11.5	30.6	13.8	13.4	8.6	9.3	7.9	13.4	8.3	8.4	9.5	9.1
Cyprus	-	-	-	-	0.7	1.4	0.5	0.7	0.5	0.4	1.1	0.8	0.1	0.2
Singapore	-	-	1.7	1.8	1.0	1.9	0.6	0.4	1.6	1.6	2.7	2.5	0.1	0.2
Other	-	-	4.2	8.6	13.8	15.3	21.9	22.2	9.5	15.6	16.9	19.4	49.3	36.5
Total Non OECD	-	-	36.0	53.4	58.7	52.2	37.3	38.6	31.4	52.1	43.5	45.0	71.2	54.4
Total	-	-	592 999	81 803	362 562	319 277	37 300	31 271	60 669	143 421	8 917	20 880	20 521	244 614

NOTES: See pages following Table XIII(d)
I: Imports; E: Exports.
Values in percentage of total trade except for Total (which is in '000 metric tons).

SOURCE: National Delegations' replies to the Annual Seaborne Trade Questionnaire

NOTES TO TABLES XIII(a)-(d)

A. GEOGRAPHICAL REGIONS

Other OECD Europe

Austria
Switzerland
Iceland
Turkey
Yugoslavia
Greenland (if not incl. elsewhere)
Faroe Islands ("   "   )
North Sea Offshore ("   ")

Eastern Europe

USSR
Germany (DDR)
Poland
Czechoslovakia
Hungary
Romania
Bulgaria
Albania

Mediterranean

Gibraltar
Malta
Morocco
Algeria
Tunisia
Libya
Egypt
Cyprus
Syria
Lebanon
Israel
Jordan

Middle East

Iran
Iraq
Kuwait
Saudi-Arabia
Qatar
Bahrain
UAE
Oman
Yemen
South Yemen
Middle East n.e.s.

East Africa (7)

Sudan
Ethiopia
Djibouti
Somali Rep.
Kenya
Tanzania
Seychelles
Br. Indian Ocean Terr. (3)
Uganda
Malawi
Zambia
Burundi (5)
Rwanda (5)

Southern Africa

Angola
Zimbabwe
Mozambique
Malagasy Rep.
Réunion, Comoros and Mayotte (2)
Mauritius
Botswana (2)
Lesotho (2)
Swaziland (2)
South Africa
Namibia
Africa n.e.s.

Western Africa

Mauritania
Senegal
Gambia
Mali
Niger
Burkina Faso
Guinea-Bissau
Guinea
Sierra Leone
Liberia
Ivory Coast
Ghana
Togo
Benin
Nigeria
Cameroon
Equatorial Guinea
Chad
Centr. African Rep.
Gabon
Congo
Zaire

South Asia

Afghanistan
Pakistan
India
Bangladesh
Sri Lanka
Maldives (3)
Nepal/Bhutan
Far-East n.e.s.

South-East Asia

Burma
Thailand
Laos
Vietnam
Kampuchea
Malaysia
Indonesia
Singapore
Brunei

China Sea (Market Economy)

Philippines
Korea (Rep.)
Taiwan
Hong Kong
Macao (3)

China Sea (Centrally Planned)

Mongolia
China (PR)
North Korea

Oceania

US Terr. in Ocean (4)
Br. Terr. in Ocean
Fr. Terr. in Ocean (3)
Papua New Guinea (1)
Solomon Islands
Oceania n.e.s.

Caribbean

St. Pierre Miq. (6)
Mexico
Cuba
Haiti
Dominican Republic
Jamaica
Guatemala
Belize
Bahamas
Bermuda
Barbados
Turks and Caicos
Cayman Isles
Windward & Leeward Isles
Honduras
El Salvador
Nicaragua
Costa Rica
Panama
Canal Zone
Fr. Antilles
Neth. Antilles
Trinidad & Tobago
Colombia
Venezuela
Guyana
Surinam
French Guiana
America n.e.s.

South America West

Ecuador
Peru
Bolivia
Chile

South America East

Brazil
Paraguay
Argentina
Uruguay
Falkland Islands

Notes

Puerto Rico and Virgin Isles: included with United States
Azores and Madeira: incl. with Portugal
n.e.s.: not explicitly specified

(1) UK: incl. with Australia
(2) UK: incl. with East Africa
(3) UK: incl. with S-E Asia
(4) UK: incl. with China Sea
(5) UK: incl. with West Africa
(6) UK: incl. with Canada
(7) Portugal, Australia: incl. with Middle East

B. **TREATMENT OF 'IN TRANSIT' CARGO (WITHOUT TRANSHIPMENT)**

Included: Belgium (L/U), Canada, Finland, Germany, Greece, Italy, Portugal, Sweden, United States.
Excluded: Australia, Belgium (O/D), Denmark, France, Japan, Netherlands, New Zealand, Spain, Norway, United Kingdom (unless they involve a commercial transaction within the United Kingdom).

It should be noted that where transit cargo is included, it relates to cargo passing through the ports of a country with an origin/destination outside that country. It does not relate to cargo passing through the ports of another country with origin/destination in the respondant country: e.g., cargo discharged in Hamburg for Switzerland is included in German statistics; cargo discharged in Rotterdam for Germany is not included in German statistics.

C. **UNITS**

All quantities are in thousand metric tons. All countries use gross tonnage, except France, Japan, Portugal, Norway and United Kingdom which give net tonnage and Netherlands and Belgium/Luxemburg (Loading/Unloading basis) which give tare weight (i.e., including container or vehicle weight.)

D. **SOURCES OF DATA**

General Declarations: Australia, Canada, Finland, Germany, Greece, Netherlands, New Zealand, Spain, Sweden, Belgium (L/U).
Customs returns: Belgium (O/D), Denmark, France, Japan, Norway, Portugal, United States, United Kingdom.

Generally, but not always, the difference is reflected by whether the replies are 'Origin/Destination' or 'Loading/Unloading'. For this reason, users of these tables are strongly urged NOT to combine data derived from different types of return as they are almost always incompatible. Similarly, the import figures of one country can be very different from the corresponding exports of another because of differences in definition.

E. **AVAILABILITY OF MATERIAL**

The complete data for all participating countries, covering the years 1981-1985, is available on magnetic tape, on application to OECD Data Dissemination and Reception Unit, at an appropriate fee.

Table XIV

DEVELOPMENT OF WORLD FLEET
(Ships of 100 grt and over)

MID-YEAR	TOTAL				OIL TANKERS					ORE AND DRY BULK CARRIERS					OTHER VESSEL TYPES				
	GRT		DWT		GRT			DWT		GRT			DWT		GRT		DWT		
	MILL.	% CHANGE IN YEAR	MILL.	% CHANGE IN YEAR	MILL.	% CHANGE IN YEAR	% OF WORLD FLEET	MILL.	% CHANGE IN YEAR	MILL.	% CHANGE IN YEAR	% OF WORLD FLEET	MILL.	% CHANGE IN YEAR	MILL.	% CHANGE IN YEAR	% OF WORLD FLEET	MILL.	% CHANGE IN YEAR
1960	129.8	3.9	..	..	41.5	9.4	32	..	..	..	..	..	..	..	88.3	1.4	68	..	..
1961	135.9	4.7	..	..	43.8	5.7	32	..	..	..	..	..	..	..	92.1	4.2	68	..	..
1962	140.0	3.0	..	..	45.3	3.3	32	..	..	..	..	..	..	..	94.7	2.8	68	..	..
1963	145.9	4.2	..	..	47.1	4.1	32	..	..	..	..	..	..	..	98.8	4.3	68	..	..
1964	153.0	4.2	..	..	50.6	7.3	33	..	..	16.7	..	11	..	..	85.8	1.0	56	..	..
1965	160.4	4.8	..	..	55.0	8.9	34	..	..	18.8	12.6	12	..	..	86.6	1.2	54	..	..
1966	171.1	6.7	..	..	60.2	9.4	35	..	..	23.3	24.1	14	..	..	87.6	1.2	51	..	..
1967	182.1	6.4	..	..	64.2	6.6	35	..	..	29.1	24.8	16	..	..	88.8	1.4	49	..	..
1968	194.2	6.6	..	..	69.2	7.8	36	..	..	34.9	20.0	18	..	..	90.1	1.4	46	..	..
1969	211.7	9.0	..	..	77.4	11.8	37	..	..	41.8	19.8	20	..	..	92.5	2.7	43	..	..
1970	227.5	7.5	338.8	..	86.1	11.3	38	148.5	..	46.7	11.6	20	76.3	..	94.7	2.4	42	114.0	..
1971	247.2	8.7	376.2	11.0	96.1	11.6	39	169.4	14.0	53.8	15.3	22	89.0	16.6	97.3	2.7	39	117.9	3.4
1972	268.3	8.6	414.1	10.1	105.1	9.3	39	188.4	11.3	63.5	18.0	24	106.9	20.2	99.7	2.5	37	118.7	0.7
1973	289.9	8.0	452.5	9.3	115.4	9.7	40	209.7	11.3	72.6	14.4	25	123.3	15.3	101.9	2.2	35	119.5	0.6
1974	311.3	7.4	494.0	9.2	129.5	12.2	42	238.4	13.7	79.4	9.3	25	135.6	10.0	102.4	0.5	33	120.0	0.4
1975	342.2	9.9	553.4	12.0	150.1	15.9	44	281.6	18.1	85.5	7.7	25	146.8	8.2	106.6	4.1	31	125.0	4.2
1976	372.0	8.7	608.3	9.9	168.2	12.1	45	320.0	13.6	91.7	7.2	25	158.1	7.7	112.1	5.2	30	130.3	4.2
1977	393.7	5.8	648.8	6.7	174.1	3.5	44	335.3	4.8	100.9	10.0	26	174.4	10.3	118.6	5.8	30	139.1	6.8
1978	406.0	3.1	670.4	3.3	175.0	0.5	43	339.1	1.1	106.5	5.6	26	184.5	5.8	124.4	4.9	31	146.8	5.5
1979	413.0	1.7	681.5	1.7	174.2	-0.5	42	338.3	-0.2	108.3	1.7	26	188.5	2.2	130.5	4.9	32	154.7	5.4
1980	419.9	1.7	690.9	1.4	175.0	0.5	42	339.8	0.4	109.6	1.2	26	191.0	1.3	135.3	3.7	32	160.1	3.5
1981	420.8	0.2	697.2	0.9	171.7	-1.9	41	335.5	-1.3	113.1	3.2	27	199.5	4.5	136.0	0.5	32	162.2	1.3
1982	424.7	0.9	702.0	0.7	166.8	-2.8	39	325.2	-3.1	119.3	5.5	28	211.2	5.9	138.6	1.9	33	165.6	2.1
1983	422.6	-0.5	694.5	-1.1	157.3	-5.7	37	306.1	-5.9	124.4	4.3	30	220.6	4.5	140.9	1.7	33	167.8	1.3
1984	418.7	-0.9	683.3	-1.6	147.5	-6.2	35	286.8	-6.3	128.3	3.2	31	228.4	3.5	142.9	1.4	34	168.1	0.2
1985	416.3	-0.6	673.7	-1.4	138.4	-6.1	33	268.4	-6.4	134.0	4.4	32	237.3	3.9	143.9	0.7	35	168.0	-0.1
1986	404.9	-2.7	647.6	-4.0	128.4	-7.2	32	247.5	-7.8	132.9	-0.8	33	235.2	-0.9	143.6	-0.2	35	164.9	-1.8

NOTE: Ore and dry bulk carriers (which include combination carriers) are included with 'Other vessel types' for the period prior to 1963.
.. signifies data not published in Lloyd's Register of Shipping Statistical Tables or calculated therefrom.
The Great Lakes fleets of Canada and the United States, and the United States reserve fleet are included.

SOURCE: Lloyd's Register of Shipping: Statistical Tables.

Table XV(a)

WORLD FLEET AS AT MID-1986 IN GRT AND DWT
(Ships of 100 grt and over)

COUNTRY OF REGISTRATION	TOTAL FLEET		INCREASE OR DECREASE SINCE MID-1985		OIL TANKERS		INCREASE OR DECREASE SINCE MID-1985	
	'000 GRT	'000 DWT	'000 GRT	'000 DWT	'000 GRT	'000 DWT	'000 GRT	'000 DWT
Australia	2 368.5	3 653.6	280.2	559.5	661.9	1 136.1	74.0	134.2
Austria	124.8	210.6	-9.4	-15.9	-	-	-	-
Belgium	2 419.7	3 916.5	19.4	62.9	266.5	462.6	34.2	42.4
Canada	3 160.0	3 829.7	-183.8	-245.6	278.8	424.5	-2.5	-4.4
Denmark	4 651.2	6 805.2	-291.0	-614.2	2 044.3	3 902.1	-154.4	-266.2
Finland	1 469.9	1 907.8	-504.1	-946.0	597.0	1 095.7	-329.4	-629.6
France	5 936.3	9 305.3	-2 301.1	-4 407.3	2 602.7	5 150.7	-1 742.9	-3 461.0
Germany (FR)	5 565.2	7 744.6	-611.8	-1 496.3	748.0	1 407.6	-645.7	-1 299.0
Greece	28 390.8	51 294.3	-2 640.7	-4 061.8	10 258.5	20 667.1	892.8	1 940.2
Iceland	176.4	161.6	-3.9	-6.9	2.7	5.2	-	-
Ireland	149.3	148.9	-44.7	-77.6	7.7	13.3	-0.8	-1.4
Italy	7 896.6	12 407.1	-946.6	-1 966.0	2 560.8	4 665.6	-1 040.3	-2 095.0
Japan	38 487.8	59 979.0	-1 452.3	-3 472.2	12 364.6	23 140.8	-1 724.8	-3 476.0
Netherlands (1)	4 324.1	5 993.9	22.8	44.5	931.1	1 658.2	189.5	331.4
New Zealand	314.2	344.8	18.3	10.6	73.5	116.7	-	-
Norway	9 294.6	14 202.7	-6 044.0	-11 518.8	3 304.1	6 254.3	-3 958.9	-7 901.5
Portugal	1 114.4	1 747.1	-322.5	-658.6	533.4	1 013.6	-326.8	-705.8
Spain	5 422.0	9 286.0	-834.2	-1 534.0	2 371.8	4 935.3	-534.3	-1 069.7
Sweden	2 516.6	3 037.4	-645.3	-1 193.4	503.9	931.8	-390.4	-763.3
Switzerland	346.2	550.7	4.2	14.9	2.0	3.8	2.0	3.8
Turkey	3 423.7	5 712.5	-260.7	-579.3	1 036.9	1 917.5	-545.4	-1 104.4
United Kingdom	11 567.1	16 871.6	-2 776.4	-4 923.1	4 394.1	8 170.0	-1 543.0	-2 867.6
United States	19 900.8	28 850.6	383.2	-142.0	7 296.4	14 702.5	-175.4	-304.8
Total OECD	159 020.2	247 961.5	-19 144.4	-37 166.6	52 840.7	101 775.0	-11 925.5	-23 497.7
Algeria	881.7	1 018.5	-465.7	-924.7	119.1	194.8	-475.2	-935.8
Argentina	2 117.0	3 171.2	-340.3	-397.5	654.0	1 078.9	-187.5	-262.6
Bahamas	5 985.0	10 600.4	2 077.7	3 738.1	4 200.9	8 059.6	1 191.0	2 323.2
Bermuda	1 208.3	1 759.7	227.6	298.9	301.2	504.5	80.7	87.5
Brazil	6 212.3	10 277.9	154.9	238.3	1 937.7	3 530.8	103.3	170.2
Bulgaria	1 385.0	1 989.1	62.8	99.4	316.6	516.2	4.9	7.8
Cayman Islands	1 389.9	2 121.7	976.1	1 539.4	737.5	1 187.3	691.3	1 110.4
Chile	566.9	907.5	112.4	205.7	15.0	24.6	-	-
China (PR)	11 567.0	17 424.0	998.8	1 506.0	1 700.6	2 749.6	224.7	343.9
Cuba	958.6	1 274.2	-6.5	38.0	68.2	103.3	-	-
Cyprus	10 616.8	18 763.0	2 420.7	4 463.7	4 480.8	8 695.7	1 153.7	2 287.0
Ecuador	437.7	611.6	-6.2	-13.2	157.4	282.2	-2.2	-4.4
Egypt	1 063.0	1 484.9	110.4	177.8	98.8	164.5	1.5	2.8
Germany (DR)	1 518.9	1 923.6	84.5	107.6	35.9	63.3	-	-
Gibraltar	1 612.9	2 999.0	1 029.6	1 978.1	855.7	1 697.9	689.2	1 357.6
Honduras	555.2	827.1	198.6	310.9	67.3	118.3	16.5	24.7
Hong Kong	8 179.7	13 664.5	1 321.6	2 331.9	883.9	1 596.9	443.9	838.0
India	6 540.1	10 691.0	-64.4	-69.9	1 813.8	3 156.4	96.5	162.5
Indonesia	2 085.6	2 927.1	149.2	253.4	617.2	1 055.3	126.4	216.1
Iran	2 911.4	5 064.3	531.3	1 199.8	1 241.9	2 471.8	323.7	741.2
Iraq	1 016.3	1 699.6	4.4	13.7	776.9	1 439.8	29.8	51.0
Israel	556.6	679.2	6.9	21.7	1.0	1.9	-	-
Korea (North)	407.3	615.3	-105.3	-214.1	58.8	115.8	-112.4	-224.9
Korea (South)	7 183.6	11 561.9	14.7	-211.0	976.8	1 853.9	-25.5	-122.7
Kuwait	2 580.9	4 121.3	231.0	615.5	1 629.4	2 941.8	339.6	746.0
Lebanon	484.6	766.8	-20.4	-23.2	14.1	23.2	-	-
Liberia	52 649.4	101 587.6	-5 529.5	-11 964.6	28 674.5	59 631.6	-2 911.0	-6 665.7
Libya	825.2	1 459.6	-28.6	-54.1	708.0	1 341.0	-37.1	-68.3
Malaysia	1 743.6	2 506.6	-29.5	-76.1	237.5	402.9	13.4	22.6
Malta	2 014.9	3 415.4	159.1	426.6	515.2	998.1	186.2	371.7
Mexico	1 520.2	2 206.6	53.0	129.1	605.7	1 028.0	65.3	135.4
Morocco	416.5	595.4	-44.4	-84.1	10.1	19.1	-51.5	-91.9
Nigeria	563.9	809.3	120.5	202.2	223.2	435.6	68.9	137.2
Pakistan	434.1	623.2	-16.9	-31.5	43.4	89.9	-0.9	-0.9
Panama	41 305.0	68 349.4	630.8	1 082.7	9 191.8	17 996.0	778.1	1 598.2
Peru	754.2	997.1	-63.9	-99.5	147.5	251.5	-35.3	-63.6
Philippines	6 922.5	11 668.6	2 328.5	4 097.6	655.8	1 262.1	93.6	165.4
Poland	3 457.2	4 694.2	141.9	254.3	317.7	552.0	-0.5	-1.1
Romania	3 233.9	4 843.3	210.1	340.7	383.7	699.8	-	-
Saint Vincent	509.9	833.2	274.7	473.7	82.6	147.9	82.6	147.9
Saudi Arabia	2 978.0	4 954.6	-159.2	-299.7	1 604.3	3 040.8	26.4	1.7
Singapore	6 267.6	10 603.7	-237.0	-583.6	1 653.0	3 197.4	-396.4	-801.1
South Africa	599.5	661.7	-33.0	-11.5	39.0	63.8	1.3	1.2
Sri Lanka	622.2	972.0	-12.5	-2.2	139.9	262.4	2.3	14.0
Taiwan	4 272.8	6 583.1	-54.7	-114.3	581.2	1 056.6	-47.0	-97.5
Thailand	533.1	772.4	-53.2	-91.0	62.5	110.8	-84.3	-147.5
United Arab Emirates	653.5	1 018.9	-215.1	-504.8	371.7	652.3	-256.9	-528.4
USSR	24 960.9	28 145.6	215.5	-7.7	4 086.9	6 255.4	-504.1	-790.6
Venezuela	998.3	1 428.6	13.4	6.8	470.3	769.4	-27.7	-41.6
Yugoslavia	2 872.6	4 476.3	173.3	295.9	308.2	536.9	91.0	172.2
Rest of World (2)	4 758.8	6 526.3	239.3	437.3	711.8	1 318.7	133.7	276.8
World Total	404 910.3	647 638.6	-11 358.2	-26 053.2	128 425.8	247 523.3	-10 022.5	-20 831.9

1. Including the Netherlands Antilles.
2. No country included in 'Rest of World' has more than 400 000 grt under its flag.
SOURCE: Lloyd's Register of Shipping: Statistical Tables

Table XV(b)

WORLD FLEET: ANALYSIS BY PRINCIPAL TYPES AS AT MID-1986
(Ships of 100 grt and over)

'000 grt

COUNTRY OF REGISTRATION	OIL TANKERS	% OF TOTAL	ORE AND DRY BULK (1)	% OF TOTAL	GENERAL CARGO (2)	% OF TOTAL	MISCEL-LANEOUS (3)	% OF TOTAL	TOTAL
Australia	661.9	28	1 185.0	50	257.1	11	264.5	11	2 368.5
Austria	-	-	63.0	50	61.8	50	-	-	124.8
Belgium	266.5	11	1 415.8	58	366.9	15	370.5	16	2 419.7
Canada	278.8	9	1 851.4	59	178.7	5	851.1	27	3 160.0
Denmark	2 044.3	44	290.2	6	1 711.7	37	605.0	13	4 651.2
Finland	597.0	41	121.1	8	393.8	19	358.0	32	1 469.9
France	2 602.7	44	957.2	16	1 587.4	27	789.0	13	5 936.3
Germany (FR)	748.0	13	558.7	10	3 555.2	64	703.3	13	5 565.2
Greece	10 258.5	36	13 201.9	46	4 116.8	15	813.6	3	28 390.8
Iceland	2.7	2	-	-	64.8	36	108.9	62	176.4
Ireland	7.7	5	-	-	75.1	50	66.5	45	149.3
Italy	2 560.8	32	3 059.1	39	1 136.5	14	1 140.2	15	7 896.6
Japan	12 364.6	32	13 894.8	36	5 742.8	15	6 485.6	17	38 487.8
Netherlands(4)	931.1	22	523.8	12	2 033.2	47	836.0	19	4 324.1
New Zealand	73.5	24	12.8	4	160.7	51	67.2	21	314.2
Norway	3 304.1	36	2 479.4	27	1 055.9	11	2 455.2	26	9 294.6
Portugal	533.4	48	230.6	21	191.5	17	158.9	14	1 114.4
Spain	2 371.8	44	1 174.9	22	1 003.2	18	872.1	16	5 422.0
Sweden	503.9	20	271.4	11	1 116.4	44	624.9	25	2 516.6
Switzerland	2.0	1	264.2	76	64.7	19	15.3	4	346.2
Turkey	1 036.9	30	1 352.7	40	826.2	24	207.9	6	3 423.7
United Kingdom	4 394.1	38	2 149.7	19	2 543.6	22	2 479.7	21	11 567.1
United States	7 296.4	37	2 020.3	10	7 265.7	36	3 318.4	17	19 900.8
Total OECD	52 840.7	33	47 078.0	30	35 509.7	22	23 591.8	15	159 020.2
Algeria	119.1	13	57.5	7	211.1	24	493.9	56	881.7
Argentina	654.0	31	514.6	24	734.8	35	213.6	10	2 117.0
Bahamas	4 200.9	70	901.7	15	443.9	8	438.5	7	5 985.0
Bermuda	301.2	25	319.1	26	261.1	22	326.9	27	1 208.3
Brazil	1 937.7	31	2 802.3	45	1 154.5	19	317.8	5	6 212.3
Bulgaria	316.6	23	572.1	41	366.3	27	130.0	9	1 385.0
Cayman Islands	737.5	53	283.4	21	282.5	20	86.5	6	1 389.9
Chile	15.0	3	313.7	55	141.8	25	96.4	17	566.9
China (PR)	1 700.6	15	3 871.5	33	5 386.0	47	608.9	5	11 567.0
Cuba	68.2	7	61.9	7	663.9	69	164.6	17	958.6
Cyprus	4 480.8	42	3 739.2	35	2 199.8	21	197.0	2	10 616.8
Ecuador	157.4	36	11.2	3	234.3	53	34.8	8	437.7
Egypt	98.8	9	343.1	32	494.0	47	127.1	12	1 063.0
Germany (DR)	35.9	3	352.7	23	881.9	58	248.4	16	1 518.9
Gibraltar	855.7	53	618.1	38	129.3	8	9.8	1	1 612.9
Honduras	67.3	12	96.2	17	360.6	65	31.1	6	555.2
Hong Kong	883.9	11	6 089.6	74	904.3	11	301.9	4	8 179.7
India	1 813.8	28	2 943.4	45	1 454.0	22	328.9	5	6 540.1
Indonesia	617.2	30	128.8	6	981.2	47	358.4	17	2 085.6
Iran	1 241.9	43	1 109.0	38	415.1	14	145.4	5	2 911.4
Iraq	776.9	76	-	-	111.7	11	127.7	13	1 016.3
Israel	1.0	0	74.1	14	474.6	85	6.9	1	556.6
Korea (North)	58.8	14	64.1	16	237.4	58	47.0	12	407.3
Korea (South)	976.8	14	4 269.1	59	1 206.6	17	731.1	10	7 183.6
Kuwait	1 629.4	63	-	-	514.0	20	437.5	17	2 580.9
Lebanon	14.1	3	130.8	27	281.7	58	58.0	12	484.6
Liberia	28 674.5	54	18 028.3	34	2 388.0	5	3 558.6	7	52 649.4
Libya	708.0	86	-	-	71.7	9	45.5	5	825.2
Malaysia	237.5	14	456.3	26	582.8	33	467.0	27	1 743.6
Malta	515.2	26	952.5	47	498.8	25	48.4	2	2 014.9
Mexico	605.7	40	311.5	20	142.9	9	460.1	30	1 520.2
Morocco	10.1	2	124.8	30	78.7	19	202.9	49	416.5
Nigeria	223.2	40	-	-	294.6	52	46.1	8	563.9
Pakistan	43.4	10	12.0	3	356.3	82	22.4	5	434.1
Panama	9 191.8	22	17 400.0	42	11 066.5	27	3 646.7	9	41 305.0
Peru	147.5	19	190.4	25	246.0	33	170.3	23	754.2
Philippines	655.8	9	4 804.7	69	1 073.6	16	388.4	6	6 922.5
Poland	317.7	9	1 499.4	43	1 236.7	36	403.4	12	3 457.2
Romania	383.7	12	1 589.6	49	993.8	31	266.8	8	3 233.9
Saint Vincent	82.6	16	297.6	59	123.3	24	6.4	1	509.9
Saudi Arabia	1 604.3	54	372.9	13	541.9	18	458.9	15	2 978.0
Singapore	1 653.0	26	2 477.8	40	1 721.5	27	415.3	7	6 267.6
South Africa	39.0	6	124.7	21	298.5	50	137.3	23	599.5
Sri Lanka	139.9	22	242.1	39	230.0	37	10.2	2	622.2
Taiwan	581.2	13	1 998.1	47	1 570.0	37	123.5	3	4 272.8
Thailand	62.5	12	28.5	5	382.0	72	60.1	11	533.1
United Arab Emirates	371.7	57	8.6	1	230.1	35	43.1	7	653.5
USSR	4 086.9	16	3 433.3	14	8 370.2	34	9 070.5	36	24 960.9
Venezuela	470.3	47	85.6	8	305.9	31	136.5	14	998.3
Yugoslavia	308.2	11	1 182.1	41	1 304.3	45	78.0	3	2 872.6
Rest of World(5)	711.8	15	542.1	11	2 711.0	57	793.9	17	4 758.8
World Total	128 425.8	32	132 908.1	33	92 854.3	23	50 722.1	12	404 910.3

1. Including combination carriers. 2. Including container ships and passenger/cargo ships.
3. Including fishing vessels, fish factory and carrier ships, chemical and other non-oil tankers, liquefied gas carriers, transporters of barges, vehicles or livestock, passenger ships and ferries, research ships and other non-trading vessels.
4. Including Netherlands Antilles 5. No country in this group has more than 400 000 grt under its flag.

SOURCE: Lloyd's Register of Shipping, Statistical Tables.

Table XVI(a)

SIZE DISTRIBUTION OF WORLD FLEET AS AT MID-1986
(in terms of gross register tonnage)

SIZE GROUPS (GRT)	WORLD FLEET			OIL TANKERS		ORE AND BULK CARRIERS		GENERAL CARGO		OTHERS	
	SHIPS	'000 GRT	%	'000 GRT	%	'000 GRT	%	'000 GRT	%	'000 GRT	%
100 – 499	38 116	9 446.6	2.3	478.3	0.4	–	–	2 138.8	3.0	6 829.5	9.5
500 – 999	7 724	5 793.5	1.4	754.1	0.6	–	–	1 594.8	2.2	3 444.6	4.8
1 000 – 1 999	5 844	8 605.3	2.1	948.2	0.7	–	–	3 873.7	5.4	3 783.4	5.3
2 000 – 3 999	5 950	17 635.6	4.4	1 693.0	1.3	–	–	8 713.6	12.0	7 229.0	10.1
4 000 – 5 999	2 728	13 425.3	3.3	1 251.6	1.0	–	–	7 956.6	11.1	4 217.1	5.9
6 000 – 6 999	949	6 141.0	1.5	289.8	0.2	361.9	0.3	3 883.4	5.4	1 605.9	2.2
7 000 – 7 999	717	5 390.7	1.3	505.7	0.4	525.9	0.4	3 107.2	4.3	1 251.9	1.7
8 000 – 9 999	2 268	20 764.9	5.1	741.7	0.6	2 273.3	1.7	15 085.7	21.0	2 664.2	3.7
10 000 – 14 999	3 549	43 034.5	10.6	4 617.4	3.6	14 012.8	10.5	17 370.6	24.1	7 033.7	9.8
15 000 – 19 999	2 445	42 079.1	10.4	8 686.5	6.8	22 878.8	17.2	4 238.8	5.9	6 275.0	8.8
20 000 – 29 999	1 887	45 228.8	11.2	8 408.0	6.5	27 444.0	20.7	1 673.9	2.3	7 702.9	10.8
30 000 – 39 999	1 186	40 921.5	10.1	9 057.9	7.1	23 277.6	17.5	1 144.8	1.6	7 441.2	10.4
40 000 – 49 999	517	22 810.5	5.6	9 691.3	7.5	7 361.4	5.5	906.8	1.3	4 851.0	6.8
50 000 – 59 999	308	16 783.6	4.1	7 829.1	6.1	5 499.8	4.1	256.7	0.4	3 198.0	4.5
60 000 – 69 999	273	17 718.0	4.4	8 705.2	6.8	8 010.3	6.0	–	–	1 002.5	1.4
70 000 – 79 999	181	13 537.3	3.4	4 980.2	3.9	8 025.2	6.0	–	–	531.9	0.7
80 000 – 89 999	117	9 928.7	2.5	3 361.7	2.6	5 655.0	4.3	–	–	912.0	1.3
90 000 – 99 999	60	5 696.1	1.4	1 256.4	0.9	3 294.4	2.5	–	–	1 145.3	1.6
100 000 – 109 999	56	5 883.2	1.5	4 643.3	3.6	727.9	0.6	–	–	512.0	0.7
110 000 – 119 999	91	10 556.6	2.6	8 828.1	6.9	1 728.5	1.3	–	–	–	–
120 000 – 129 999	112	14 004.9	3.5	13 136.5	10.2	868.3	0.7	–	–	–	–
130 000 – 139 999	75	10 144.1	2.5	9 468.5	7.4	675.7	0.5	–	–	–	–
140 000 and over	113	19 380.5	4.8	19 093.3	14.9	287.3	0.2	–	–	–	–
Total	75 266	404 910.3	100.0	128 425.8	100.0	132 908.1	100.0	71 945.5	100.0	71 630.9	100.0

NOTE: "Ore and Bulk Carriers" include combination carriers; "General Cargo" is defined in the same way as in Tables XVI(b) and XVII.

SOURCE: Lloyd's Register of Shipping

Table XVI(b)

SIZE DISTRIBUTION OF WORLD FLEET AS AT MID-1986
(in terms of deadweight tonnage)

SIZE GROUPS (GRT)	WORLD FLEET			OIL TANKERS		ORE AND BULK CARRIERS		GENERAL CARGO		OTHERS	
	SHIPS	'000 GRT	%	'000 GRT	%	'000 GRT	%	'000 GRT	%	'000 GRT	%
200 – 749	18 784	6 020.7	0.9	414.1	0.2	5.2	0	1 945.4	1.9	3 656.0	5.8
750 – 1 499	7 949	8 648.7	1.3	1 020.7	0.4	3.3	0	3 256.6	3.2	4 368.1	7.0
1 500 – 2 499	4 655	8 923.1	1.4	1 450.2	0.6	23.3	0	4 150.9	4.1	3 298.7	5.3
2 500 – 4 999	5 254	18 673.9	2.9	2 499.5	1.0	159.2	0.1	11 680.8	11.4	4 334.4	6.9
5 000 – 7 999	3 493	22 253.2	3.4	2 677.2	1.1	244.3	0.1	15 046.4	14.8	4 285.3	6.8
8 000 – 9 999	1 265	11 319.1	1.8	714.5	0.3	432.2	0.2	7 386.7	7.3	2 785.7	4.4
10 000 – 11 999	1 093	11 952.4	1.9	696.0	0.3	838.1	0.3	7 751.1	7.6	2 667.2	4.2
12 000 – 14 999	1 840	24 722.9	3.8	1 005.2	0.4	1 946.2	0.8	18 876.3	18.6	2 895.2	4.6
15 000 – 17 999	1 736	28 088.0	4.3	2 839.6	1.2	5 269.1	2.2	17 003.9	16.8	2 975.4	4.7
18 000 – 24 999	1 990	42 575.1	6.6	6 395.5	2.5	19 372.2	8.2	11 357.1	11.1	5 450.3	8.7
25 000 – 39 999	3 120	98 519.2	15.2	20 521.2	8.3	62 881.0	26.7	2 385.6	2.3	12 731.4	20.3
40 000 – 59 999	1 133	54 333.0	8.4	13 643.8	4.7	32 471.5	13.8	692.0	0.7	9 525.7	15.2
60 000 – 79 999	842	57 008.9	8.8	13 939.2	5.6	39 871.2	16.9	–	–	3 198.5	5.1
80 000 – 99 999	381	33 472.9	5.2	25 984.3	10.5	6 950.5	3.0	–	–	528.1	0.8
100 000 – 124 999	268	30 549.6	4.7	10 527.1	4.2	19 910.7	8.4	–	–	111.8	0.2
125 000 – 149 999	262	35 578.1	5.5	17 478.2	7.1	18 099.9	7.7	–	–	–	–
150 000 – 174 999	148	23 854.1	3.7	9 200.6	3.7	14 653.5	6.2	–	–	–	–
175 000 – 199 999	36	6 739.7	1.0	2 737.0	1.1	4 002.6	1.7	–	–	–	–
200 000 – 224 999	31	6 731.3	1.0	4 124.0	1.7	2 607.3	1.1	–	–	–	–
225 000 – 249 999	107	25 084.9	3.9	22 032.2	8.9	3 052.7	1.3	–	–	–	–
250 000 – 274 999	156	41 349.2	6.4	39 219.4	15.8	2 129.8	0.9	–	–	–	–
275 000 – 299 999	65	18 339.9	2.8	17 503.2	7.1	836.8	0.4	–	–	–	–
300 000 and over	89	32 900.6	5.1	32 900.6	13.3	–	–	–	–	–	–
Total	54 697	647 638.6	100.0	247 523.3	100.0	235 770.6	100.0	101 532.7	100.0	62 812.0	100.0

NOTE: 'Ore and Bulk Carriers' include combination carriers.
'General Cargo' includes single deck and multideck vessels but excludes passenger/cargo ships, fully cellular container ships and specialised carriers of vehicles, lighters or livestock.
The deadweight figures include only those ships for which Lloyd's Register of Shipping records a deadweight value in excess of 200 dwt. The oil tanker and dry bulk carrier figures relate to the same ships as given in the gross register tonnage table and hence exclude a number of bulk carriers of less than 6 000 grt (c. 8 000 dwt).

SOURCE: Lloyd's Register of Shipping

Table XVII

AGE DISTRIBUTION OF WORLD FLEET AS AT MID-1986

in grt

AGE RANGE (YEARS)	WORLD FLEET			OIL TANKERS			ORE AND BULK CARRIERS			GENERAL CARGO			OTHERS		
	SHIPS	'000 GRT	%	'000 GRT	%		'000 GRT	%		'000 GRT	%		'000 GRT	%	
Under 5	10 215	77 931	19.3	13 226	10.3		37 155	28.0		11 000	15.3		16 550	23.1	
5 - 10	15 065	90 502	22.4	26 886	20.9		27 792	20.9		17 800	24.7		18 024	25.2	
10 - 15	15 230	135 390	33.4	66 936	52.1		38 524	29.0		14 399	20.0		15 531	21.6	
15 - 20	13 752	57 335	14.2	11 744	9.2		21 396	16.1		13 769	19.1		10 426	14.6	
20 - 25	8 281	23 650	5.8	5 451	4.2		5 865	4.4		7 320	10.2		5 014	7.0	
25 - 30	4 792	10 268	2.5	2 658	2.1		1 040	0.8		3 943	5.5		2 627	3.7	
Over 30	7 931	9 834	2.4	1 524	1.2		1 136	0.8		3 714	5.2		3 460	4.8	
Total	75 266	404 910	100.0	128 425	100.0		132 908	100.0		71 945	100.0		71 632	100.0	

in dwt

AGE RANGE (YEARS)	WORLD FLEET			OIL TANKERS			ORE AND BULK CARRIERS			GENERAL CARGO			OTHERS		
	SHIPS	'000 DWT	%	'000 DWT	%		'000 DWT	%		'000 DWT	%		'000 DWT	%	
Under 5	8 803	116 478	18.0	22 682	9.2		64 827	27.5		13 739	13.5		15 230	24.2	
5 - 10	11 233	143 751	22.2	51 108	20.6		49 130	20.8		26 001	25.6		17 512	27.9	
10 - 15	11 106	239 553	37.0	134 817	54.5		69 549	29.5		20 933	20.6		14 254	22.7	
15 - 20	9 867	90 194	13.9	22 453	9.1		38 366	16.3		20 347	20.0		9 058	14.4	
20 - 25	5 457	32 905	5.1	9 472	3.8		10 250	4.4		10 005	9.9		3 178	5.1	
25 - 30	3 167	13 360	2.0	4 477	1.8		1 742	0.7		5 470	5.4		1 671	2.7	
Over 30	5 064	11 397	1.8	2 515	1.0		1 936	0.8		5 037	5.0		1 909	3.0	
Total	54 697	647 638	100.0	247 524	100.0		235 770	100.0		101 532	100.0		62 812	100.0	

NOTE: 'Ore and Bulk Carriers' include combination carriers.
'General Cargo' includes single deck and multideck vessels but excludes passenger/cargo ships, fully cellular container ships and specialised carriers of vehicles, lighters or livestock.
The deadweight figures include only those ships for which Lloyd's Register of Shipping record a deadweight value. The oil tanker and dry bulk carrier figures relate to the same ships as given in the gross register tonnage columns. They exclude a number of dry bulk carriers of less than 6 000 grt (c. 8 000 dwt).

SOURCE: Lloyd's Register of Shipping

Table XVIII(a)

AGE DISTRIBUTION OF PRINCIPAL FLEETS AS AT MID-1986
(Ships of 100 grt and over)

COUNTRY	UNDER 5 YEARS	5-10 YEARS	10-15 YEARS	15-20 YEARS	20-25 YEARS	25-30 YEARS	30 YEARS AND OVER	TOTAL TONNAGE
	PER CENT OF TOTAL TONNAGE							'000 GRT
Australia	36	34	21	6	1	1	1	2 368.5
Austria	-	52	48	-	-	-	-	124.8
Belgium	42	39	14	3	1	0	1	2 419.7
Canada	11	13	14	18	21	10	13	3 160.0
Denmark	28	26	36	6	2	1	1	4 651.2
Finland	23	27	26	15	6	1	1	1 469.9
France	17	23	52	4	2	1	1	5 936.3
Germany (FR)	36	31	18	10	3	1	1	5 565.2
Greece	11	21	38	19	7	2	2	28 390.8
Iceland	4	16	34	26	12	6	2	176.4
Ireland	12	44	24	8	5	4	3	149.3
Italy	6	19	38	19	8	6	4	7 896.6
Japan	31	24	35	9	1	0	0	38 487.8
Netherlands	35	29	35	6	1	1	2	4 324.1
New Zealand	11	40	35	6	5	2	1	314.2
Norway	24	29	35	7	1	2	2	9 294.6
Portugal	22	2	37	23	6	3	7	1 114.4
Spain	12	32	38	11	3	2	2	5 422.0
Sweden	33	34	19	10	2	1	1	2 516.6
Switzerland	25	32	40	2	1	-	0	346.2
Turkey	7	15	41	23	7	3	4	3 423.7
United Kingdom	13	27	39	12	5	3	1	11 567.1
United States	11	27	20	10	7	6	19	19 900.8
Total OECD	20	25	33	12	4	2	4	159 020.2
Argentina	9	30	17	20	18	3	3	2 117.0
Bahamas	10	27	48	13	1	1	0	5 895.0
Brazil	22	40	25	6	2	3	2	6 212.3
Bulgaria	15	32	20	15	13	3	2	1 385.0
Cayman Islands	5	6	14	19	48	6	2	1 389.9
China (PR)	18	14	22	16	15	10	5	11 567.0
Cyprus	3	10	44	33	8	1	1	10 616.8
Germany (DR)	13	27	16	22	15	6	1	1 518.9
Gibraltar	0	25	56	11	7	1	0	1 612.9
Hong Kong	38	22	33	6	1	0	0	8 179.7
India	20	17	39	15	8	1	0	6 540.1
Indonesia	17	20	26	15	7	6	9	2 085.6
Iran	26	13	48	10	1	1	1	2 911.4
Korea (South)	19	15	34	25	5	1	1	7 183.6
Kuwait	25	46	22	5	1	0	1	2 580.9
Liberia	13	22	52	12	1	0	0	52 649.4
Malaysia	24	31	31	7	2	2	3	1 743.6
Malta	0	11	15	39	26	6	3	2 014.9
Mexico	18	23	28	23	4	2	2	1 520.2
Panama	30	17	29	14	5	3	2	41 305.0
Philippines	34	13	26	21	3	1	2	6 922.5
Poland	14	19	36	22	6	2	1	3 457.2
Romania	37	28	23	6	5	1	0	3 233.9
Saudi Arabia	9	7	46	20	9	6	3	2 978.0
Singapore	22	25	42	9	1	1	0	6 267.6
Taiwan	32	25	18	24	1	0	0	4 272.8
USSR	15	20	20	21	18	5	1	24 960.9
Yugoslavia	14	28	20	22	10	4	2	2 872.6
Rest of the World(1)	11	27	25	17	10	6	4	19 895.4
World Total (grt)	19	22	34	14	6	3	2	404 910.3
World Total (number of ships)	14	20	20	18	11	6	11	75 266

1. No country included in this category has more than 1 250 000 grt.

SOURCE: Lloyd's Register of Shipping

Table XVIII(b)

AGE DISTRIBUTION OF PRINCIPAL TANKER FLEETS AS AT MID-1986
(Ships of 100 grt and over)

COUNTRY	UNDER 5 YEARS	5-10 YEARS	10-15 YEARS	15-20 YEARS	20-25 YEARS	25-30 YEARS	30 YEARS AND OVER	TOTAL TONNAGE
	PER CENT OF TOTAL TONNAGE							'000 GRT
Australia	35	20	35	10	-	-	-	661.9
Austria	-	-	-	-	-	-	-	-
Belgium	58	36	3	-	1	1	1	266.5
Canada	3	33	17	20	10	7	10	278.9
Denmark	21	33	46	0	0	0	0	2 044.3
Finland	14	5	46	26	9	-	0	597.0
France	2	7	88	1	1	1	-	2 602.7
Germany (FR)	6	22	41	26	5	0	0	750.0
Greece	6	22	49	16	4	2	1	10 258.5
Iceland	44	-	-	18	38	-	-	2.7
Ireland	-	72	-	-	18	-	10	7.7
Italy	9	8	56	10	6	8	3	2 560.8
Japan	10	25	59	6	0	0	0	12 364.6
Netherlands	47	1	36	1	6	8	1	931.1
New Zealand	29	-	71	-	-	-	-	73.5
Norway	17	27	47	9	0	0	0	3 304.1
Portugal	36	2	53	9	0	-	-	533.4
Spain	6	35	51	6	1	1	0	2 371.8
Sweden	16	52	24	5	2	0	1	503.9
Switzerland	59	-	-	-	-	-	41	2.0
Turkey	2	25	55	10	5	3	2	1 036.9
United Kingdom	9	26	47	11	5	2	0	4 394.1
United States	5	31	27	9	6	11	11	7 296.4
Total OECD	10	24	49	9	3	3	2	52 842.8
Bahamas	6	28	54	11	1	0	0	4 200.9
Brazil	14	33	31	9	3	9	1	1 937.7
Cayman Islands	-	-	8	23	66	2	1	737.5
China (PR)	15	9	34	7	22	8	5	1 700.6
Cyprus	3	8	59	19	10	1	-	4 480.8
Gibraltar	-	44	56	0	0	-	0	855.7
Hong Kong	28	27	30	15	0	0	0	883.9
India	38	5	48	7	2	-	0	1 813.8
Iran	4	7	89	0	0	0	0	1 241.9
Iraq	-	43	57	0	-	0	-	776.9
Korea (South)	2	5	84	4	2	2	1	976.8
Kuwait	31	45	23	0	0	-	1	1 629.4
Liberia	7	20	67	6	0	-	0	28 674.5
Libya	-	5	95	-	-	-	-	708.0
Panama	15	17	53	6	6	2	1	9 191.8
Philippines	1	19	48	25	2	1	4	655.8
Saudi Arabia	4	0	59	20	9	8	0	1 604.3
Singapore	9	22	61	7	1	0	0	1 653.0
Taiwan	13	31	27	28	1	0	-	581.2
USSR	16	24	17	14	22	6	1	4 086.9
Rest of the World(1)	15	9	37	16	8	3	2	7 191.6
World Total (grt)	11	21	52	9	4	2	1	128 425.8
World Total (number of ships)	14	21	25	16	10	7	7	6 490

1. This includes all non-Member countries with less than 650 000 grt except for Taiwan (for which Lloyd's provides a breakdown)

SOURCE: Lloyd's Register of Shipping

Table XVIII(c)

AGE DISTRIBUTION OF PRINCIPAL DRY BULK CARRIER FLEETS AS AT MID-1986
(Ships of 6 000 grt and over)

COUNTRY	UNDER 5 YEARS	5-10 YEARS	10-15 YEARS	15-20 YEARS	20-25 YEARS	25-30 YEARS	30 YEARS AND OVER	TOTAL TONNAGE '000 GRT
	PER CENT OF TOTAL TONNAGE							
Australia	47	46	7	-	-	-	-	1 185.0
Austria	-	50	50	-	-	-	-	71.5
Belgium	47	37	16	-	-	-	-	1 415.7
Canada	12	14	11	17	23	11	11	1 851.4
Denmark	73	14	13	-	-	-	-	290.2
Finland	22	61	6	11	-	-	-	126.6
France	47	26	24	1	2	-	-	957.2
Germany (FR)	56	15	21	8	-	-	-	558.6
Greece	18	20	35	19	7	1	0	13 201.9
Italy	4	22	38	21	8	6	1	3 059.1
Japan	43	23	25	9	-	-	-	13 894.8
Netherlands	29	46	25	-	-	-	-	530.9
Norway	29	25	44	2	-	-	-	2 479.4
Portugal	20	-	24	56	-	-	-	230.6
Spain	11	28	39	21	1	-	-	1 174.9
Sweden	33	19	48	-	-	-	-	274.4
Switzerland	30	21	49	-	-	-	-	264.2
Turkey	2	8	47	32	11	-	-	1 352.7
United Kingdom	22	38	35	4	-	1	0	2 149.7
United States	18	24	14	3	-	4	37	2 020.3
Total OECD	28	23	30	12	4	1	2	47 089.1
Bahamas	18	17	40	25	-	-	-	901.7
Brazil	26	53	20	1	-	-	0	2 802.3
China (PR)	22	16	21	20	18	3	0	3 871.5
Cyprus	3	10	34	47	6	-	-	3 739.2
Hong Kong	42	20	32	5	1	-	-	6 089.6
India	15	17	39	16	11	1	1	2 943.4
Iran	61	14	10	14	-	1	-	1 109.0
Korea (South)	27	15	26	30	2	-	-	4 269.1
Liberia	22	23	37	18	2	-	-	18 023.3
Malta	-	-	9	58	29	3	1	952.4
Panama	40	16	22	16	5	1	0	17 400.0
Philippines	44	11	25	19	1	-	-	4 804.7
Poland	23	12	41	23	1	-	-	1 499.4
Romania	51	22	15	8	4	-	-	1 589.6
Singapore	34	21	38	6	1	0	-	2 477.8
Taiwan	35	12	22	31	-	-	-	1 998.1
USSR	19	44	26	9	1	1	-	3 433.3
Yugoslavia	16	24	31	15	11	2	1	1 182.1
Rest of the World(1)	17	18	29	20	13	2	1	6 727.5
World Total (grt)	28	21	29	16	4	1	1	132 908.1
World total (number of ships)	25	22	25	18	6	2	2	5 274

1. No country in this category has more than 650 000 grt.

NOTE: These figures include combination carriers.

SOURCE: Lloyd's Register of Shipping

Table XIX

TONNAGE LOST AND SCRAPPED
(Ships of 100 grt and over)

YEAR	VESSEL TYPE	TANKERS(1) SHIPS	'000 GRT	BULK CARRIERS(2) SHIPS	'000 GRT	GENERAL CARGO(3) SHIPS	'000 GRT	OTHER SHIPS	'000 GRT	TOTAL SHIPS	'000 GRT
1983	Lost	20	488.6	26	409.6	192	517.9	102	56.5	340	1 472.6
	Scrapped	375	11 849.1	99	2 133.5	575	2 532.3	261	243.9	1 310	16 758.8
	Total	395	12 337.7	125	2 543.1	767	3 050.2	363	300.4	1 650	18 231.4
1984	Lost	27	1 562.5	17	270.8	182	439.6	101	81.0	327	2 353.9
	Scrapped	300	9 653.1	161	3 204.0	967	4 551.4	357	342.4	1 785	17 750.9
	Total	327	11 215.6	178	3 474.8	1 149	4 991.0	458	423.4	2 112	20 104.8
1985	Lost	19	776.1	22	405.0	162	406.7	104	63.4	307	1 651.2
	Scrapped	277	11 293.9	252	5 351.9	1 063	4 882.7	768	700.8	2 360	22 229.3
	Total	296	12 070.0	274	5 756.9	1 225	5 289.4	862	764.2	2 667	23 880.5

YEAR	FLAG	OECD SHIPS	'000 GRT	OPEN REGISTRIES(4) SHIPS	'000 GRT	EASTERN EUROPE(5) SHIPS	'000 GRT	REST OF THE WORLD SHIPS	'000 GRT	TOTAL SHIPS	'000 GRT
1983	Lost	156	661.9	88	568.6	11	28.9	85	213.2	340	1 472.6
	Scrapped	699	6 776.7	275	6 231.9	104	321.4	232	3 428.8	1 310	16 758.8
	Total	855	7 438.6	363	6 800.5	115	350.3	317	3 642.0	1 650	18 231.4
1984	Lost	152	757.0	72	909.8	7	79.8	96	607.3	327	2 353.9
	Scrapped	869	7 783.9	392	5 179.6	149	342.0	375	4 445.4	1 785	17 750.9
	Total	1 021	8 540.9	464	6 089.4	156	421.8	471	5 052.7	2 112	20 104.8
1985	Lost	126	526.1	46	586.6	4	18.6	131	519.9	307	1 651.2
	Scrapped	933	8 974.4	412	7 976.5	547	522.6	463	4 755.8	2 360	22 229.3
	Total	1 059	9 500.5	458	8 563.1	551	541.2	599	5 275.7	2 667	23 880.5

1. Including liquefied gas and chemical carriers.
2. Including combination carriers.
3. Including container and ro/ro ships.
4. Bahamas, Cyprus, Lebanon, Liberia, Panama.
5. Albania, Bulgaria, German Democratic Republic, Poland, Romania, USSR.

SOURCE: Lloyd's Register of Shipping: Casualty Returns.

Table XX(a)

PERSONNEL EMPLOYED IN THE MERCHANT MARINES OF OECD MEMBER COUNTRIES: BY OCCUPATION
(Employed on vessels of 100 grt and over, excluding fishing vessels)

Persons employed

COUNTRY	AT END-YEAR 1985					AT END-YEAR 1986				
	MASTER AND DECK OFFICERS (1)	ENGINE ROOM OFFICERS (2)	DECK AND ENGINE ROOM RATINGS	CATERING STAFF (3)	MISCEL-LANEOUS (4)	TOTAL	MASTER AND DECK OFFICERS (1)	ENGINE ROOM OFFICERS (2)	DECK AND ENGINE ROOM RATINGS	CATERING STAFF (3)	MISCEL-LANEOUS (4)	TOTAL
Australia	1 442	1 562	3 150	1 460	745	8 359	1 342	1 459	3 046	1 460	623	7 930
Austria	58	36	152	38	–	284	64	40	173	38	–	315
Belgium	899	748	1 077	405	3	3 132	881	688	984	372	3	2 928
Canada	..	..	..	..	..	..	..	..	..	..	..	..
Denmark	2 689	2 118	3 332	2 669	179	10 987	2 510	1 816	2 922	2 350	181	9 779
Finland	987	762	2 185	3 115	378	7 427	891	661	1 843	3 162	384	6 941
France	1 814	1 204	3 886	1 448	–	8 352	1 554	953	3 179	1 121	–	6 807
Germany	5 724	3 137	9 879	2 916	1 617	23 273	5 139	2 739	8 289	2 590	1 713	20 470
Greece	..	..	..	..	..	..	..	..	..	..	..	31 934(5)
Iceland	..	..	..	..	..	..	..	..	..	..	..	..
Ireland	..	..	..	..	..	..	..	..	..	..	..	..
Italy	..	..	..	..	..	..	..	..	..	..	..	..
Japan	..	..	..	..	..	62 132	..	..	..	..	..	59 349(6)
Netherlands(7)	6 787			6 338		13 349(8)	3 901	2 784	5 239	2 249	45	14 218(8)
New Zealand	350	378	956	552	–	2 236	365	369	976	513	–	2 223(9)
Norway	6 501	4 667	9 385	9 551	1 368	31 472	5 272	3 663	7 493	8 287	1 180	25 895
Portugal	434	362	1 397	534	186	2 913	..	..	..	..	..	..
Spain	2 974	2 823	9 221	4 703	200	19 921	2 965	2 805	9 215	4 671	217	19 873
Sweden(10)	2 363	1 678	4 294	3 650	228	12 213	..	..	..	..	..	..
Switzerland	144	97	331	81	–	653	127	83	275	78	–	563
Turkey	..	..	..	..	..	..	3 474	2 834		7 578	–	13 886
United Kingdom	7 005	7 785	9 552	10 236	444	35 022	5 844	6 291	9 057	8 589	–	29 781
United States	..	..	..	..	..	..	..	..	..	..	..	..

1. Including radio officers, apprentices and cadets
2. Including apprentices and cadets
3. Including pursers
4. Including surgeons
5. As at 20th September 1986
6. As at 1st October 1986
7. As at 31st March of each year
8. Due to change in calculation criteria, 1985 and 1986 figures are not comparable
9. As at 31th October 1986
10. As at 30th September 1985

SOURCE: National Delegations to OECD

Table XX(b)

PERSONNEL EMPLOYED IN THE MERCHANT MARINES OF OECD MEMBER COUNTRIES: BY NATIONALITY
(Employed on vessels of 100 grt and over, excluding fishing vessels)

Persons employed

COUNTRY	AT END-YEAR 1985					AT END-YEAR 1986				
	OWN NATIONALS	OTHER OECD	OTHER COUNTRIES	TOTAL	PERCENTAGE CHANGE IN TOTAL SINCE 1984	OWN NATIONALS	OTHER OECD	OTHER COUNTRIES	TOTAL	PERCENTAGE CHANGE IN TOTAL SINCE 1985
Australia	4 895	3 490		8 385	-1	5 842(1)	2 088		7 930	-5
Austria	1		254	284	-15	1	37	277	315	+11
Belgium	2 489	504	139	3 132	-2	2 332	474	122	2 928	-6
Canada	..	..	..	..	..	..	..	..	..	..
Denmark	9 766	341	880	10 987	-5	8 846	305	628	9 799	-12
Finland	7 255	140	32	7 427	-11	6 794	126	21	6 941	-7
France	8 228	1	123	8 352	-16	6 695	2	110	6 807	-19
Germany	18 500	4 773		23 273	0	16 301	4 169		20 470	-12
Greece						28 791	3 143		31 934(5)	..
Iceland	..	..	..	..	..	..	..	..	..	..
Ireland	..	..	..	..	..	..	..	..	..	..
Italy	..	..	..	..	..	..	..	..	..	..
Japan	..	..	..	63 132	..	..	..	..	59 349(2)	-6
Netherlands(6)	9 797	3 552		13 349	-7	10 071	4 147		14 218	(3)
New Zealand	2 236	0	0	2 236	-5	2 223	0	0	2 223(7)	-1
Norway	24 985	3 023	3 464	31 472	-4	20 199	2 435	3 261	25 895	-19
Portugal	2 913	0	0	2 913	-39	..	..	..	..	..
Spain	19 921	0	0	19 921	-15	19 873	0	0	19 873	0
Sweden(4)	10 271	1 942		12 213	-4	..	..	..	..	..
Switzerland	275	139	239	653	-5	210	122	231	563	-14
Turkey	..	..	..	..	..	..	..	..	8 248	..
United Kingdom	28 980	3 021		32 001	-16	29 781	..	..	29 781	-7
United States	..	..	..	..	..	..	..	..	..	..

1. Increase over previous years reflects the addition of naturalised persons not previously included with Australian-born nationals
2. As at 1st October 1986
3. Due to change in calculation criteria, 1985 and 1986 figures are not comparable
4. As at 30th September 1985
5. As at 20th September 1986
6. As at 31st March of each year
7. As at 31st October 1986

SOURCE: National Delegations to OECD

Table XXI

DEVELOPMENT OF DRY CARGO AND TANKER VOYAGE CHARTER FREIGHT INDICES
(Quarterly and annual averages)

YEAR	DRY CARGO (1)					TANKERS (2)				
	1st Quarter	2nd Quarter	3rd Quarter	4th Quarter	Annual Average	1st Quarter	2nd Quarter	3rd Quarter	4th Quarter	Annual Average
1970	110	122	125	120	119	136	148	236	264	196
1971	97	81	73	73	81	167	98	74	90	107
1972	67	67	72	91	74	70	63	86	115	84
1973	115	144	161	226	162	147(140)	197(188)	305(293)	285(245)	234(217)
1974	233	231	205	203	218	213(199)	143(150)	107(97)	117(111)	145(139)
1975	159	143	130	136	142	67	72	79	77	74
1976	123	133	139	142	134	75	70	71	78	74
1977	135	131	131	135	133	84	68	60	76	72
1978	134	140	139	147	140	70	72	88	158	97
1979	150	168	196	204	179	156	158	171	180	166(89)
1980	204	221	203	224	213	80	70	55	78	71
1981	220	202	186	174	196	54	56	41	38	47
1982	167	169	147	152	159	39	42	50	42	43
1983	166	174	173	172	170	44	42	50	49	46
1984	173	176	167	174	173	48	51	46	47	48
1985	171	172	160	165	167	45	39	38	44	41
1986	158	156	154	162	158	45	51	60	44	50

1. Index based on 28 routes, July 1965 to June 1966 = 100; includes tankers in the grain trade.

2. Expressed in terms of Worldscale=100. The Worldscale schedule was revised annually until 1980 and thereafter twice a year. The approximate average changes at the beginning of the years since 1970 have been as follows: 1971:+3%, 1972:+5%, 1973:-2%, 1974:nil, 1975:+38%, 1976:+10%, 1977:+2%, 1978:+6%, 1979:+2%, 1980:+15%, mid-1980:+25%, 1981:nil, mid-1981:+13%, 1982:-7%, mid-82:-4%, 1983:-1%, mid-83:nil, 1984:+1%, mid-84:+4%, 1985:+2%, mid-85:-1%, 1986:+1%, mid-86:-6%. The single N.S.N. Index was discontinued at the end of 1974. The values in brackets for 1973 and 1974 are those published in the German Tanker Voyage Index. The German Index, which had previously been unweighted, has been recalculated for the period from 1980 using the proportions of ship sizes used during that year. The comparable value for 1979 as a whole is given in brackets.

SOURCE: Tanker Index to 1974 and Dry Cargo Index: Norwegian Shipping News/Shipping News International. Tanker Index from 1973: Statistiches Bundesamt, Weisbaden.

Table XXII

DRY CARGO VOYAGE AND TRIP CHARTER AND LINER FREIGHT INDICES

	VOYAGE CHARTER INDEX(1)			TRAMP TRIP CHARTER INDEX(2)			LINER FREIGHT INDEX(3)		
	1984	1985	1986	1984	1985	1986	1984	1985	1986
January	173	170	166	100	106	89	137	164	141
February	173	172	152	97	101	86	137	168	136
March	173	171	157	106	100	81	135	167	132
April	182	177	158	111	100	79	141	158	134
May	178	172	158	115	102	82	147	160	132
June	168	166	153	107	90	78	145	159	132
July	166	161	151	94	86	70	152	153	128
August	168	158	148	103	78	70	153	150	125
September	167	158	163	100	82	90	158	152	125
October	171	166	161	104	88	93	160	147	124
November	178	165	164	113	96	88	157	145	125
December	175	164	161	109	90	86	162	143	124
Yearly average (unweighted)	173	167	158	105	95	83	148	156	130

1. Based on tramp voyage rates on 28 routes, arranged in five bulk commodity groups with approximate weight aimed to give worldwide coverage, July 1965 to June 1966 = 100. Includes tankers in the grain trade.

2. Based on the weighted average of all trip charters (i.e. on a basis of payment per day or per dwt per day of charter) for ships of more than 12 000 dwt fixed for dry cargo on the Baltic Exchange and reported in the 'Daily Freight Register' (1976=100).

3. Based on liner rates for containerised and non-containerised general cargo and bulk cargo carried by Conference shipping lines to and from those North Sea ports in the Antwerp/Hamburg range which are of major importance to the German economy. They are not restricted to German flag vessels (1980=100).

SOURCE: Voyage Charter Index: Norwegian Shipping News/Shipping News International. Trip Charter Index: General Council of British Shipping. Liner Freight Index: Statistiches Bundesamt, Weisbaden.

Table XXIII

DRY CARGO TIME CHARTER FREIGHT INDICES

	1984		1985		1986	
	NORWEGIAN SHIPPING NEWS (1)	GENERAL COUNCIL OF BRITISH SHIPPING (2)	SHIPPING NEWS INTER-NATIONAL (1)	GENERAL COUNCIL OF BRITISH SHIPPING (2)	SHIPPING NEWS INTER-NATIONAL (1)	GENERAL COUNCIL OF BRITISH SHIPPING (2)
January	177		210		162	
February	176		195		159	
March	191	117	197	115	146	92
April	191		166		151	
May	185		175		145	
June	176	128	175	116	144	85
July	167		166		134	
August	187		157		149	
September	169	114	178	91	153	88
October	176		166		166	
November	180		174		160	
December	192	134	177	102	157	95
Yearly average (unweighted)	180	123	178	106	152	90

1. Based on average rates for all fixtures for oil-fired steamers and motor vessels in the 10 000 to 50 000 dwt range, excluding charters of more than a year (1971=100).

2. The quarterly values are based on the weighted average rates of all vessels in excess of 12 000 dwt reported fixed during the quarter for periods up to 24 months other than specialised ships such as timber carriers, ro/ro ships, etc. (1976=100).

SOURCE: Norwegian Shipping News/Shipping News International; General Council of British Shipping.

Table XXIV

TANKER VOYAGE FREIGHT INDICES

Worldscale points

	1984									1985									1986								
	NSN					SB				SNI					SB				SNI					SB			
	A	B	C	D	E	C	P	TOTAL		A	B	C	D	E	C	P	TOTAL		A	B	C	D	E	C	P	TOTAL
January	28	58	98	135	125	39	144	47		34	53	81	104	117	38	105	43		32	64	84	128	135	41	117	47
February	23	64	92	141	145	38	153	47		36	53	93	120	117	38	123	45		26	56	76	128	156	35	154	45
March	33	62	89	135	136	40	127	50		30	55	79	111	120	39	122	46		27	59	96	149	159	37	136	44
April	29	56	92	135	130	38	122	45		35	54	73	109	120	33	109	39		30	54	99	132	143	35	137	43
May	33	56	92	121	133	47	132	54		26	54	74	112	117	34	108	40		32	74	100	164	155	44	130	51
June	69	61	91	116	132	46	140	54		23	49	67	105	112	32	109	38		50	79	94	129	168	51	153	59
July	56	53	77	118	124	43	127	49		22	43	62	107	109	30	93	35		38	68	97	160	154	48	140	56
August	29	49	72	111	109	41	104	45		26	48	72	113	102	32	89	37		46	81	110	143	149	64	139	70
September	27	53	80	121	125	36	126	43		34	59	87	115	112	37	94	41		38	71	102	133	146	46	144	54
October	30	56	92	123	136	41	134	49		31	61	83	119	120	32	96	37		23	51	90	143	137	34	131	41
November	31	58	96	129	121	41	118	47		41	76	104	142	151	40	121	47		26	59	90	137	141	30	134	38
December	32	56	94	124	119	40	126	46		43	78	97	138	166	40	124	47		29	67	99	134	153	43	148	51
Yearly average (unweighted)	35	57	89	126	128	41	129	48		32	57	81	116	122	35	108	41		33	65	95	140	150	42	139	50

NOTE: The Worldscale schedule is revised twice a year, 1984:+1%, mid-1984:+4%, 1985:+2%, mid-1985:-1%, 1986:+1%, mid-1986:-6%. NSN (Norwegian Shipping News)/Shipping News International) categories are as follows: A: VLCC/ULCC (over 150 000 dwt); B: medium sized crude carriers (60-150 000 dwt); C: small crude carriers/product carriers (30-60 000 dwt); D: handy-sized dirty (black product carriers under 30 000 dwt); E: handy-sized clean (white product carriers under 30 000 dwt). SB (Statistiches Bundesamt): C: Crude; P: Products (black and white transported in vessels under 80 000 dwt).

SOURCE: Norwegian Shipping News/Shipping News International; Statistiches Bundesamt, Wiesbaden.

OECD SALES AGENTS
DÉPOSITAIRES DES PUBLICATIONS DE L'OCDE

ARGENTINA - ARGENTINE
Carlos Hirsch S.R.L.,
Florida 165, 4° Piso,
(Galeria Guemes) 1333 Buenos Aires
Tel. 33.1787.2391 y 30.7122

AUSTRALIA-AUSTRALIE
D.A. Book (Aust.) Pty. Ltd.
11-13 Station Street (P.O. Box 163)
Mitcham, Vic. 3132   Tel. (03) 873 4411

AUSTRIA - AUTRICHE
OECD Publications and Information Centre,
4 Simrockstrasse,
5300 Bonn (Germany)   Tel. (0228) 21.60.45
Local Agent:
Gerold & Co., Graben 31, Wien 1   Tel. 52.22.35

BELGIUM - BELGIQUE
Jean de Lannoy, Service Publications OCDE,
avenue du Roi 202
B-1060 Bruxelles   Tel. (02) 538.51.69

CANADA
Renouf Publishing Company Ltd/
Éditions Renouf Ltée,
1294 Algoma Road, Ottawa, Ont. K1B 3W8
Tel: (613) 741-4333
Toll Free/Sans Frais:
Ontario, Quebec, Maritimes:
1-800-267-1805
Western Canada, Newfoundland:
1-800-267-1826
Stores/Magasins:
61 rue Sparks St., Ottawa, Ont. K1P 5A6
Tel: (613) 238-8985
211 rue Yonge St., Toronto, Ont. M5B 1M4
Tel: (416) 363-3171
Sales Office/Bureau des Ventes:
7575 Trans Canada Hwy, Suite 305,
St. Laurent, Quebec H4T 1V6
Tel: (514) 335-9274

DENMARK - DANEMARK
Munksgaard Export and Subscription Service
35, Nørre Søgade, DK-1370 København K
Tel. +45.1.12.85.70

FINLAND - FINLANDE
Akateeminen Kirjakauppa,
Keskuskatu 1, 00100 Helsinki 10   Tel. 0.12141

FRANCE
OCDE/OECD
Mail Orders/Commandes par correspondance :
2, rue André-Pascal,
75775 Paris Cedex 16
Tel. (1) 45.24.82.00
Bookshop/Librairie : 33, rue Octave-Feuillet
75016 Paris
Tel. (1) 45.24.81.67 or/ou (1) 45.24.81.81
Principal correspondant :
Librairie de l'Université,
12a, rue Nazareth,
13602 Aix-en-Provence   Tel. 42.26.18.08

GERMANY - ALLEMAGNE
OECD Publications and Information Centre,
4 Simrockstrasse,
5300 Bonn   Tel. (0228) 21.60.45

GREECE - GRÈCE
Librairie Kauffmann,
28, rue du Stade, 105 64 Athens   Tel. 322.21.60

HONG KONG
Government Information Services,
Publications (Sales) Office,
Beaconsfield House, 4/F.,
Queen's Road Central

ICELAND - ISLANDE
Snæbjörn Jónsson & Co., h.f.,
Hafnarstræti 4 & 9,
P.O.B. 1131 - Reykjavik
Tel. 13133/14281/11936

INDIA - INDE
Oxford Book and Stationery Co.,
Scindia House, New Delhi 1   Tel. 331.5896/5308
17 Park St., Calcutta 700016   Tel. 240832

INDONESIA - INDONÉSIE
Pdii-Lipi, P.O. Box 3065/JKT.Jakarta
Tel. 583467

IRELAND - IRLANDE
TDC Publishers - Library Suppliers,
12 North Frederick Street, Dublin 1.
Tel. 744835-749677

ITALY - ITALIE
Libreria Commissionaria Sansoni,
Via Lamarmora 45, 50121 Firenze
Tel. 579751/584468
Via Bartolini 29, 20155 Milano   Tel. 365083
Sub-depositari :
Editrice e Libreria Herder,
Piazza Montecitorio 120, 00186 Roma
Tel. 6794628
Libreria Hœpli,
Via Hœpli 5, 20121 Milano   Tel. 865446
Libreria Scientifica
Dott. Lucio de Biasio "Aeiou"
Via Meravigli 16, 20123 Milano   Tel. 807679
Libreria Lattes,
Via Garibaldi 3, 10122 Torino   Tel. 519274
La diffusione delle edizioni OCSE è inoltre
assicurata dalle migliori librerie nelle città più
importanti.

JAPAN - JAPON
OECD Publications and Information Centre,
Landic Akasaka Bldg., 2-3-4 Akasaka,
Minato-ku, Tokyo 107   Tel. 586.2016

KOREA - CORÉE
Kyobo Book Centre Co. Ltd.
P.O.Box: Kwang Hwa Moon 1658,
Seoul   Tel. (REP) 730.78.91

LEBANON - LIBAN
Documenta Scientifica/Redico,
Edison Building, Bliss St.,
P.O.B. 5641, Beirut   Tel. 354429-344425

MALAYSIA - MALAISIE
University of Malaya Co-operative Bookshop
Ltd.,
P.O.Box 1127, Jalan Pantai Baru,
Kuala Lumpur   Tel. 577701/577072

NETHERLANDS - PAYS-BAS
Staatsuitgeverij
Chr. Plantijnstraat, 2 Postbus 20014
2500 EA S-Gravenhage   Tel. 070-789911
Voor bestellingen: Tel. 070-789880

NEW ZEALAND - NOUVELLE-ZÉLANDE
Government Printing Office Bookshops:
Auckland: Retail Bookshop, 25 Rutland Street,
Mail Orders, 85 Beach Road
Private Bag C.P.O.
Hamilton: Retail: Ward Street,
Mail Orders, P.O. Box 857
Wellington: Retail, Mulgrave Street, (Head
Office)
Cubacade World Trade Centre,
Mail Orders, Private Bag
Christchurch: Retail, 159 Hereford Street,
Mail Orders, Private Bag
Dunedin: Retail, Princes Street,
Mail Orders, P.O. Box 1104

NORWAY - NORVÈGE
Tanum-Karl Johan
Karl Johans gate 43, Oslo 1
PB 1177 Sentrum, 0107 Oslo 1Tel. (02) 42.93.10

PAKISTAN
Mirza Book Agency
65 Shahrah Quaid-E-Azam, Lahore 3   Tel. 66839

PORTUGAL
Livraria Portugal,
Rua do Carmo 70-74, 1117 Lisboa Codex.
Tel. 360582/3

SINGAPORE - SINGAPOUR
Information Publications Pte Ltd
Pei-Fu Industrial Building,
24 New Industrial Road No. 02-06
Singapore 1953   Tel. 2831786, 2831798

SPAIN - ESPAGNE
Mundi-Prensa Libros, S.A.,
Castelló 37, Apartado 1223, Madrid-28001
Tel. 431.33.99
Libreria Bosch, Ronda Universidad 11,
Barcelona 7   Tel. 317.53.08/317.53.58

SWEDEN - SUÈDE
AB CE Fritzes Kungl. Hovbokhandel,
Box 16356, S 103 27 STH,
Regeringsgatan 12,
DS Stockholm   Tel. (08) 23.89.00
Subscription Agency/Abonnements:
Wennergren-Williams AB,
Box 30004, S104 25 Stockholm.
Tel. (08)54.12.00

SWITZERLAND - SUISSE
OECD Publications and Information Centre,
4 Simrockstrasse,
5300 Bonn (Germany)   Tel. (0228) 21.60.45
Local Agent:
Librairie Payot,
6 rue Grenus, 1211 Genève 11
Tel. (022) 31.89.50

TAIWAN - FORMOSE
Good Faith Worldwide Int'l Co., Ltd.
9th floor, No. 118, Sec.2
Chung Hsiao E. Road
Taipei   Tel. 391.7396/391.7397

THAILAND - THAILANDE
Sukslt Siam Cu., Ltd.,
1715 Rama IV Rd.,
Samyam Bangkok 5   Tel. 2511630

TURKEY - TURQUIE
Kültur Yayinlari Is-Türk Ltd. Sti.
Atatürk Bulvari No: 191/Kat. 21
Kavaklidere/Ankara   Tel. 25.07.60
Dolmabahce Cad. No: 29
Besiktas/Istanbul   Tel. 160.71.88

UNITED KINGDOM - ROYAUME-UNI
H.M. Stationery Office,
Postal orders only: (01)211-5656
P.O.B. 276, London SW8 5DT
Telephone orders: (01) 622.3316, or
Personal callers:
49 High Holborn, London WC1V 6HB
Branches at: Belfast, Birmingham,
Bristol, Edinburgh, Manchester

UNITED STATES - ÉTATS-UNIS
OECD Publications and Information Centre,
2001 L Street, N.W., Suite 700,
Washington, D.C. 20036 - 4095
Tel. (202) 785.6323

VENEZUELA
Libreria del Este,
Avda F. Miranda 52, Aptdo. 60337,
Edificio Galipan, Caracas 106
Tel. 32.23.01/33.26.04/31.58.38

YUGOSLAVIA - YOUGOSLAVIE
Jugoslovenska Knjiga, Knez Mihajlova 2,
P.O.B. 36, Beograd   Tel. 621.992

Orders and inquiries from countries where Sales
Agents have not yet been appointed should be sent
to:
OECD, Publications Service, Sales and
Distribution Division, 2, rue André-Pascal, 75775
PARIS CEDEX 16.

Les commandes provenant de pays où l'OCDE n'a
pas encore désigné de dépositaire peuvent être
adressées à :
OCDE, Service des Publications. Division des
Ventes et Distribution. 2. rue André-Pascal. 75775
PARIS CEDEX 16.

70712-04-1987

OECD PUBLICATIONS, 2, rue André-Pascal, 75775 PARIS CEDEX 16 - No. 43933 1987
PRINTED IN FRANCE
(76 87 01 1) ISBN 92-64-12991-X